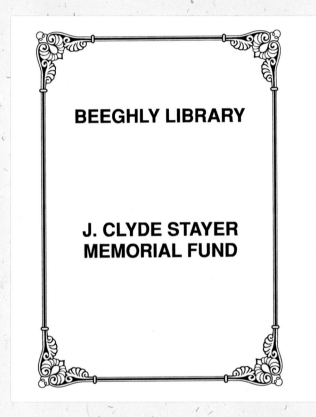

SOCIAL COMMITMENTS IN A DEPERSONALIZED WORLD

SOCIAL COMMITMENTS IN A DEPERSONALIZED WORLD

Edward J. Lawler, Shane R. Thye, and Jeongkoo Yoon

Russell Sage Foundation • New York

The Russell Sage Foundation

The Russell Sage Foundation, one of the oldest of America's general purpose foundations, was established in 1907 by Mrs. Margaret Olivia Sage for "the improvement of social and living conditions in the United States." The Foundation seeks to fulfill this mandate by fostering the development and dissemination of knowledge about the country's political, social, and economic problems. While the Foundation endeavors to assure the accuracy and objectivity of each book it publishes, the conclusions and interpretations in Russell Sage Foundation publications are those of the authors and not of the Foundation, its Trustees, or its staff. Publication by Russell Sage, therefore, does not imply Foundation endorsement.

Library of Congress Cataloging-in-Publication Data

Lawler, Edward J.
    Social commitments in a depersonalized world / Edward J. Lawler, Shane R. Thye, and Jeongkoo Yoon.
        p. cm.
    Includes bibliographical references and index.
    ISBN 978-0-87154-463-6 (alk. paper)
    1. Interpersonal relations. 2. Social groups. I. Thye, Shane R. II. Yoon, Jeongkoo. III. Title.
    HM1106.L39 2009
    302.3—dc22

                                                                        2008050600

Text design by Genna Patacsil.

RUSSELL SAGE FOUNDATION
112 East 64th Street, New York, New York 10065
10 9 8 7 6 5 4 3 2 1

Dedicated to the children in our lives:
Avery, Gyeol, Lauren, Nathan, Sam, Sang

CONTENTS

CHAPTER 2

ABOUT THE AUTHORS

Edward J. Lawler is Martin P. Catherwood professor of industrial and labor relations and professor of sociology at Cornell University.

Shane R. Thye is professor of sociology at the University of South Carolina.

Jeongkoo Yoon is professor of business administration at Ewha University, South Korea.

PREFACE

In an individualistic, market-oriented social world, the ties of people to social units—small groups, organizations, communities, nations—tend to be unsettled and problematic. Why would people in such a world attach themselves closely to groups or social units? What are the sources or bases for such ties? Are the ties purely contractual? Are they formed from the bottom up—that is, through the interactions and activities of the people themselves—or from the top down? Are some types of person-to-group ties stronger and more resilient than others? Do some promote more cooperation and sacrifice by members than others? These are long-standing issues for the social sciences (see, for example, Kornhauser 1959; Bell 1960). We suggest that they are of renewed import today given that most societies and nations in the twenty-first century are undergoing major transformations that unsettle person-to-group ties in the process. This volume theorizes how and when people create and sustain order from the bottom up, and in broad terms it revisits the Hobbesian problem of social order.

The central theme is that emotional and affective processes at the social interaction or micro level generate positive or negative sentiments about larger (macro) social units or groups. We theorize that affective sentiments about groups develop to the extent that people attribute their individual feelings to group affiliations. Once developed, affective sentiments about groups organize future interactions between particular people, making those interactions more predictable and stable. Person-to-group ties that have an affective component render the group itself an object of intrinsic or expressive value, enhancing the group's capacity to promote cooperation, trust, and collective action among its members. This volume integrates these themes under a general theory of social commitments, which are conceived as direct ties between individuals and larger social units, both local groups or organizations and larger and more distant communities or nations. The main theoretical ideas and principles used here have received direct or indirect empirical support in a program of laboratory experiments conducted by the authors (for reviews, see Thye, Yoon, and Lawler 2002; Lawler and Thye 2006). They posit a common process for social commitments regardless of the size, scale, or institutional character of the group or social unit.

This volume originated in an extensive program of theory and research conducted by the authors over approximately twenty years. It is the product of a long-term collaboration in which orders of authorship are virtually meaningless. The prior work investigated how and when people involved in social exchange generate cohesive relations and small groups. Emotion and affect are central to this process. In this research program, we developed two theories about the role of emotion or affect in exchange transactions—the theory of relational cohesion (Lawler and Yoon 1996, 1998; Lawler, Thye, and Yoon 2000) and the affect theory of social exchange (Lawler 2001; Lawler, Thye, and Yoon 2008). An important implication of these theories is that under certain structural conditions (for example, equal power, joint tasks, or shared responsibilities), repeated exchanges by the same people foster positive emotions and feelings that, in turn, produce affective ties to their relations and groups. Together these theories (and related research) suggest how transactional, instrumentally based social ties can produce more relational, group-oriented interactions and behavior through an emotional and affective process. The theory of social commitment in this volume abstracts from and develops these ideas to address a neglected or missing component in analyses of the Hobbesian problem of order—namely, the role of emotion and affect.

We stress the foundational nature of everyday emotions and feelings in local, immediate social situations. When people interact with each other, they invariably experience emotions or feelings along a negative-to-positive dimension. If their interaction goes well and produces a valued result, they are likely to feel good; if the interaction goes awry and produces a negative result (tension), they are likely to feel bad. Good feelings might include gratitude toward the other or pride in self, whereas negative feelings might include anger toward the other or shame toward self. These everyday feelings stem from "gut-level" responses (pleasure-displeasure); if positive, people strive to experience them again, whereas, if negative, they strive to avoid them. By theorizing these emotional effects, our aim is to make new linkages between experiences and interactions in groups and the collective ties that people develop toward those groups or organizations.

The theory of social commitments has broader implications for how people at a distance may generate and sustain shared affiliations in a work organization and how social divisions in a society may be bridged successfully and productively. While we trace person-to-group commitments to interactions among people in local micro situations, these interactions need not be face to face. Virtual interactions, using new computer- or Internet-based media, may be effective at supporting strong person-to-group ties, as are face-to-face interactions. The theory of social commitments suggests the structural (objective) and cognitive (subjective) conditions under which this is possible. The jointness of the task is the key structural condition, and the sense of shared responsibility is the key cognitive condition.

The chapter structure and content is as follows. The first two chapters identify and put in context the broad themes of the volume. Chapter 1 introduces and makes a case for the idea that person-to-group (P-G) ties are distinct and independent of ties or commitments between people (P-P). Chapter 2 contrasts different forms of person-to-group commitment—instrumental, affective, and normative—and places these in the context of alternative narratives about the social transformations occurring today. The premise is that human lives are becoming more and more transactional, individualized, or market-oriented and less and less relationally or socially oriented. This poses the problem of social commitment and social order and makes addressing it timely.

The next two chapters set up and present the main theoretical ideas and principles for addressing how social commitments come about and are sustained. Chapter 3 puts our approach to emotion and affect in the context of the relevant psychological and sociological literature on affect in social interaction, and this sets the stage for presenting the theory of social commitments in chapter 4. The core principles of the theory indicate that if a group presents individuals with a joint task and that task generates a sense of shared responsibility, people tend to attribute their individual feelings (positive or negative) to the group affiliation and to associate those feelings with the affiliation; this is the central micro foundation for social commitments.

Subsequent chapters use the theory or apply it to a range of issues. Chapters 5 to 7 deal with structural dimensions. Chapter 5 suggests how and when different structural ties generate the group affiliations to which people are likely to become committed. This chapter has implications for when group-oriented behavior emerges in a structure of individualized network ties. Chapter 6 analyzes "nested commitments" to local, immediate groups (for example, a work group or department) in the context of the larger organization (for example, a corporation), asking whether the former undermines the latter. The chapter elaborates the special commitment problems faced by decentralized organizations and suggests how the emotional effects of task structures and role definitions may overcome these. Chapter 7 contrasts the types of commitment that are likely to develop under hierarchy and network forms of organization. The implication is that network forms of organization have greater capacity to generate affective group ties, in part because they facilitate bottom-up emotional and affective processes.

Chapters 8 and 9 use the theory to examine select connections between micro and macro structures and processes. Chapter 8 analyzes the conditions under which micro-sociological processes legitimize macro-level social inequalities by promoting social commitments. The implication is that if people of unequal status engage in joint tasks or activities, they tend to develop shared emotions and feelings that promote social order at the micro level. Chapter 9 conceives of nationalist sentiments as a key source of order and stability for the modern nation-state and asks whether and how nation-states sustain such sentiments in the face of the internationalizing forces of globalization. The theory suggests that the perceived salience and efficacy of states are crucial.

Chapters 10 and 11 return to the broad theme of social order. Chapter 10 compares our affect-based theory of how social orders emerge to alternative approaches. It compares four fundamental mechanisms through which social interactions generate order and stability—norms, trust, identity, and affect—and argues that affect is most fundamental. The concluding chapter summarizes the important role of emotion and affect in "solving" problems of commitment and social order and explores some of our ideas about how people, groups, and organizations might use our theory to manage their social commitments.

ACKNOWLEDGMENTS

We give special thanks to the Russell Sage Foundation. They provided Edward Lawler with a visiting scholar award that enabled him to work full-time on this volume during the 2007–2008 year; in addition, the foundation offered a supportive environment with excellent staff and a great group of twenty other RSF scholars to rub elbows with. This environment contributed immeasurably to the volume.

Because it emerged out of theorizing and research that dates from the early 1990s, this volume owes a debt to many other organizations and individuals. Four grants from the National Science Foundation provided us with the tangible support to conduct the research that tested the underlying theoretical principles and thereby established a foundation for the broader, more expansive theoretical analyses of this volume. Two provosts at Cornell University, Don Randel and Biddy Martin, provided the necessary latitude and encouragement to Edward Lawler to stay deeply engaged in research while serving an eight-year stint as dean of Cornell's School of Industrial and Labor Relations, as well as financial support that allowed the three authors to convene in Ithaca, New York, every summer for many years. The School of Industrial and Labor Relations at Cornell also provided many important forms of support that contributed to this work, including physical space for our research.

Many individuals have helped us at one point or another. Four are worthy of special mention because they carefully read the entire volume. Michael Hechter, Peter Marsden, and Murray Webster gave us not only extremely valuable comments on the volume as a whole but also detailed comments on each chapter that were very helpful. Samuel Bacharach, a colleague and life-long friend of Edward Lawler's, not only provided him with much-needed encouragement to work on this project at key moments of frustration, but also read the entire volume twice. His advice on the message of the volume and how to communicate it most effectively was invaluable. David Lipsky read much of the book and provided us with timely validation of the value of the volume's main message to a broader audience, given his background in the field of industrial relations. Together, these scholars helped us correct some errors, clarify key points, frame the volume's relevance to the social order problem in an appropriate and persuasive way, and ensure that the main message was salient and up-front throughout. Beyond such assistance, they nudged us to temper the natural caution and modesty that develops in academic article writing over time and to reach for a broader audience and a more provocative rendition of the volume's message. Any errors or misjudgments we have made in this process, of course, are our own.

Several scholars gave us valuable comments on particular parts of the manuscript. Mildred Schwartz read chapter 9, the "nationalist sentiments" chapter, twice. Her trenchant criticism of the first version pushed us to revise the approach of the chapter, include material we had missed, and revise or refine the message in important ways. We certainly "own" any remaining problems or errors. Three fellow scholars at the Russell Sage Foundation (during 2007–2008) gave us comments on particular chapters. Isabela Mars provided insightful comments on chapter 9; Tamara Buckley and Erica Gabrielle Foldy gave us valuable comments on chapter 8. There certainly are many other colleagues in our departments and fields who have contributed to our work over the years leading up to this volume, but too many to mention. All three of us have had the benefit of good colleagues, stimulating intellectual environments, and supportive institutions as the seeds of this work were planted and nurtured and as the work evolved over time.

We would like to mention several students who contributed in one way or another to this project. First and foremost, Lena Hipp of Cornell University carefully read each chapter of the volume with an eagle eye, spotting gaps in our logic as well as broader issues that we needed to address; she also took on the daunting task of preparing the references. At the final stage, George Kandathil, also of Cornell, provided assistance with the references section. Many more graduate and undergraduate students helped with our research projects in one way or another, including Emily Arnold, Mouraine Baker, Brian Booth, Younhyung Cho, Jenny Craig, Lisa Dilks, Gehoon Hong, Yeji Jeong, Soyoung Jung, Michael Large, Sujung Lee, Elizabeth Mattern, Tucker McGrimmon, Jaron McKinney, Wesley Sine, and Sonja Talwar. Marty Kuhn did the programming for the laboratory experiments we conducted over the entire period leading up to this volume.

Finally, several staff members at the Russell Sage Foundation provided invaluable assistance and help through the process. The head of the press, Suzanne Nichols, helped us understand the implications of the reviewers' comments and provided a useful synthesis of ways to improve the manuscript. Cindy Buck did a nice job copyediting the manuscript, and April Rondeau did an effective job of managing the production process. Michael Remaley and Angela Gloria worked hard on the marketing. Finally, before the book project was started in earnest, Frances Benson of Cornell University Press generously read a preliminary version of chapter 1 and gave us some sage advice on book publishing.

Our families supported us in important ways, as families often do. Writing a book is an all-consuming task. Lawler's wife Joan accepted, with her usual tolerance and support, his obsession with this project for extended periods, something that is not new with her and for which she probably never receives truly appropriate appreciation or thanks. Thye's wife Dana provided a valuable sounding board for many of the ideas of the book and shouldered much more than her fair share of the "task jointness" that it takes to run a household and raise two children. We also thank Youngjoo Sohn for her support of Yoon's summer research pilgrimage to Cornell for many years. The children in our lives provided welcome distraction during this project: Lawler's two grandsons, Nathan and Sam; Thye's two daughters, Avery and Lauren; and Yoon's two sons, Sang and Gyeol. We did not always want those distractions, but we almost always needed them.

Edward J. Lawler
Shane R. Thye
Jeongkoo Yoon

CHAPTER 1

Introduction: Person-to-Group Ties

In the fall of 2007, Alex Rodriguez, a star baseball player for the New York Yankees, opted to exercise an option in his contract to become a "free agent." This allowed him to negotiate a new contract with any team prepared to bid for his services. He had two years left on his contract with the Yankees, so he did not need to do this. His stated reasons for opting out were uncertainty about the direction of the Yankee organization (which was undergoing management changes at the time) and concerns that some other players on the team whose contracts had expired might not be re-signed. The message he conveyed was that these other players were valuable and important teammates to him. The media and many fans wondered, however, why Rodriguez had not simply waited another ten days or so before declaring free agency, because the results of Yankee negotiations with the other players would have been known by then. Nathan Lawler, the eight-year-old grandson of one of the authors, insightfully captured the sentiment of most Yankee fans when he said, after seeing an ESPN report on these developments, "I don't think A-Rod cares what team he plays on." Less generous interpretations from fans were that he was "greedy," "only out for himself," and a glaring example of what was wrong with professional sports.

Fans and the general public interpreted Rodriguez's actions and statements as indicating that "being a Yankee" was not of significant value to him. He was treating his ties to the Yankees as purely transactional, that is, as purely a matter of getting the best individual deal. The response of the Yankee organization was quite negative. Representing the ownership family, Hank Steinbrenner said: "If you don't want to be a Yankee . . . we don't want you, that's the bottom line." "If we are going to make you rich and we're going to give you the privilege of being a Yankee, you've got to show us you want to be here" (Curry, Jack, and Tyler Kepner. 2007. "For Rodriguez and Yankees, It's all but over." *New York Times,* October 29, 2007). The Yankee organization made it clear that it wanted players who intrinsically valued "being a Yankee" and thus saw the affiliation as something special, something self-defining and identity-affirming. In broader conceptual terms, they expected players to form a relational tie to the organization, that is, a person-to-group tie of intrinsic or expressive value. Such ties have a significant emotional and affective component. From the Yankee organization's standpoint, what may begin as a transactional tie, formed contractually when a player joins the team, has to become a relational tie by the time of contract renegotiation. Alex Rodriguez's behavior did not convey such a relational tie, and the Yankee organization balked.

Interestingly, a contrasting message came from Wall Street, one that supported and encouraged Alex Rodriguez's transactional approach to his association with the Yankees. A subsequent article in the *New York Times* (Belson, Ken. 2007. "Rodriguez not greedy by standard of Wall St." October 30, 2007) suggested that, by Wall Street standards, Alex Rodriguez's vigorous quest for a higher salary was not only appropriate but even laudable. The article quoted James Melcher, founder and chief executive of Balestra Capital, a hedge fund in New York: "Not only do I have no problem with it, I'm cheering him on." Similarly, Daniel Alpert of Westwood Capital in New York was quoted in the *Times* article as saying: "There's nothing coldblooded about it. He's pricing himself to what the market will bear. This isn't charity." Underlying this Wall Street view is the notion that only transactional ties make sense for both employees and employers in the modern world. Whereas fans and the Yankee organization emphasized the importance of relational person-to-group ties, in which a player (employee) accords value to membership itself, the Wall Street reaction emphasized the transactional and instrumental ties of the marketplace.[1]

Negotiating an employment contract is inherently a transactional matter, and Rodriguez's behavior reflected this. Yet, over time, a group or organizational affiliation may take on intrinsic value, and this example conveys the sensitivity of organizations to the sort of commitments to them made by members or employees. Employees who credibly show such commitment may reap local benefits or rewards that compensate for the costs of not pursuing their market wage or salary, and employers that operate with a purely transactional perspective on employees may generate weaker and more fragile ties between employees and the organization, making it easy for employees to leave when they have a better financial offer. The importance of relational ties is likely to vary with the organization and its management; person-to-firm relations on Wall Street, for instance, reputedly approach the transactional extreme.

The contrasting responses to Rodriguez's actions may reflect larger, global changes in the sort of ties people develop to their work organizations. Player-team ties certainly appear to be more transactional and less relational today than thirty years ago. Similarly, prevailing employee-employer contracts are more transactional today than in the past, primarily because of the demise of the standard employment contract of the midtwentieth century, which assumed continuous, lifetime employment with the same organization and linear careers that could be accomplished internally within a given firm. The response of the Yankee organization may reflect an outdated, anachronistic conception of person-to-group ties, whereas the Wall Street response may capture appropriate practical wisdom for the twenty-first century. This raises an important and timely question: if, as many analysts suggest, the world is becoming more transactional and market-oriented, what role do person-to-group ties play?

This volume argues that there are fundamental social conditions under which transactional, purely instrumental ties to a group tend to become relational and expressive. We reframe the transactional-relational issue as a problem of social commitment and conceive this problem as bearing on the classic Hobbesian question: how is social order possible? Social commitments are construed here as distinct from purely instrumental or transactional ones in that they are non-instrumental and infused with emotion or affect. They entail person-to-group ties with an emotional or affective component and have the capacity to generate group-oriented cooperation and collaboration more effectively and efficiently than transactional ties alone.

PERSON-TO-PERSON TIES
AND PERSON-TO-GROUP TIES

People develop social commitments or ties to other people with whom they interact as well as to the small groups, organizations, and communities that constitute the larger context for their social interactions. This implies two fundamental types of social ties: those between people, or person-to-person (P-P) ties, and those between people and their social units, or person-to-group (P-G) ties. We may come to enjoy and value either or both of these ties as ends in themselves, rendering those ties relational. If we value person-to-group ties in themselves, we orient our behavior to the expectations and interests of the group; if we value ties to particular people in themselves, we orient our behavior to the expectations and interests of those people. Relational ties can involve both person-to-person and person-to-group ties.[2]

Person-to-person and person-to-group ties are likely to be interconnected, but there is not necessarily a one-to-one correspondence between them. Moreover, the valence of these ties can differ. People may be strongly committed to a group without necessarily being strongly committed to its members, and vice versa (see Prentice, Miller, and Lightdale 1994). For example, a baseball player may have strong ties to his team, such as the Yankees, but weak ties to fellow players; or he may have strong ties to many fellow team players but weak ties to the team or larger organization. The main point is that people may be attached to their group but not to the individuals in it, or they may be attached to individuals in their group but not to their group. Person-to-group ties may be harder to establish or sustain in the diverse, globalizing world of the twenty-first century as traditional group ties loosen and become more fluid and as interpersonal ties become more transitory and based on less frequent face-to-face interaction. Yet it is precisely these sorts of conditions that also make person-to-group ties a more important source of commitment and social order.

The contrast between person-to-person and person-to-group ties is implicit in classic theories of sociology that deal with how social orders come about and are maintained. George Herbert Mead (1934) differentiated interactions with specific others from interactions with a generalized other, characterizing the latter as involving the society or community. Taking the role of a generalized other tends to foster different behaviors than taking the role of specific others in a social situation because the generalized other represents the normative framework and moral fabric of the larger community as a whole. Talcott Parsons (1951) portrayed person-to-person relations and person-to-group relations as two analytically independent dimensions of social order at the macro or societal level. While he argued that social order is based on both the ties among people and their common ties to a larger social unit, Parsons emphasized the person-to-group dimension. The theorizing of Mead and Parsons implies that the person-to-group dimension is especially important to the binding together of large, dispersed populations of people who lack direct ties to one other. Direct ties to the larger unit make direct ties to other members less important as a source of order and stability.[3] The next section treats several examples from routine aspects of daily life that illustrate the distinctive roles of person-to-person and person-to-group ties, as well as how they may be interconnected.

Some Everyday Examples

In this section, we compare the social ties in a hair salon, morning coffee shop, or residential neighborhood, beginning with the hair salon.

Assume that you frequent a particular hair salon and a particular stylist. Your relationship with that particular hairdresser developed gradually through "trial and error" or repeated visits. The first time you had your hair cut at this salon, you may have been pleased with the work, so you went back. You got to know the hair stylist and the other staff in the hair salon. You developed feelings toward your own hairdresser and also toward the hair salon as a whole, based on how salon staff treated you when you made an appointment, on the appearance or "feel" of the salon, and so forth. Your tie to the particular person (the hair stylist) is likely to have developed prior to your tie or commitment to the social unit (the hair salon). This raises interesting questions: Under what conditions would you develop a commitment not only to your hairdresser but also to the salon? If your preferred hair stylist were to move to another salon in the area, would you stay with the salon or move to the other salon with your stylist? These questions boil down to an issue of whether the person-to-person social commitment is stronger for the customer than the person-to-group commitment. This issue can be generalized to organizations in which people work; to ties that clients develop to particular employees—such as a broker in a financial firm—or to the larger employer; to the communities or local neighborhoods where they live; and to their national identities or affiliations.

Next, take the example of a coffee shop that you frequent each morning, as do some other "regulars." You have all chosen this coffee shop based on its convenience, its ambience, the quality of the coffee, the friendliness of the staff, and so forth. Even in large cities where many options are available, one often finds the same people having coffee at the same place, morning after morning. Regardless of the specific basis for your repeated morning presence (the coffee, convenience, ambience), a minimal social commitment to the place itself brings you in contact with other regulars. You recognize and come to acknowledge each other, and some of you strike up conversations and form relationships.

The presence of regulars further enhances the feelings of comfort and ease among those of you who are at the coffee shop day after day. In this example, the tie to the group (the coffee shop) precedes and helps to foster person-to-person relationships among the regular customers. Moreover, while these relationships may entail rather minimal ties or commitments, they need not be deep to have important effects on patrons' behavior and loyalty. Person-to-group ties, however shallow and minimal, can foster a sense of community in places where anonymity, depersonalization, and the privatization of lives prevail.

Finally, take the example of moving to a new neighborhood. Both relations to particular neighbors and to the neighborhood are likely to develop in tandem. You do not move into the neighborhood because of a particular neighbor—as you might go to a particular hair salon because of a hair stylist—but neither does your commitment to the neighborhood develop prior to your ties to your neighbors, as with the coffee shop. You certainly choose a neighborhood when you buy a house, but your ties to the neighborhood and especially your ties to particular neighbors tend to form after your move. You may develop strong social ties to particular neighbors before your ties to the neighborhood develop, or you may become more closely tied to your neighborhood than to your neighbors. This has important consequences for how you relate to others and to the neighborhood—for example, in your willingness to give time, effort, or other valued benefits to the neighborhood as such. The neighborhood case is similar to that of new employees entering an organization: differences in the ties to coworkers and the organization can be quite important.

A comparison of these examples suggests that the interrelationships of person-to-person and person-to-group ties are complex and vary significantly. In the case of the hair salon, the person-to-person tie fosters the person-to-group tie. The former occurs within the latter, and the group (the hair salon) makes possible the valued person-to-person tie. In the coffee shop, the person-to-group tie generates person-to-person ties by bringing people who do not know each other together in the first place. In the neighborhood case, the person-to-person and person-to-group ties do not form in any particular sequence or causal order. Either could emanate from the other, or both could emerge simultaneously. Our theory of social commitments emphasizes the role of person-to-group ties without necessarily presuming a particular causal order vis-à-vis person-to-person ties. The theory of social commitments indicates how and when social interactions generate person-to-group ties de novo, but also how and when they make salient and activate an already existing person-to-group tie.

The hair salon, coffee shop, and neighborhood examples also illustrate the subtlety and pervasiveness of micro social orders, that is, relatively stable and smooth ongoing patterns of behavior and interaction at the local level. People can anticipate what is likely to happen in each situation, their expectations are generally confirmed, and the confirmation of their expectations further solidifies the micro order. A key reason for this is simply that each situation is experienced repeatedly by a given person with at least some of the same others. If the same people interact repeatedly, chances are that they will develop standard, stable, and predictable ways of dealing with each other (Homans 1950; Collins 2004) and also standard, predictable ways of dealing with the overarching social unit. We treat micro-level social orders as involving repeated interaction between two or more people in which they (1) orient their behavior to others or to the group; (2) experience emotions, both positive or negative; (3) perceive a social unit (group); and (4) develop affective sentiments about other members and the social unit in the course of repeated interaction (see Lawler, Thye, and Yoon 2008). These four dimensions can be applied to most everyday situations. They also can be extended to social order at the macro level.

THE PROBLEM OF SOCIAL ORDER AND PERSON-TO-GROUP TIES

Thomas Hobbes's (1651/1985) analysis of the problem of social order implicitly involved both person-to-person and person-to-group ties. His fundamental argument was that because the human species is prone to avarice, force, aggression, and malfeasance, people are highly vulnerable to each other. The social world in a hypothetical "state of nature" without person-to-group ties was conceived as precarious, dangerous, and anarchic. Without the external constraint of (sovereign) authority, the ties among people in a population (person-to-person ties) would descend into a "war of all against all." For Hobbes, facing a war of all against all, the human species is saved by its instinct for self-preservation and capacity for reason. These qualities lead individuals to rationally form ongoing human associations and communities that, in our terms, create strong person-to-group ties in the form of social contracts wherein people accept group constraints in exchange for individual protection and safety. These associations are contractual and transactional in form. In sum, the source of the problem was at the person-to-person level, but it could not be solved there. Contractual person-to-group ties were necessary to reduce chaos and disorder at the person-to-person level.[4]

Contractual solutions to the problem of social order have important appeal, in part because transactional ties are integral to the daily experience of most people and in part because implicit contracts are often as important and binding as explicit ones (see Hechter 1987; Coleman 1990). In a modern version of the Hobbesian contractual solution, Michael Hechter (1987) offers a theory of solidarity indicating that the more dependent people are on a group for goods they cannot produce alone or in other combinations, the more extensive are their obligations to that group. People accept and comply with norms defining their obligations to the extent that they receive individual benefits from the collective or joint goods produced by the group. Hechter's theory emphasizes person-to-group ties and conceives of these as purely transactional. People tie themselves to and remain in a group only insofar as it provides them with individual benefits better than could be obtained elsewhere (either from acting alone or in other groups). Rational-choice principles—such as profit maximization—shape and govern contractual ties.

There also are notable noncontractual, nonrational solutions to the problem of order, offered by Peter Berger and Thomas Luckmann (1966), Randall Collins (1981, 2004), Thomas Scheff (1990), Philip Selznick (1992), Dennis Wrong (1994), and others. These have an implicit or explicit institutional theme, indicating that standard ways of doing things become taken for granted, assumed, and normative. Here repetition of a practice or pattern of interaction occurs for its own sake, because "this is what people do in this situation." In short, it is expected. From an institutional framework, social order emerges from and is manifest in patterns and practices that are sustained and reproduced in social interaction (Collins 1981). Clubs, neighborhoods, professional associations, corporations, communities, and nations all reveal regular patterns of human interaction that reflect local or larger institutional practices and ties, formal or informal, and the social interactions within them. In fact, Wrong (1994, 5) boils down the problem of social order to "the predictability of human conduct on the basis of common, stable expectations." This is a micro translation of the larger social order, which posits consistency and convergence between the micro and macro social realms of human experience (see also Collins 1975, 1981).[5]

Macro and micro realms, however, may be divergent or unconnected as well as convergent. Social order should be especially resilient when the local micro processes activate, translate, and reproduce macro structural patterns and cultural beliefs (see Lawler, Ridgeway, and Markovsky 1993; Berger, Ridgeway, and Zelditch 2002). In turn, such orders are weakened if there is a disjuncture or lack of connection between the micro and macro realms. Anyone who has worked in a highly decentralized organization has probably seen up close the disconnect and disjuncture between the macro organization (the corporation or company) and the local unit (the division, department, or work team). If there is a disconnect or divergence between micro and macro conditions, one would expect this to be manifest in the relationship that people have to the local micro group versus the larger macro group.

In this volume, we theorize how and when person-to-group ties forge connections and resolve disjuncture between local micro conditions and more distant macro conditions. These also are conditions under which people transform rationally based contractual ties into noncontractual relational ties. This chapter concludes with an overview of the theoretical argument.

AN OVERVIEW OF THE ARGUMENT

The main line of argument is that person-to-group ties are produced and reproduced through recurrent social interactions between those who share a group affiliation. Local, immediate person-to-person ties give rise to or activate existing person-to-group ties that essentially define and interpret the overarching similarities among people who share the group affiliations, even if they do not or never will interact with many of them. For example, national and ethnic identities may be contingent in part on social interactions with only a few others who share that identity, but in a context that makes the identity salient and valued. Moreover, person-to-group ties are likely to be infused with emotion and affect for one very simple reason: when people interact with others, they tend to experience mild, everyday feelings, and under some conditions people associate these feelings with a shared group affiliation or membership. This emotional or affective component is a distinctive feature of our theory, and it enables us to explain how and when person-to-group ties transcend transactional beginnings and become relational and expressive.

Our theorizing of person-to-group ties interweaves three basic themes regarding individual emotions, repeated interactions, and joint tasks or activities. The first theme is that emotion and affect play a role in person-to-group ties or social commitments. Emotion and affect ostensibly give commitments considerable resilience and strength, in part because of their visceral, gut-level quality. Further, emotion-based commitment is strong because emotions typically are associated with meanings and identities created and reproduced in local micro situations—that is, in interaction with other people. Emotion and affect also are important because they are subject to only limited social controls from above. Organizations, communities, and nations may exercise control over what people see and do in public settings, but they have decidedly less control over what people feel and how they interpret and use their feelings in their local, immediate interactions. Larger social units also cannot fully control the inferences that people make about their ties to larger social units such as their work organization, community, or nation.

The second theme is that repetitive social interaction with the same others has enormous social impact. It is almost a truism to say that people who repeatedly or recurrently interact adjust their behaviors, cognitions, and feelings to one another in subtle and not-so-subtle ways. While people significantly influence one another in the process, these interactions are also a potential source of independence from larger social units, whether these are voluntary associations, work organizations, or nations. A central component of our theoretical argument is that micro-level social interactions are prime engines for emotion and affect. It is therefore noteworthy that the major social transformations associated with globalization free large numbers of people to interact (or attempt to interact) with a very wide range of other people in different places around the world. The question for us is to explain how and when people's everyday emotions lead to enduring affective sentiments about their groups, organizations, communities, or nations, which can be construed as a form of voluntary, noncontractual constraint on individual action.

The third theme is that joint activity is fundamental to understanding the emotional aspects of social interactions and social commitments. Social interactions tend to have an instrumental basis because joint activities involve some sort of implicit or explicit exchange or transfer of benefits by each party to the other—for example, reciprocity. We develop the argument that these interactions, even if purely instrumental, produce emotions that transform the instrumental tie into an expressive tie. Thus, there is a common, underlying emotional or affective process that explains how people form and maintain social commitments across different types of social units, from small groups to work organizations to communities to nations. Our theory integrates the implied rational, instrumental foundation of exchanges between people and between people and organizations with the nonrational emotional or affective experiences of people involved in social interaction and exchange.

In sum, we aim to understand how people develop and sustain person-to-group social commitments. What exogenous structural or cultural conditions enhance the opportunity for or possibility of such ties? What endogenous interaction processes lead to the actualization of strong or weak person-to-group ties or commitments? At the heart of our theory are endogenous emotional and affective mechanisms that promote and sustain person-to-group ties that are valued in themselves. This is essentially a social process that is common to groups of virtually any type or size, from small work groups to nation-states. Thus, we adopt a "generalizing strategy" that has the merit of yielding relatively simple, parsimonious, broadly applicable principles. Such principles can help us understand in general terms how people themselves create order in the context of apparent chaos and, in the process, strengthen overarching commonalities across vastly different populations. These principles also help to analyze and frame how organizational policies may overcome the fragmentation and internal conflicts endemic to large, complex, multinational, and decentralized organizations.

CHAPTER 2

Narratives of Social Transformation

The millennial change to the twenty-first century has ushered in a plethora of broad analyses and commentaries on the life of people today, the futures that are plausible and probable, and how existing social institutions might adapt in response. A pervasive theme of these analyses is that the world is in the midst of truly fundamental transformations across virtually all realms of human activity—political, economic, social, and environmental. What do these analyses foretell? The common view is that the twenty-first century is introducing a new age and a new order with an uncertain trajectory and the expectation of radical changes in how people live. The classic problem of social order is an underlying, often unstated or implicit, question or issue in such analyses.

There may be few comparable historical periods of simultaneous transformation across so many areas of life. The Reformation and Renaissance periods of the sixteenth-century Enlightenment are two clear examples, and the subsequent period of industrialization in the nineteenth century is another. Early sociological theorists such as Karl Marx (1867/1967), Émile Durkheim (1915), and Max Weber (1918/1968) provided trenchant analyses of the transition to industrial society; developing big ideas to grapple with big societal problems, they focused on what the new industrial order would look like and what would hold it together. Today there also is no shortage of scholars, journalists, and other social analysts attempting to understand and interpret in general terms the interrelated problems and global prospects for societies of the twenty-first century (see, for example, Ritzer 1995; Putnam 2000; Haas 2000; Friedman 2005; Stiglitz 2006; Laitin 2007).

Major social transformations of the past almost invariably shook up, unsettled, or even unhinged the relationships of people to their communities and redefined them in fundamental ways. One can argue that the social transformations under way today are similarly "shaking up" the connections people have to standard, traditional groupings, such as work organizations, unions, voluntary associations, local community groups, and nations. Robert Putnam (2000, 2007) provides a provocative, if controversial, argument that network ties to and trust in other people (social capital) are declining and social isolation is concomitantly on the rise. His argument is based on downward trends in participation or involvement in voluntary associations (clubs), local communities, and national political affairs (see Putnam 2000). More recently, Putnam (2007) has extended his thesis, arguing that people tend to "hunker down," especially in more ethnically diverse communities. He finds evidence, based on a survey of forty-one U.S. communities, that people trust others less, have fewer close friends, are less involved in their community, and spend more time watching television. Miller McPherson, Lynn Smith-Lovin, and Matthew Brashears (2006), using data from the General Social Survey (GSS), affirm that people's networks of close ties (those whom they confide in) have become smaller and more kin-based in the last twenty years (specifically between 1985 and 2004). Declines in social capital or close person-to-person ties occur at the micro level and are manifest in the daily lives of people, but importantly, these trends ostensibly are generated by macro social tendencies. The general implication of the evidence is that people today are leading more individualized and privatized lives.

Many, if not most, elements of the current social transformations are attributed to globalization and its correlates. Broad-sweeping characterizations of a "radically changing world" can be found in most eras, not just the current one, and they often entail hyperbolic visions of the future that come to nothing. In the midst of such an era, the facts about ongoing trends are hard to discern and invariably a matter of interpretation. Broad claims can be construed as socially constructed narratives that tell plausible stories about the changing world by interweaving a range of observations, impressions, and interpretations. Facts or empirical claims are raw material, but these are arranged, ordered, and interconnected within an overarching interpretive frame. For example, one narrative may presume convergence and consistency between macro-level and micro-level conditions and processes, whereas another may presume fundamental tensions that create a significant problem of social order.

This chapter has two main parts. In the first, we argue that there is a prevailing, if not consensual, narrative about current social transformations. This narrative assimilates a range of facts and observations about how people organize their lives and careers, how employers treat employees, how citizens relate to their countries, and so forth. We term this an *individualization narrative.* It envisions and idealizes a thoroughly transactional world. An alternative narrative, which we term the *social-relational narrative,* envisions a quite different world and raises fundamental questions about the individualization narrative. These alternative narratives are important to highlight because they assume different types of social ties between people and social units and approach the larger problem of social order in a different way. In the second part of the chapter, we identify and compare different forms of person-to-group ties (commitment)—instrumental, affective, and normative—and show how the three are interrelated. This discussion frames our subsequent analyses of how transactional ties become relational ones.

WHAT IS CHANGING?

In this section, we document several changes or trends commonly associated with the transition from the twentieth to the early twenty-first century. These observations serve as grist for narrative mills. Evidence can be marshaled to support each of these points, although it is important to note that some are controversial and under debate. Most telling is the confluence and interrelatedness of these observations and what they tell us about the way our society is changing.

- Traditional employment contracts that provide job security have all but disappeared. At best, employers commit to enhancing employees' transferable (generalized) skills that they can take elsewhere when they are no longer needed. People fend for themselves in job markets and in their careers more than ever.
- Globalization, particularly in the area of technology, promotes more access to more information for more people around the world than ever before. Access to information is being "democratized," and the world is becoming "flatter" (Friedman 2005), which has important implications for political systems (Haas 2000).
- Because of available technological resources (the Internet), people can now connect with and form relations with many more people across geographic

and social boundaries. They are in contact with many others who are different from themselves. Yet individuals tend to have weak, fragile, and ever-changing social ties.

- Our daily lives are increasingly personalized, individualized, or privatized. People join fewer voluntary associations (Putnam 2000); they form and maintain fewer close ties, and significant numbers of people report not having anyone to confide in about important matters (McPherson, Smith-Lovin, and Brashears 2006). Technological innovations such as Xboxes, home gyms, and iPods facilitate and support private, personal time spent alone.

- There is an erosion of the capacity of the nation-state to provide equal access to the means of developing human and social capital. Nations struggle to protect their citizens from random disasters (such as hurricanes) and nonrandom threats (such as terrorism) and to mobilize citizens on behalf of collective goals (Haas 2000).

- Whereas inequalities between nations of the world are declining in some respects, social inequalities within many nations are becoming more pronounced. Significant populations are excluded from the opportunities generated by the other trends cited here—for example, access to employers that promote their skills and access to technologies for acquiring information are limited.

- Global warming is accelerating. It is estimated that by 2100 the earth's temperatures will rise up to eleven degrees Fahrenheit, causing extreme weather patterns, drought, glacial retreat, species extinction, and increased disease (Wigley and Raper 2001). This exerts more pressure on nation-states to organize collective action, on individuals to voluntarily change their behaviors, and on corporations to address social goals.

Thus, there are good reasons for believing that both the macro and micro conditions of social life are changing significantly and at the same time. Several of the observations involve micro conditions that directly affect people and how they relate to each other, while others involve macro conditions that imply a change in fundamental person-to-group ties. At the micro level, people experience on a regular, if not daily, basis greater access to information and expanded opportunities for interacting with others, but they form fewer close personal ties. At the macro level, large-scale social entities (nations, corporations, international organizations) face more difficult challenges but also more substantial constraints and more limited capacities to address them effectively (see, for example, Haas 2000; Scharpf and Schmidt 2000b; Fukuyama 2004). The relationships of people to their work organizations, local communities, and nations are presumably looser or more distant than they were even twenty years ago. Putnam (2000, 2007) frames the attendant problems of social order as being due to the fact that looser person-to-group ties promote weaker person-to-person ties, that is, interpersonal trust, reciprocity, and networks. We frame the problem as due to a macro-micro disconnect within which person-to-person interaction and ties do not produce and reproduce strong person-to-group ties.[1]

Implicit in the loosening or weakening of participation in or ties to traditional groupings (Putnam 2000) is also a growth of individual autonomy, freedom, and initiative. In being "freed" from extant ties—to corporations, communities, nations—people have more opportunities to create and sustain ties of their choice. This point is exemplified by the capabilities of the Internet, which enables people to become less dependent on particular social units. This reduces the capacity of given groups (communities, corporations, unions, nations) to mobilize collective action and to address some of the larger macro problems associated with the transformations. Thus, by reframing social transformations as a growing separation, disconnection, or disjuncture between the micro and macro conditions of human existence, it makes sense that person-to-group ties are both a fundamental part of the problem and, important for our purposes, a part of the solution. Alternative narratives, built around the observations listed in this section, offer different analyses and point to distinct ways in which problems of commitment and social order may play out in the twenty-first century.

NARRATIVES ABOUT SOCIAL TRANSFORMATIONS
What Is a Narrative?

According to *Webster's Unabridged Dictionary* (1997), a *narrative* is a story or account of events, experiences, actions, or trends based on factual as well as interpretive elements (see also Hall 1999). The concept of a narrative is most often associated with cultural analyses in sociology or postmodernist textual analyses in the humanities (Abbott 2007; Hall 1999). Narratives are not truths or descriptions, but rather conceptual devices that allow one to interweave objective conditions with subjective interpretations. Narratives are analogous to lenses: they bring into focus and sharpen some aspects of the world while downplaying or ignoring other aspects, and they impose coherence through extrapolation, reduction, and selective accentuation. We believe the idea of a narrative is a useful way to characterize broad-sweeping interpretations of the changes in the twenty-first century, in part because the factual bases are disputable and it is impossible to tell which interpretations are valid. Moreover, narratives create social realities that people act on as if they were true. Narratives have real consequences.

Many, if not most, interpretations of the social transformations of the twenty-first century converge around what can be termed an individualization narrative—namely, the broad idea that human lives are becoming individualized, privatized, and marketlike. The next section elaborates this individualization story about the contemporary world and compares it to an alternative narrative that we term the social-relational narrative. The idea here is that current trans-formations run counter to and "bump up" against the fundamental social nature of the human species.

The Individualization Narrative

From this interpretive framework, people today are construed as having a highly individualized and privatized existence in which they are focused on their own personal lives, caring little about the lives of others, caring even less about the employers they work for, the governments that ostensibly serve their needs and desires, or the communities in which they reside. Outside of a few close per-sonal ties, life within this narrative is likened to a grand spot market. Within this market environment, individuals pursue their own valued objects, goals, and experiences; instrumentalism, self-interest, and individual gratification reign supreme; ties to others and to organizations are transactional or contractual rather than emotional or relational; and trust and confidence in institutions is low. Market logic organizes and shapes most of human activity, and social interac-tions and ties are primarily instrumental transactions wherein individuals exchange valued goods.

Within this narrative, corporations dominate as mechanisms for achieving individualistic, personalized goals but have minimal social value beyond that. One implication is that corporations have little capacity to draw on reservoirs of symbolic support and commitment to promote collective action, because the ties of people to corporations are purely transactional, as are their ties to other people. At the societal level, economics trumps politics; at the individual level, the "I" trumps the "we" as individuals vie to maximize personal self-interest. An individualization narrative is implicit or explicit in much contemporary discourse about emerging trends of the twenty-first century. The narrative itself can have powerful effects on how people think about their social world, their place within it, and their ties to others. The bases of social order here are necessarily transactional, contractual, and, as we argue, precarious without significant person-to-group ties.

Changes in technology promote the infusion of market logic and individualization into new areas. Consider, for example, how many people now use the Internet to build personal relationships. Recent surveys in the United States suggest that more than 20 million people visit at least one online dating service each month.[2] *Online Dating Magazine* estimates that over 120,000 marriages take place each year as a result of online activity; the magazine also reports that one-third of adult Americans say they know someone who has used an online dating service. This typifies the individualization narrative in that dating and romance are market commodities that individuals consume in digital spot markets. Furthermore, corporate interest in such commoditization is driven by the revenue that accompanies private consumption.

Consider also the access that children have to computer games. The evidence indicates that children become conversant with computer technology at a young age and spend considerable time on websites. Many of these have significant educational value, but what is noteworthy is that spending time on a computer is a solitary, individualized activity. Miniclip is a website that provides a variety of games for children to play. These games provide performance feedback, and children can move through them at different levels of play. The games may promote various skills and transmit cultural values (having to do with individual performance and achievement), but typically children play alone. Another website, Webkins, allows children to play games alone or to find partners via the Internet. Here they learn that the Internet can be used to make contact with other people and interact with them. Overall, new technologies make possible more individualized and personalized lives in which contacts with many others are readily available, but these contacts and resulting ties are often shallow and episodic.

These examples also suggest a significant flowering of human choice, potential, and development. The individualization narrative is a story of individual freedom and expanding repertoires of human choice, occurring in the context of economic complexity, efficiency, and productivity. Individualization and privatization reverberate through modern lives. In fact, in this conceptual frame, relational ties are a threat to efficiency, if not also a reflection of individual innocence or stupidity. Recall in chapter 1 the response of Wall Street fund managers to Alex Rodriguez's decision to opt out of his baseball contract with the New York Yankees. In markets, ties to others or to organizations are a source of inefficiency, stickiness, or market failure; in organizations, they are a source of inertia or politicized behavior; and in nations, they are a source of political corruption.

As an illustration, witness the growth of legal and quasi-legal institutions and rules designed to prevent insider trading, the awarding of government contracts to political leaders' campaign donors, and noncompetitive contracting with suppliers, all of which involve relational ties that increase benefits to some at the expense of others. The common problem here is that relational ties among people ostensibly lead to favoritism, the abuse of power, and mutual back-scratching. The standard solution to such problems is to limit, monitor, or regulate the formation of relational ties, which often leads to an expanded administrative and legal apparatus (Anechiarico and Jacobs 1996).[3] The objective is to nurture and promote individualized action based on market principles.

Transactional ties are dynamic, malleable, and responsive to market principles. This narrative or characterization of the social world raises the question of whether people should or even can form and sustain social commitments to social units—from small groups to organizations, communities, and nations—as their lives become increasingly individualized and privatized. What groups or social entities provide people with a larger sense of meaning or foster a valued identity for individuals? Do the social objects of commitment, attachment, and the like take different forms, or do they become more and more localized? If so, how can larger overarching institutions and communities remain important sources of commitment, community, and individual sacrifice? How can organizations muster the power to mobilize individuals around collective purposes? An individualization narrative implies purely transactional answers to these sorts of questions and assumes that contractual ties (person-to-person or person-to-group) are sufficient to achieve collective as well as individual purposes in groups and organizations. In a larger sense, it suggests contractual solutions to the problem of social order.

The Social-Relational Narrative

The alternative narrative emphasizes the inherently social nature of the human species and our remarkable tendency to transform purely transactional ties into relational ties whereby the other and the relationship become objects of value in themselves. This narrative is less obvious, more subtle, and not as consistent with the market zeitgeist of the age as the individualization narrative.

From a social-relational narrative, the earlier observations reflect forces that run counter to the essential social or relational dimensions of human evolution, social history, and accumulated human experience. As social beings, people care about others and their community; their behavior is guided by other-regard and community-regard as well as self-interest. People are responsive to each other because they interact with each other and do things jointly in groups, organizations, communities, and nations. In the pursuit of common goals, individuals necessarily form relational ties. This tendency may stem from the evolutionary fitness of social relations and social organization (Turner 2002), from genetic machinery or wiring, or from the sedimentation of cultural and institutional practices over human history. Regardless of the sources, the social-relational narrative suggests that, in relations and groups, people's regard for others and for the interests of overarching organizations and communities reign supreme. Viewed from the social-relational narrative, individualization is depersonalizing and isolating. The transactional world envisioned by the individualization narrative is highly problematic in the context of a social-relational narrative.

A social-relational narrative implies that if organizational or institutional changes constrain or eliminate the relational ties in some areas, these are likely to reemerge at a subterranean level or in other realms of life where people have the opportunity to form and sustain such ties. People create and sustain relations or relational ties wherever they interact frequently with others. It is well known, for example, that social-relational ties start very shortly after birth. In fact, neonates synchronize their bodily movement with the structure and intonation of human voice within just a few hours following birth (Condon and Sanders 1974). Parent-child attachments shape human experience and learning from the very beginnings of life and constitute important components of human evolutionary adaptation (Baumeister and Leary 1995; Turner 2002). In the longer term, therefore, the social-relational dimension of human experience cannot be denied.

One implication of this, consistent with a variety of sociological research on economy and society (Swedberg 2003), is that people are likely to create tacit or implicit relations even in the purest of markets or privatized spheres. Thus, whereas social-relational ties to others and to social units may be suppressed by market forces or by rules, laws, and formal procedures, these institutional mechanisms have delimited effects as even these situations are penetrated by relational ties. Social relations have a chameleonic character, changing shape, color, and form as people mutually influence each other and nurture the relational side of social life.

A social-relational narrative, unlike an individualization one, implies a fundamental tension between individual, personal spheres of life and organizational, institutional spheres. Such tension has been a theme of sociology from the early days of the discipline (Durkheim 1893/1997; Weber 1918/1968; Marx 1867/1967; Simmel 1964). With an individualization narrative, this tension essentially disappears or becomes insignificant. The explanation for this is the alignment of interests between individuals and organizations. The aligning of the interests of individuals with the group is a standard solution to the problem of collective goods or, more generally, to the problem of social order. Adam Smith (1776/2007, 18) summarized the idea succinctly in his *Wealth of Nations,* writing: "It is not from the benevolence of the butcher, the brewer, or the baker, that we expect our dinner, but from their regard to their own interest. We address ourselves, not to their humanity but to their self-love, and never talk to them of our own necessities but of their advantages."

In contrast, the social-relational narrative interprets these trends as reflecting a growing separation and tension between everyday micro-sociological processes and large-scale macro processes. Thus, the micro and macro realms of human existence are diverging in the social-relational narrative, whereas they are converging in the individualization narrative. The implication of a greater disconnect between the macro and micro realms is that social relations and ties become more controllable from within at the micro level (endogenously), but less controllable from without at the macro level (exogenously). This also means that the capacity of larger institutions and organizations to control social and relational ties is diminished, whereas the autonomy and capacity of individuals to shape their local micro ties at will are enhanced. Paradoxically, individuals have more autonomy and freedom from macro-organizational constraints in a social-relational narrative than in an individualization narrative.

Applied to the forces of globalization, the individualization narrative extols the benefits of "freeing" individuals from existing institutional constraints, whereas the social-relational narrative emphasizes the problem of generating socially meaningful ties under these conditions. Thomas Friedman (2005) suggests, for example, that the most important change associated with globalization is the "leveling" or "democratizing" of access and opportunity in the areas of knowledge, finance, and employment. Increasing economic (corporate) globalization, in conjunction with Internet-related means and flows of communication, ostensibly empowers individuals in new and important ways across national and cultural boundaries. At the same time, these trends are weakening the control capacities of nations, corporations, and international organizations. New technologies of communication contribute to a growing disjuncture between the micro conditions of human lives and the macro conditions of their larger institutions. Thus, given the social transformations under way, traditional institutions and organizations such as nations, state governments, corporations, and unions may not have the same capacity to structure activities and influence members and citizens and to effectively shape events as they did in a more nationalized and regionalized world.

In this regard, the evidence on "declining social capital" in American society concerns primarily ties to such traditional formal groups and organizations—political, religious, and economic (see Putnam 2000). There are good reasons, however, for surmising that other groupings that are more informal, flexible, and fluid, as well as less visible, are being generated as people are "freed" from certain constraints as a result of globalization and associated processes. Internet technologies are an important piece of this. In fact, the emergence of these new groupings figures in one of the main lines of critique directed at Putnam's "declining social capital" thesis (see Stolle and Hooghe 2004). Putnam's (2000, 2007) concept of social capital is primarily about person-to-person ties; while these may emanate from common group memberships, he neglects to consider the direct ties that people may feel to group or organizational entities as such. Strong person-to-group ties may reduce one's sense of social isolation, regardless of how extensive and deep one's person-to-person ties are to other members. With strong person-to-group ties that bind large populations, fewer close personal ties or sparser interpersonal networks may not have the negative effects often attributed to them.[4]

In our theorizing, person-to-group ties are produced and reproduced endogenously through the social interactions of people working to achieve individual and collective ends. Person-to-group ties have a person-to-person foundation and, in this sense, an important bottom-up dimension. Virtual social interactions, involving brief episodes, may be sufficient to sustain such ties.[5] Thus, the relevant group objects of commitment may remain nations, corporations, professions, unions, or other historic social groupings, but even these have to be endogenously generated and regenerated by individuals interacting in ways that affirm and produce shared or joint benefits that they cannot accomplish in their individualized and privatized social worlds. If nations, corporations, unions, or communities make this likely, people will give due attention to the welfare of those social units. If not, ties to such social units will lack the capacity to generate sacrifice when it is needed for positive collective purposes. With this issue in mind, the next section contrasts different forms of commitment.

FORMS OF COMMITMENT

The best-known conceptual framework for forms of person-to-group commitment was provided in the work of Rosabeth Kanter (1968, 1972). She contrasted three forms of commitment: continuance, normative, and affective. *Continuance commitment* is the propensity of actors to remain a member of the group or organization because of the individual benefits they derive from membership or the opportunity costs of leaving the group or organization. Continuance is instrumental commitment and entails a rational choice. The strength of this form of commitment is contingent on the value of the benefits received from the focal group vis-à-vis what is available elsewhere. Among the three everyday examples discussed in chapter 1, the hair salon and the coffee shop should foster minimal continuance commitment because there are many alternative sources of the benefits they provide and it is easy to move to other salons or coffee shops. Instrumental or continuance commitment should be stronger in a neighborhood because, while there may be equal or better neighborhoods, the costs of moving are typically significant.

Continuance or instrumental commitments imply a market-oriented and transactional relationship between the group and the individual (Emerson 1972b): a group or organization benefits individuals, and they, in turn, contribute something to the organization or group. People stay or continue their relationship to or membership in a group or organization as long as it provides benefits better than could be found elsewhere. Such ties therefore are relatively shallow and potentially unstable. A "better offer" readily produces an exit from the current group or organization. One reason is that the existing group or organization adds no value itself to individuals' rational calculus of where to find the best outcomes. Instrumental commitments are the dominant form assumed by the individualization narrative, which essentially envisions a world of rational actors without group-oriented loyalties. Insofar as people develop continuance commitments to an organization at all, there is nothing special or attractive about that organization beyond the instrumental benefits received by individual members; it is a purely transactional tie. Normative and affective commitments differ from continuance commitment in that the group or organization takes on value in itself.[6]

Normative and affective commitments involve relational ties, meaning that they are partly or wholly non-instrumental. *Normative commitment* is defined as a sense of moral or normative obligation to a group or organization (Kanter 1968, 1972; Meyer, Allen, and Gellatly 1990). This form of commitment involves a belief that it is right and proper to conform to the rules and to serve group or collective interests. People with a normative commitment are motivated not by their own individual interest per se, but by their sense of duty and obligation to the collective goals. Such social commitments are institutionally based and grounded in taken-for-granted elements of the social situation. It may be possible to trace such commitments to a rational foundation (see Hechter 1990); however, there is no decision or explicit choice necessarily implied because this form of commitment reflects "the way things are" and "the way most people think they should be." Normative commitments legitimate a group or organization, its mission or goals, and its structure (hierarchy) for achieving these (Selznick 1992). The organization, its mission, and its structure are thereby cast in moral terms.

The strength of normative social commitments reflects the degree to which people perceive an affinity between themselves and a group's or organization's mission, values, and goals. Applied to the three everyday examples in chapter 1, the hair salon and coffee shop may reveal taken-for-granted practices or norms that make those units more attractive than otherwise (Berger and Luckmann 1966), but these effects are probably small. A neighborhood, however, should promote stronger normative commitment, especially if there is a formal or informal association of residents that organizes collective efforts and invokes community norms. Employees in a corporation develop stronger normative commitments to the degree that they come to understand and believe in the mission of the corporation and view the corporation as representing or instantiating larger values they concur with. In this way, normative commitments tend to be cognitive, although, as suggested later, they can have either an instrumental or an affective foundation.

An *affective commitment* involves an emotional tie to the group or organization (Lawler 1992). Such a tie is indicated to the degree that affiliation or membership is valued in its own right, as an end in itself. This intrinsic value of membership is based on the positive feelings (such as pleasure, enjoyment, enthusiasm, elation) generated by participation in group activities, as well as the degree to which the group or organization is self-defining and self-enhancing. With an affective commitment, the group membership or affiliation has become an expressive object, defining who one is or wants to be, and a symbol or emblem for a set of valued associations with similar others. Being a member is a positive statement about who one is, what one has done or accomplished, and one's status and prestige. Individual feelings can be construed as internal, self-generated rewards and punishments, and affective commitments develop when these are associated with group memberships or affiliations (see Lawler 2001).

We conceive of social commitments as person-to-person or person-to-group ties that have significant affective and normative components. People value the ties as ends in themselves—that is, they are expressive and self-defining, at least to some degree. At the same time, social commitments have instrumental components because of the structural interdependencies and incentives that make social interactions profitable or beneficial for individuals. Instrumental conditions account for the initiation of interaction and the formation of a transactional tie. We contend, however, that the rational-choice, self-interest-oriented, transactional elements are insufficient to produce what we define as a social commitment, which requires expressive elements, in particular emotion and affect.

It should be evident that the individualization narrative treats instrumental commitments as the most effective method of connecting persons and groups (the aligning of interests), whereas a social-relational narrative implies that normative and affective ties are most effective (the aligning of values and emotions). In the context of widespread individualization of human lives, instrumental, transactional ties become dominant and crowd out normative and affective ties or commitments. Social commitments appear as anachronisms, except in very small groups with dense patterns of interaction and close personal ties among members (for example, families or friendship groups). In the context of a social-relational narrative, however, it is assumed that people seek and find social commitments beyond their close, personal ties with particular others, searching among either extant, available groups or ones that are self-generated and emergent. Thus, if there is a decline in the areas of life where people can create and sustain social commitments, then they will find ways to re-create these commitments elsewhere, or they will transform instrumental ties into normative or affective ones. Instrumental commitments may become partly emotional or affective if group membership is a persistent source of positive feelings and emotions, and they may become partly normative if the membership is a source of moral obligation. This raises a question about whether there are causal connections between the three forms of commitment. The next section introduces the interrelationships that frame subsequent analyses in this volume.

How Are Forms of Commitment Interrelated?

There is an important body of research on the three forms of commitment in the field of organizations (see, for example, Mathieu and Zajac 1990; Lawler 1992; Yoon and Thye 2002). Reviews of this research literature support the notion that there are multiple dimensions of commitment, while also indicating that the tripartite distinction proposed by Kanter does not hold up in all cases. The research tends to almost universally find two operative dimensions of organizational commitment: one instrumental (transactional) and one non-instrumental (relational). The relational form involves either normative or affective commitments or some combination of the two. An extensive review and meta-analysis by John Meyer, Natalie Allen, and Ian Gellatly (1990) demonstrates, however, that the affective dimension is the most consistent and reliable counterpoint to the instrumental dimension of commitment. Based on these results and a recent theoretical elaboration of organizational commitment (Yoon and Lawler 2006), we treat instrumental and affective forms of commitment as most fundamental, and normative commitments as derivative of these two forms. This has the merit of distinguishing, but also integrating, rational and nonrational foundations for normative constraints. Moreover, we argue that instrumental commitments set the stage for affective commitments—a central claim or assumption in subsequent chapters of this volume. The interconnections are portrayed in figure 2.1.

The figure illustrates that social units are fundamentally both instruments through which individuals achieve goals and promote their rational self-interests and expressive entities in that they reflect positive feelings about who individuals are in given social situations. In other words, organizations and communities are sources of payoff, profit, and reward, but they also invoke positive feelings and emotional experiences, along with related identities. You may enjoy the salary and benefits from your university position, but you may also especially enjoy being a Hawkeye, Bear, or Gamecock. Using still other terms for these benefits, the former are interest-based and the latter are identity-based, and they have been shown to have distinct effects on individual and collective behavior (see Anthony 2005). Finally, the distinction between instrumental and expressive dovetails with the differences between transactional and relational ties and between rational-choice and institutional approaches to norms, as well as with a key distinction made by Parsons (1951) in his analysis of social relations.[7]

Figure 2.1   Interrelationship of Forms of Commitment

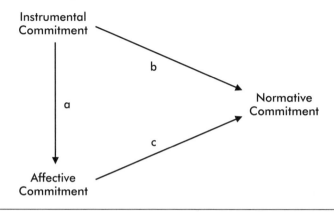

Source: Authors' compilation.

Overall, there are good theoretical reasons for presuming that the instrumental and expressive are distinctive and more fundamental than the normative, but also that they give rise to normative social commitments.

The idea that norms have an instrumental or expressive foundation has a long history in sociology and social psychology (Weber 1918/1968; Durkheim 1915; Parsons 1951; Collins 1975). Link *b* in figure 2.1 reflects the idea that norms and normative commitments develop from instrumental conditions that make joint efforts and collective goods difficult to achieve without external enforcement, that is, without monitoring and sanctioning of those who shirk their collective responsibility (Hechter 1987; Coleman 1990). People invest in enforcement mechanisms insofar as the subsequent benefits outweigh the costs they incur to support group norms. Link *c* suggests that norms also may emerge and be maintained owing to affective sentiments about shared memberships or common affiliations with other people. Finally, link *a* posits a causal path from instrumental to affective commitment in order to represent the "fact" that affective ties may emerge as a by-product of the instrumental conditions that bring the same people together around joint efforts or tasks. Figure 2.1 captures our argument that affective and rational-choice processes are complementary foundations for the emergence of social institutions (Hechter 1990).[8]

The upshot is that the simple, parsimonious framework in figure 2.1 conceptualizes and elaborates further the social commitment dimension of the problem of social order. Social commitments involve the strength of links *a* and

c, that is, the degree to which instrumental commitments give rise to affective ones and affective ones generate stronger normative commitments. It is this general process that leads actors to accord expressive value to social units. The individualization narrative presumes that only link b is important and that it overrides links a and c in most areas of life. With the social-relational narrative, links a and c represent an important antidote or counterpoint to the widespread individualizing or privatizing of people's lives. Thus, if instrumental conditions generate affective ties to persons and social units, as we argue, then it is plausible that this also is how social-relational ties with non-instrumental properties develop even in the context of a highly individualized social context. If affective processes also promote group-based self-definitions and stronger identification with particular social units, then actions that serve the group interests are partly about who one is, not just about what one gets. Links a and c, therefore, are pathways through which people create and sustain social commitments in the context of an increasingly individualized social world. On the most general level, these pathways represent our proposed solution to the problem of commitment and social order. Future chapters flesh out the theoretical foundations for this general solution. In the next chapter, we elaborate the role of emotion and affect in order to put our theoretical position about the centrality of affect in context and to set the stage for presenting the theory of social commitments in chapter 4.

CONCLUSIONS

Modern modes of communication have made it possible for separated or isolated individuals to find and interact with others who have a common interest, to activate multiple group memberships or affiliations, to organize their work and leisure activities, and to regularly cross national and cultural boundaries, both cognitively and behaviorally (if not physically). These activities involve empowered individuals who make choices or decisions for themselves, who have ties to larger organizations but are not captive to them, and who cannot be controlled by institutional constraints and rules without their consent. In such a world, social commitments—in particular the ties of people to social units—become more problematic. There is essentially a looser connection between the micro and macro realms of human experience, and the micro realms loom as especially important given the expanded choices and opportunities available to individuals. At the micro level, people themselves generate and sustain social commitments in highly individualized and privatized social worlds. It is therefore plausible that in the modern world larger problems of social order are manifest and resolved as much at the local or micro level as at the macro level.

A disjuncture between the micro-level experiences of individuals and the macro conditions of their lives raises the classic question of Thomas Hobbes (1651/1985): "How is social order possible?" There are many reasons and pieces of empirical data suggesting that the social world is undergoing a major transformation in the early part of the twenty-first century. Many of these changes are at the macro level—for example, increasing economic globalization and political interdependence among societies or states, along with new communication technologies—but these are coterminous with changes at the micro level, such as the increasing choices and opportunities for people to interact with diverse others and to move from place to place or from organization to organization. For Hobbes, the "freeing" of individuals from traditional constraints would be a source of chaos and disorder, because this would unleash the self-interested, avaricious, and distrustful impulses of humanity. A new social contract would be needed to bridge and realign the micro and macro conditions of people's lives. Indeed, contractual solutions of one sort or another have received considerable attention over the last twenty years or so (see, for example, Hechter 1987; Coleman 1990; Fehr and Gintis 2007)—during the very same period when the major social transformations became more apparent and obvious, as well as a topic of conversation, analysis, and debate.

In contrast, we suggest a noncontractual solution to the problem of social order, reconceiving it as primarily a problem of person-to-group ties or commitments. In these terms, contractual solutions focus on instrumental, rationally based action and incentives to motivate and sustain behaviors that serve collective interests while also serving individual interests. The operative term here is *alignment*—specifically of individual and group interests. Alignment tends to require mutual adjustments (implicit or explicit negotiation) on the part of both individuals and groups, and as long as the terms of the contract are observed, order and stability ensue. This sort of solution is not stable in the long term, however, because structures and related incentive conditions are likely to change, giving either the organization or the individual the motivation to leave or to terminate the contractual tie. Our noncontractual solution proposes that the person-to-group tie can withstand such exogenous forces, in particular changes in the incentives upon which social order is based, insofar as the group itself becomes intrinsically and expressively valued, that is, people develop a social commitment to the group. Emotion and affect are integrally involved in this process.

Thus, subsequent chapters analyze the conditions under which social commitments tend to develop and be sustained. Just as Hobbes's people in a "state of nature" come to realize that they can receive protection by forming an association, people in our theorizing realize that they benefit by interacting with certain others. The incentives may involve something as simple as good coffee in the morning (see chapter 1) or as important as a career in the health services industry. We assume that a decision to join an organization or to interact with particular others is, at the inception, a rational, profit-maximizing choice. Beyond inception, however, other social processes become important if people interact with others repeatedly in the same group and if they experience everyday positive feelings (joy, pleasure, enthusiasm) as a result. Our concern is with understanding these other social processes, specifically those that build on and complement, but also transcend, the rational-instrumental.

CHAPTER 3

Affect in Social Interaction

The twentieth-century bank robber and escape artist Willie Sutton, the original "Slick Willie," robbed nearly one hundred banks during his thirty-year career, from 1920 to 1952.[1] When asked why he robbed banks, Sutton famously responded: "Because that's where the money is!" This quote, now known as "Sutton's Law," expresses a simple principle that has found its way into speeches and articles on topics ranging from bond issues to medical practice, religious matters, and, in surprisingly few cases, bank robberies. Simply put, it directs one to check the most obvious answers first.[2] However, Sutton never actually gave this amusing and suggestive reply to the question of why he robbed banks. The quote was manufactured by an aspiring young reporter who needed to sharpen his story. What Willie Sutton actually said when asked why he robbed banks was, "Because I enjoyed it. I loved it. I was more alive when I was inside a bank, robbing it, than at any other time in my life. I enjoyed everything about it so much that one or two weeks later I'd be out looking for the next job." The final irony about Sutton's Law is that even though it suggests that one should check the obvious, the real reason Sutton robbed banks was completely non-obvious. His commitment to robbing banks was measured, not in legal tender, but in emotional currency.

The story of Willie Sutton illustrates the power of emotions to motivate behavior. On any given day people are likely to experience a wide variety of feelings, including elation, frustration, sadness, joy, guilt, and happiness. The emotions produced may be fleeting or persistent, mild or intense, displayed or inhibited, and they can be triggered by any number of sources. Emotions are peculiar in that, for the most part, neither they nor our reactions to them are typically under our voluntary control. For example, you probably could not work yourself into a rage, but once enraged, you might not be able to control your behavior. By the same token, it is not likely that you could will yourself out of depression or experience intense fear by simply thinking of a fearful event. Emotions are fundamentally triggered by social situations and our interactions with individuals or things in our environment. When we feel an emotion, we feel it all over, that is, from "head to toe" (Damasio 1999).

In broader terms, the Willie Sutton story suggests that people are fundamentally emotional, affective beings. If anything is clear from recent work in neuroscience, it is this point (see, for example, LeDoux 1996; Damasio 1999). People continually feel and emote; what they see, how they see it, and their response to what they see are all intertwined with their emotional states. Emotions entail neurological, cognitive, and behavioral elements, and they are implicated in virtually everything people do.[3] Antonio Damasio's (1999) analysis of neurological research affirms the centrality of the emotional dimension to human lives. Of particular note, his analysis indicates that when people "feel feelings," they become aware of the distinction between self and the world external to them. This means that emotional states of the brain are intricately involved in the formation of the self, which is a counterpoint to the long history of cognitively oriented analyses of self and identity in psychology and sociology. Damasio claims further that when a stimulus enters the brain, an emotional response to it tends to precede the cognitive processing of that stimulus, suggesting the inseparability of the emotional from the cognitive (Damasio 1999). In opening a 2003 work, Damasio makes a general observation about the relative neglect of emotional phenomena:

> Feelings of pain or pleasure or some quality in between are the bedrock of our minds. We often fail to notice this simple reality because mental images of the objects and events that surround us, along with the images of the words and sentences that describe them, use up so much of our overburdened attention. But there they are, feelings of myriad emotions and related states, the continuous musical line of our minds. . . .
>
> Given the ubiquity of feelings, one would have thought that their science would have been elucidated long ago—what feelings are, how they work, what they mean—but this is hardly the case. (Damasio 2003, 3)

If emotions are such a central feature of the human species, they also should be crucial to understanding the problems of social order associated with periods of major social transformation. Affectively based solutions to the problem of social order, however, would need to address a difficult, micro-to-macro issue: how do feelings experienced at the individual level become relevant to people's feelings or sentiments about a group, organization, community, or nation?

Émile Durkheim (1915) and George Homans (1950) both had answers to this question, though from quite different perspectives. Focusing on order (solidarity) at the macro level, Durkheim emphasized the emotions people experience in joint activities that reflect and celebrate a larger community. More specifically, his argument, based on knowledge of the preliterate societies of his day, was that collective religious activity (rituals) are an integrating force owing to the emotional effects (effervescence, uplift, excitement) of repeated ritual activity done in concert with others. These joint activities affirm the objective and overarching nature of the group affiliation (society), making it salient as an external force or constraint (Durkheim 1915).

Homans (1950) examined how relations form, a micro variant of the problem of order. He argued that three dimensions, applicable to any social situation, account for the emergence of stable relationships: the nature of the activities that people are engaged in; how often they interact with each other; and the sentiments of affection or sympathy that people develop toward one another. The strength of social relations is based on the frequency of interaction directed at task activities and the affective sentiments that people develop toward each other as a result of those interactions. Durkheim and Homans considered affective ties crucial to macro or micro orders, respectively, but for Homans these ties were between people (P-P ties), whereas for Durkheim the ties were person-to-group (P-G ties). Despite their theoretical differences, they shared the general idea that social orders are based on repeated social activities that foster positive affect.

This chapter analyzes various roles played by affect in social interactions at the micro level. An extensive body of theory and research on emotion has emerged in psychology and sociology, especially over the last thirty years. Yet there are many unresolved issues about the concept and role of emotions. There is little consensus on how many emotions there are, or which ones are fundamental (Kemper 1987; Watson and Tellegen 1985; Izard 1991; Scheff 1990), on how cognition and emotion are interrelated (Forgas, Williams, and Wheeler 2001), or on which emotions are culturally specific and which have universal, cross-cultural features (Izard 1991; Scherer 1984).[4] Some of these issues are rather fundamental to an understanding of emotional phenomena. This chapter is not intended to address all or even most of these issues, but rather aims to cut a pathway through these conceptual issues to set the context for chapter 4, where we theorize how and when emotions promote person-to-group commitments. Thus, it is a selective review of psychological and sociological literature on emotion. The goals of the chapter are to point the reader to relevant themes in the literature, identify the varied effects that emotions have in social situations, and place our own approach and focus in this larger theoretical context. To achieve these objectives, we identify and compare different approaches to the role of affect in social interaction.

APPROACHES TO UNDERSTANDING AFFECT

We adapt a classificatory framework put forth in a previous paper (Lawler and Thye 1999). This framework organizes work on emotions around affect's three points of entry into social interactions: interaction context (affect as built into cultural norms or structural positions), interaction process (affect as a part of how people communicate and interpret information as they interact), and interaction outcomes (affect as a product of the interaction). Affect at any of these junctures could have effects on social order at micro levels. Using this tripartite distinction, we identify six approaches, two of which fall within each of these rubrics. We briefly introduce these approaches and then elaborate them later in the chapter.

The interaction context includes cultural norms about the expression of emotion and structural arrangements that are likely to produce feelings. A normative approach (Hochschild 1979, 1983) holds that emotions are shaped by norms or rules of behavior and specifies which emotions are appropriate to express and which are not in a given context. A structural approach (Collins 1975; Kemper 1978) examines how status or power positions (say, between manager and employee) affect the emotions that are felt or expressed in interactions and the impact of these feelings on the capacity of people in a hierarchy to work together. The common idea of interaction-context approaches is that cultural and structural patterns have direct effects on the sort of emotions people are likely to feel, and especially on those they are likely to express. The interaction context contains the constraints and opportunities for emotional expressions.

Interaction-process approaches analyze the role of affect in information processing and signaling. One goal is to examine emotions as signals, to others or to self. The signaling function of emotions may reveal intentions and communicate trustworthiness or affirm self-other identities in social interactions (Heise 1979; Frank 1988). A second goal is to examine how and when emotions generate cognitive adjustments in interpreting information, such as becoming more optimistic or pessimistic about future events or engaging in more global processing of information (see Isen 1987; Bower 1991). Overall, emotions—whether felt or expressed—inform people of how their interaction is progressing and what they can expect in the future.[5]

An interaction-outcome approach implicitly or explicitly addresses the effects of emotions on social cohesion. Our own approach falls here. The idea is that any social interaction can go well or badly, from a casual contact between a customer and clerk to a conversation between a boss and employee. Thus, a success-failure dimension is applicable broadly to any episode of social interaction and not limited to explicit task activities. If an interaction episode goes well, people feel good; if it goes badly, they feel bad. The social-cohesion approach contends that outcome-generated affect, under some conditions, triggers perceptions and sentiments about social units or groups that may strengthen or weaken social commitments (Collins 1981; Lawler and Yoon 1996). We theorize this process in the next chapter. An attribution approach (Weiner 1986) examines how people interpret or ascribe causes to these feelings; we suggest that social units are a plausible cause of individual feelings. The following sections identify exemplars of the theory and research associated with each approach.[6]

Interaction-Context Approaches

A normative approach to the interaction context capitalizes on the insight that most, if not all, social situations evoke expectations about the sort of emotions that are appropriate to experience or publicly display (Hochschild 1979). The norms for displaying emotions in a courtroom, poker game, wedding, funeral, or riot are socially defined and circumscribed. Emotion norms for business meetings typically call for dispassionate problem-solving. Displays that are consistent with the emotion norms both affirm and reestablish those norms while creating an emotional tone or prevailing emotional environment that affects all the individuals who are involved.

Those who adopt the normative approach tend to view emotions as socially constructed, displayed, and managed in the context of the roles, positions, identities, or categories that people occupy (Clark 1990; Gordon 1990). The norms are exogenous (cultural) expectations that are translated and used by people in their local interactions. Emotion norms can be thought of as well-worn scripts.[7] Why do people who attend faith healing revivals physically collapse or produce writhing displays of emotion when the minister touches them? Is it really the case that everyone touched is so overwhelmed that they can no longer control their body? Probably not! It is much more likely that people collapse and put on vibrant emotional displays because that is the script for the context—behavior that is expected and affirmed by others who did the same thing before them. To act otherwise creates a breach that violates the emotion norms for that context.

Much of the research on emotion in the normative tradition has focused on situations that elicit emotion but, unlike this example, prohibit it from being displayed. When there is a discrepancy between the emotions we experience and those we may appropriately display, we experience what Peggy Thoits (1985, 1990) calls "emotional deviance," and we tend to regulate or control our feelings through "emotion management." In her study of airline attendants, Arlie Russell Hochschild (1979, 1983) documents the frequent experience of strong emotions by flight attendants as a result of the behavior of rude travelers; however, because of occupational norms, they are trained to inhibit or mask their true feelings. She finds that flight attendants "manage" their emotions and deal with this tension in two primary ways: deep acting, which occurs when individuals consciously attempt to regulate their physiological activity ("just calm down and breathe slowly") or shift their focus of attention ("just ignore it and you will feel better"); and surface acting, which involves changing one's outward behavior with the hope of altering inner feelings. For example, flight attendants who force themselves to smile after being insulted report that they actually feel better.

New research on emotion from neuroscientists documents the mechanisms for how this works. When one smiles, the muscles at the corners of the mouth, brow, and forehead are activated. This action causes the brain to release endorphins that trigger a neuron-chemical response with analgesic effects, such as reducing pain and providing a sense of overall well-being (Damasio 1999). Thus, when emotion norms and felt emotions are at variance, coping strategies can regulate feelings by altering the body or brain physiology. Hochschild's work suggests that emotion norms on airplanes contribute to the local social order by increasing the predictability and stability of emotion displays for both airline employees and customers.

A structural approach to interaction context starts with the idea that emotions emanate in part from power and status positions. Individuals with more power or status are likely to experience different emotions than individuals with lower power or status, and under some conditions they may be more likely to express them. The general hypothesis is stated succinctly by Randall Collins (1975): giving orders makes people feel "up" or "good"; taking orders makes them feel "down" or "bad." Distinct emotional reactions such as these are an obvious threat to order-related phenomena, such as cooperation, collaboration, and cohesion. In this sense, emotions may be important to an understanding of the negative effects of social inequality on social order at the micro or even macro levels. We address this general issue in chapter 8.

Research on networks of social exchange has examined the effects of power on emotion. Power is defined as a structurally based potential that allows some people to benefit at the expense of others (Emerson 1972b; Willer and Anderson 1981). The classic example of a structural power difference is a teenage dating network, A-B-C, in which the centrally located B has the option of dating two people who each have no dating alternatives. Assuming that B can date only one person on any given night, A or C must always be excluded because they have no alternatives, but B will always have a partner, assuming that A and C would prefer to go on a date rather than stay at home. B is in a position of high power. The hypothesis is that such structural power positions have an impact on the emotions that people experience in interactions with each other.

Willer, Lovaglia, and Markovsky (1997) tested this proposition directly. They measured the emotions of all three actors in a setting where the three people in the A-B-C network could exchange resources with one another. The results show that B tended to report strong positive emotions following exchanges, while A and C reported negative emotional reactions (for similar findings, see Lawler and Yoon 1993, 1996). Edward Lawler and Jeongkoo Yoon (1996) observe further that unequal power in an exchange situation reduces the capacity of people to reach solutions and develop cohesive relations. The research program of Linda Molm (1997) adds that it is not just power that matters, but the source or basis of power. She compared rewards and punishments across a series of experiments and found that a unit of punishment decreases satisfaction more than a unit of reward increases satisfaction. In short, negative outcomes have stronger emotional effects than positive outcomes, a finding that is consistent with research on collective action (Komorita and Parks 1996), exchange networks (Thye, Lovaglia, and Markovsky 1997), and behavioral economics (Thaler 1980). Overall, research documents different emotional responses for those in higher and lower power positions in a network and also suggests that these emotional reactions pose a problem of order at the micro level.

Such effects also emerge under status inequalities. Cecilia Ridgeway and Cathryn Johnson (1990) assert that people with positive status characteristics (for example, those who are highly educated or have prestigious occupations) are assumed to be more competent and that, as a result, they receive more positive feedback from group interactions and encounter fewer disagreements from others. Lower-status individuals tend to receive more criticism for expressing their ideas overall and to blame themselves for the criticism. Thus, differential performance expectations not only are a basis for differential influence but also promote patterns of feedback that lead higher-status individuals to experience more positive feelings and less negative ones than lower-status individuals.

Theodore Kemper (1978, 1987, 1990) has developed an overarching theory directed at both power and status inequalities. He emphasizes changes in power and status. People whose power or status increases feel positive emotions, whereas those whose power or status decreases feel negative emotions. Kemper predicts distinct emotions for power or status. With regard to changes in power, he argues that an increase in relative power results in feelings of security, whereas a decrease in relative power leads to fear or anxiety. With regard to status, an increase yields satisfaction or happiness, while a decrease produces shame, anger, or depression. (Kemper 1978, 1990). The shift in a person's power or status can happen in two principal ways: directly if the person's own power or status goes up, and indirectly if the power or status of another person is reduced. In both scenarios, the result is positive feelings.[8] Overall, Kemper addresses how power and status dynamics in the context of social inequality generate contrasting emotional reactions by lower- and higher-ranking persons. His theory pinpoints some of the emotionally based obstacles to cooperation and threats to social order given inequalities of status and power.

To summarize, there are two broad themes that treat emotions as an integral part of an interaction context. The normative theme indicates that social contexts are imbued with norms or informal rules about the emotions that are experienced and expressed. It points to the capacity of the social context to shape the emotions that people experience and display in interaction with others in that context. Common or coordinated emotional feelings are one basis for predictable, orderly patterns of social interaction. The structural theme points, however, to an important obstacle or challenge to orderly patterns of social interaction: power and status hierarchies generate different emotional responses from those who are higher or lower in the structure. People in advantaged positions experience positive feelings, whereas those in disadvantaged positions experience negative feelings. This is a divisive force insofar as these structural conditions reduce the capacity of those at different levels of hierarchy to collaborate and engage in collective action.

Interaction-Process Approaches

Applied to interaction processes, emotions serve as information that people process or use to make inferences about the other, the self, and the situation. As people interact with others, they sense their own emotional reactions and use this as information to make inferences about themselves and others. They also interpret the other person's emotional states and make inferences about that person's intentions and future behavior. A person who becomes angry when mildly criticized by a friend may infer that he and the friend are drifting apart, or perhaps that he overreacted and needs to do something to repair the tie. A colleague rolling her eyes as you make a point in a group discussion conveys displeasure unconsciously or unintentionally. The orienting assumption of interaction-process approaches is that emotions convey meaningful information to self and other and that they also have an impact on how people interpret information.

This section describes research that treats emotions as signals to self, as signals to the other, and as sources of cognitive adjustment.

SIGNALS TO SELF   Recent work in evolutionary sociology and neurobiology suggests a fundamental role for emotions in the history of human development. Jonathan Turner (2000, 2007) claims that the human capacity to emote in differentiated and fine-grained ways is what distinguished early hominids from other great apes. Emotions, he asserts, operated as a catalyst that allowed for the evolution among early hominids of higher-level phenomena such as speech, culture, and organization. The capacity to detect one's own affective states and also recognize the affective cues of others were crucial to such evolutionary developments. In short, emotional sophistication allowed our ancestors (but not other apes) to increase their capacity to organize socially, an important requirement as apes and monkeys were forced to move out of the trees and into the savannah.

Recent work in neurobiology dovetails with Turner's general claim. Damasio (1999; Damasio et al. 2000) suggests that neurological secretions in the brain (such as dopamine, epinephrine, or oxytocin) generate the "feeling of feelings" and that these are the foundation for human consciousness. Emotions bring about an awareness of the self juxtaposed with external objects or events—they make us socially aware. One implication is that this capacity for emotions promotes not only feelings directed at the self (pride, depression) but also feelings directed at others (gratitude, fear). Broadening and extending this point, we find it plausible that neurological processes foster awareness of and attention to the group affiliations that are part of the context within which emotions are experienced, and that they therefore bear on person-to-group ties or commitments.

Affect control theory from sociology explicitly construes emotions as signals to the self about ongoing social interactions with one or more others. The theory assumes that individuals carry with them a set of fundamental meanings about themselves, other persons, objects, and behaviors (Smith-Lovin and Heise 1988; Robinson and Smith-Lovin 2006). Fundamental meanings refer to the evaluation, potency, and activity of a person, object, or action. For example, most individuals probably believe that doctors, birthday cakes, and volunteer work are somewhat positive, strong, and active. Transient meanings are impressions gleaned in particular situations, and these may be consistent or inconsistent with fundamental meanings. Interactions with a doctor, for example, may not be consistent with fundamental meanings, as when a doctor acts too friendly or appears uncertain of his knowledge. Overall, the theory explains in some detail how individuals manage their behavior to maintain fundamental meanings in the context of social interactions—that is, how they resolve inconsistencies between fundamental and transient meanings. Emotions are crucial signals to the self in this process.

A key assertion of affect control theory is that individuals occupy roles with identities and these role identities are the baselines from which they interpret or infer transient meanings and experience emotions. Identities tend to determine which emotions they will experience. An emotional reaction occurs when an individual experiences an event and then assesses how well it fits her or his fundamental meanings of the people, identities, and actions involved. When the fit between the individual's fundamental understanding and transient impressions is good, the emotions felt are consistent with the identity. To illustrate, consider a community volunteer (a person with a positive self-identity) who receives an award recognizing her service (experiences a positive, confirming event). Here the fundamental meaning associated with the identity is consistent with the positive transient meaning, and the theory predicts that the feelings states associated with that identity will ensue. The larger implication is that social orders are generally more stable and enduring at the micro level when fundamental sentiments and transient impressions are consistent for all those in interaction and when adjustments are made quickly in response to inconsistencies. If roles and identities are undergoing substantial change, as is typical during major social transformations, one would expect inconsistencies and disorder to be a more common experience in local interactions.[9]

SIGNALS TO OTHERS   The communication of emotion to others is the focus of Robert Frank's (1988, 1993) theory of moral sentiments. He suggests that emotional expressions can resolve problems of social order (cooperation) posed by a social dilemma by fostering prosocial behaviors reciprocated over time (Frank 1988). The reason is that emotional reactions such as love, sorrow, and sympathy are powerful incentives that help to keep self-interest in check. A wife who is considering an affair, for example, may refrain out of love or respect for her husband. Workers who receive cash payments may nevertheless report all income to the Internal Revenue Service out of fear, guilt, or a sense of national loyalty. Individuals may work on community projects or contribute to public goods because of strong affective ties to their home, block, neighborhood, or city. In this way, emotional and affective processes short-circuit and regulate the desire for immediate self-gratification and lead individuals to adopt a longer time horizon and a more relational orientation.

In Frank's theory, however, the experience of emotion itself is not sufficient to fully solve problems of social commitment. A solid marriage is possible only if both people eschew external temptations. Long-term committed relationships emerge when (1) each party experiences commitment-inducing emotions, and (2) those emotions can be detected by others with the same capacity. Micro-level social interactions are central here. The first trait gives people the capacity to control passing temptations; the second ensures that individuals with high "moral fiber" are likely to locate similar others. Frank argues that individuals communicate their emotional makeup through subtle behavioral gestures and cues that have developed through evolutionary mechanisms. Emotions regulate interpersonal temptations, and long-term committed relationships prosper only when emotional reactions are coordinated at the dyadic level. Frank provides a persuasive argument for the importance of emotional expressions to the development of trust and commitment in repeated interactions among the same people.

To summarize, approaches that construe emotions as signals to self or signals to others treat affect as a fundamental element or by-product of social interaction. Theory and research in evolutionary psychology and neurobiology suggest that the capacity of people to experience emotions underlies the development of human consciousness—that is, the awareness of self, other, and larger social units. Recent research suggests how and when one's emotions reveal signals to self about the consistency of one's identity and behavior in a situation, and to the other about one's trustworthiness in a social dilemma. As signals, emotional states are subtle mechanisms that allow people to spot problems early and make adjustments in their behavior to deal with them. Emotional states also appear to play a crucial role in cooperative, coordinated social activity. In fact, one can argue that emotion signals are one of the foundations of the human capacity for complex social organization (Turner 2002).

COGNITIVE ADJUSTMENTS   A large body of psychological research examines how emotions influence social cognition, defined as the ways in which people encode, store, retrieve, and activate information about themselves and others. Affect, feelings states, and moods all have an impact on how people process information. It is well established that individuals in a positive mood perceive, encode, interpret, and remember events in a more positive light than individuals in a negative mood (Bower 1981, 1991; Isen 1987; Isen and Geva 1987). As an example, Alice Isen and her colleagues (Isen and Geva 1987; Isen and Patrick 1983) have shown that subjects in a positive mood tend to have better recall for positive trait adjectives such as "kind" and "friendly" learned at an earlier point in time. People in a given affective state also have better recall for material learned while in that same mood state, a phenomenon known as state-dependent learning. Thus, if you learn the name of a new neighbor while depressed and then later forget the name, you are more likely to recall it while in a depressed state than in a happy one. These examples suggest some of the subtle ways in which affective states bear on cognitive judgments about people and events.

Affective states also have important effects on how people anticipate or predict future events. William Wright and Gordon Bower (1992) found that, compared to subjects in a neutral mood, those in a good mood overestimated the probability of positive events and underestimated the probability of negative events. Subjects in a bad mood did just the opposite—they overestimated the probability of negative events and saw positive events as less likely. Eric Johnson and Amos Tversky (1983) reported comparable biases with respect to how people estimate frequencies. Subjects in a bad mood tended to overestimate the frequency of other bad events. Finally, still others have observed that positive affect promotes risk-taking, especially when the potential for loss is small or inconsequential (Isen and Patrick 1983; Isen and Geva 1987). Such research as a whole affirms that affective states shape interpretations and judgments (see Forgas, Williams, and Wheeler 2001). What is not so well understood is *why* moods alter judgments and decisions.[10]

To conclude, for our purposes, there are two noteworthy implications of theory and research on the interplay of affect and information-processing. First, positive feelings heighten or prime other positively charged cognitions, and negative feelings prime negatively charged cognitions. This implies that if people feel positively in the context of a positively valued group affiliation, the positive features of the group will be more salient and they will be more likely to act on behalf of that group. Second, if positive affect leads to an overestimation of positive future events in a situation, it is a relatively small leap to suggest that positive affect will promote cooperation in a relation or enhance a person's expectation of cooperation by others. These are additional ways in which emotions at the individual level in local, micro situations have consequences that bear on social order.

Interaction-Outcome Approaches

Social-cohesion approaches analyze how the emotions that result from interaction bear on cohesion, solidarity, and social order at the group level. This approach is a backdrop for the theory of social commitments (see chapter 4). A social-cohesion approach to emotion rests on two ideas. The first is that mutual dependencies or interdependencies are a structural foundation for social cohesion (Emerson 1972a, 1972b; Hechter 1987; Molm and Cook 1995; Lawler and Yoon 1996). To the degree that people in a social unit are dependent on one another for things of value, they have incentives to interact and exchange with each other (Emerson 1972a, 1972b; Lawler and Yoon 1996). This notion that individuals band together because they need one another to produce tools, agriculture, and other commodities is as old as sociology itself. The second idea, originated by Durkheim (1915), is that joint activities generate uplift, elation, confidence, and other emotions that affirm and objectify social ties or larger group memberships. Building on the early work of Durkheim, Homans, and Emerson, two recent theories elaborate further how and why affect generates cohesion and order: the theory of interaction ritual chains (Collins 1981, 2004) and the theory of relational cohesion (Lawler and Yoon 1996; Thye, Yoon, and Lawler 2002). Durkheim's analysis of religious ritual is the backdrop for Collins's (1975, 1981) theory, whereas Homans's (1950) analysis of work groups and Emerson's (1972b) power dependence theory are the backdrop for relational cohesion theory.

In his theory of interaction ritual chains, Collins argues that repeated or recurrent interaction is the micro foundation for social order, because social interactions generate emotional energy (feelings of uplift and confidence) that people carry from situation to situation. A successful, uplifting interaction at time 1 in a given situation has an effect on interaction at time 2 in a different situation. Such interactions make the relevant group affiliation more salient and an important source of order if and when the individuals are engaged in joint activities, have a common focus, or experience a similar emotional response to their activities, and these emotions become stronger over time as the activities are repeated. Under such conditions, Collins (1989, 18) argues, people begin to "feel like members of a little group, with moral obligations to one another." Thus, he specifies a rudimentary source of person-to-group ties and theorizes that these are due to the emotional effects of recurrent interactions.

The theory of relational cohesion specifies an endogenous emotional or affective process that links social structures to cohesion and commitment. The theory assumes that people are self-interested and initially form instrumental ties because of the benefits they can derive from each other. It argues that repeated exchanges by the same people under such conditions tend to introduce an expressive component into the relation, owing to the positive feelings that arise when they are able to make successful exchanges. Those who exchange more frequently experience an "emotional buzz" of satisfaction and excitement as a result of being able to achieve mutually beneficial exchanges. The emotional buzz is strongest when people are equally and highly dependent on one another (see Lawler and Yoon 1996); in this case, a more cohesive relationship is likely to develop. In sum, the endogenous process involves three moments in a sequence: exchange-to-emotion-to-cohesion.[11] The theory takes the form of a causal chain, as shown in figure 3.1.

Neither of these theories clearly answers an important question: how do an individual's emotions become associated with a group? Attribution approaches from psychology, though they also fail to address this issue, help to move us toward an answer. The main idea is that people attribute credit and blame to self, other, or situation depending on the results of a task—specifically, they blame others or the situation for failure and give credit to the self for success (see, for example, Kelley 1967). Such attributions are likely to have emotional

Figure 3.1   Endogenous Process in Relational Cohesion Theory

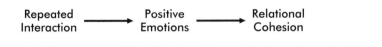

Repeated Interaction → Positive Emotions → Relational Cohesion

Source: Authors' compilation.

effects (see Weiner 1986). For example, imagine that you are working with a friend to refurbish an old boat. If you are successful and you primarily credit yourself, you should experience pride. If you believe that the other person really completed the task, you should experience gratitude toward your friend.

Bernhard Weiner (1986) theorizes these sorts of situations. He aims to understand how people interpret the often vague and global feelings they experience in interaction with others. When people experience a successful or blocked goal opportunity (winning the game, losing a promotion), the result is a generalized or global emotional response, in the form of feelings of pleasure or displeasure. Weiner terms these global feelings "primitive" emotions because they are elicited by the outcome of an interaction but are not associated with anything in particular. They are "outcome-dependent" and "attribution-independent," but such primitive emotions are important because people are motivated to understand and interpret the causes of them.

Attributions of credit and blame for global emotions are simply interpretations of what or who caused these feelings. For example, the general sense of sadness following a bad job interview may be transformed into more specific emotions with a target or cause, such as shame, if attributed to self, or anger, if attributed to the other. An important feature of specific emotions—in contrast to global or primitive emotions—is that they have targets, normally self, other, or situation. The target actually determines the specific emotion that emerges. Pride results from attributions of positive events to self; gratitude results from attributions of positive events to the other; shame results from negative events attributed to self; anger results from negative events attributed to arbitrary or illegitimate acts of others. Overall, by differentiating global from specific emotions and elucidating the specific types of attributions that lead from one to another, Weiner (1986) articulates a rich image of how more global and more specific emotions unfold in social interaction over time.

As with other attribution theories, however, Weiner's emphasis remains on attributions to individuals. A key point in our argument is that the objects or targets of attributions may include social units, in addition to self, other, and situation. Social-unit attribution may be directed at small work groups, local departments or divisions in an organization, the organization itself, a corporation, a neighborhood, a community, a nation, and so forth. If social units are targets or perceived causes of emotions and feelings, then presumably emotion attributions can have effects on compliance, cohesion, solidarity, and social order (Markovsky and Lawler 1994; Lawler and Yoon 1996; Lawler and Thye 2006). Social-unit attributions may forge a link between an individual's micro-level experiences and feelings from social interaction and one or more group affiliations—from small groups to work organizations to communities and nations.

The idea of social-unit attributions of emotion is new, so there are no frameworks for dealing with them in the emotions literature. We developed a simple framework, which is presented in table 3.1. It distinguishes global and specific emotions, following Weiner (1986), and treats the group or social unit as a distinct social object. We introduce the framework here and then use it in the next chapter as we develop the theory of social commitments.

As the table indicates, we assume that three primary social objects are viable targets for affect: self, other, and social unit. Global emotions are generalized feelings of pleasure or displeasure, such as feeling good or feeling bad, feeling up or feeling down (Lawler 2001; Lawler and Thye 2006). Specific emotions are discrete and defined with reference to the target social object that the global emotions are associated with. If global feelings of pleasure are attributed to one's own action, the emotion is pride in self; if they are attributed to the other, the emotion felt is gratitude toward that other; if negative global feelings occur and are attributed to oneself, the emotion is shame; if attributed to the other, the emotion is anger. Finally, emotions attributed to a social unit foster affective

Table 3.1   Emotions Directed at Various Social Objects

Social Object	Valence of Global Emotion	
	Positive	Negative
Self	Pride	Shame
Other	Gratitude	Anger
Social unit	Affective attachment	Affective detachment

Source: Adapted from *American Journal of Sociology* (Lawler 2001).

attachments to or detachments from that particular group. Social-unit attributions for pleasant feelings strengthen person-to-group ties, and such attributions for unpleasant feelings should weaken person-to-group ties.

CONCLUSIONS

This chapter classifies work on emotion into six categories that draw particular attention to the role of affect in social interactions. Normative approaches sensitize us to the fact that interaction contexts necessarily entail emotion norms that shape the experience and public expression of emotions and lead people to manage their emotions in ways that fit their situational roles or positions. This tends to make possible greater coordination and cooperation than otherwise would occur. Structural approaches stress hierarchies of power or status, positing positive emotions and feelings for those with high power or status and negative feelings for those with low power or status. Differential affective responses are a potential problem for commitment and social order that strong person-to-group ties may resolve (see chapter 8 for further analysis of this point). Information-oriented approaches portray emotions as meaningful cues or signals within an interaction process that reveal identities, intentions, and trustworthiness. Positive affect affirms identities, makes people more optimistic about future events, and, if expressed, communicates more trustworthiness in social dilemmas. Finally, outcome-oriented approaches emphasize the social-cohesion effects of emotions. Outcomes make people feel good or bad, and these feelings tend to generate a greater sense of cohesion with the other people involved, in part because of emotion attributions. Overall, these six approaches point to several theoretical junctures, or points of entry, for affect to play an important role in social interaction. The discussion also puts our theory of social commitments in the context of the larger bodies of literature on emotion.

Finally, there are some broad implications for the problem of social order that can be extracted from the material covered in this chapter. Most of these are directed at the micro level, but once identified, these implications can bring to mind micro conditions that underlie larger macro problems of order. Consider three conditions that could resolve a potential obstacle or threat to micro social order. First, the emotions that people feel and express correspond with contextual norms and identities, which enable them to effectively coordinate their behaviors. Second, people openly and mutually send emotional signals that convey trustworthiness and enable trustworthy people in a population to find each other. Third, people experience positive feelings from their interactions with others, and they attribute these feelings to a larger group affiliation. One can argue that the major social transformations of the early twenty-first century render all of these conditions more problematic than in the past. The point, however, is that the mainly micro-level work on emotion reviewed here can expand our thinking about the role of affect as a source of social order. The remainder of this volume focuses on the third solution presented here.

CHAPTER 4

A Theory of Social Commitments

Commitments entail beliefs and feelings about a group, and they are manifest in choices to stay with, invest in, or sacrifice for a relationship, group, organization, or community. These choices can be based on purely instrumental considerations, in which case people perceive a transaction between themselves and the group. They give to the group and receive benefits in return, and as such, their person-to-group tie is transactional. Social commitments, as we conceive them, have something more—namely, a tie that involves feelings and sentiments about the group or group affiliation and beliefs about the normative or moral properties of the group. With this kind of person-to-group tie, a person's group affiliation has expressive or intrinsic value. Individuals experience positive feelings in the group and believe in what the group stands for, and the group represents for them a particularly important source of identity (self-definition). This chapter presents a theory about how and when commitments become social in this sense.

To illustrate the phenomenon of interest, consider financial managers in investment firms. This profession is highly pecuniary, with respect to both the job responsibilities involved and the individual incentives for accomplishing them. Financial managers can reap extraordinary monetary rewards; in fact, it is not unusual for them to earn tens or even hundreds of millions of dollars. Moreover, their ties to a firm tend to be purely transactional in nature, in part because monetary units (dollars) provide a precise measure of their individual performance and worth to the firm. With this in mind, the case of David Swenson, the head of Yale University's endowment, is an interesting counterpoint (Fabrikant, Geraldine. 2007. "For Yale's Money Man, A Higher Calling." *New York Times,* February 18, 2007). Over twenty years ago, he accepted 80 percent less pay than he could have earned elsewhere to manage the Yale endowment, and he has done so with enormous success, generating annual return rates that exceed virtually every other university and garnering a strong national reputation. Why has Swenson been willing to forgo tens of millions of dollars to stay at Yale? In the *New York Times* article, he explains that it is the sense of mission he feels at a university: "One of the things I care most deeply about is that notion that anyone who qualifies for admission can go to Yale, and financial aid is a large part of this." A colleague, whom he attracted to Yale and trained in the business, said of David Swenson: "He has this love of investments that is contagious . . . [and] . . . he taught us that we were in the business of making money for financial aid for students." From Swenson's point of view, dollars and cents are an inadequate measure of winning and losing.

If groups or organizations are contexts in which people do things that make them feel good, these emotions may rub off on the social unit. This seems to have happened for David Swenson, given what he and his colleagues say about him. People like Swenson stay, invest in, and make sacrifices for an organizational affiliation because the mission or activities they participate in give them an "emotional buzz" or "uplift." Their tie to the organization is partly expressive and defines who they are to themselves and others; they derive enormous satisfaction from the person-to-group tie itself. Emotions operate like a subsidy that offsets the opportunity costs of staying with a given affiliation. The theory of social commitments put forth in this chapter aims to understand how this happens.[1]

The theory is organized around a simple observation: people are affective beings who respond emotionally to their experiences in relationships, groups, and organizations, and this sometimes has a bearing on how they define their ties to those social units. In absolute terms, social commitments vary and can entail minimal, loose ties or very strong, close ties. Compare the everyday contexts in which group commitments may form that we used for illustrative purposes in chapter 1. One of these was a morning coffee shop that people frequent on a routine basis, despite many good alternatives perhaps just around the nearest corner. Commitments to the coffee shop are minimal in an absolute sense, especially compared to the commitments that the same people develop to their ethnic community, religious group, or work organization. The latter can command much greater sacrifice than the morning coffee shop, for both instrumental reasons (the costs of exiting) and affective reasons (the group is self-defining). Nevertheless, we propose that the general conditions and processes that generate social commitments to the morning coffee shop and to other more important groups are similar—in other words, although the sacrifices made by David Swenson and someone who stops at the same coffee shop each morning are radically different, the nature and sources of their commitment behavior are common in some respects. Social commitments to particular retail outlets, coffee shops, community groups, professional associations, work organizations, ethnic affiliations, and national identities all reflect the same underlying principles and processes. The absolute strength and form of person-to-group ties vary widely across groups of different types or size, but the fundamental causes of these ties, we argue, are the same.

The theory of social commitments steps off from and further develops two previous theories about the role of emotion and affect in social exchange relations. One is the theory of relational cohesion (Lawler and Yoon 1993, 1996; Lawler, Thye, and Yoon 2000), which we explained in chapter 3. That theory indicates how power and dependence relations generate cohesion and order in relations through positive emotions. It is a counterpoint to uncertainty-reduction explanations for the emergence of relations in markets or social exchange. The second theory, the affect theory of social exchange (Lawler 2001, 2006), offers widely applicable propositions about when positive feelings are attributed to social units of whatever form or type, suggesting the importance of joint tasks or activities (for more detailed, technical reviews, see Thye, Yoon, and Lawler 2002; Lawler and Thye 2006). This chapter presents a theory that extrapolates and generalizes from this prior work, and subsequent chapters then use the theory to analyze a range of phenomena relevant to social commitments and the problem of social order more generally.

THE THEORY
The Scope of the Theory
What does it mean to generalize or abstract the theory? Any theory has a range of possible applications, or what is often termed the "scope of the theory" (Walker and Cohen 1985). Often a theory's scope is implicit and unspecified, which tends to create unnecessary debates and disagreements about how to use

and apply a theory. Our theory has a definable scope that is quite broad. In abstract terms, our theory applies to any social context with the following properties: (1) there are minimally three persons or actors in the social situation—that is, a social network is present in some form; (2) the people involved have opportunities to interact with one another repeatedly in order to generate individual or joint benefits, and a social structure gives them an incentive to at least consider interaction and exchange with one or more others; (3) people initially decide whom to interact with on purely instrumental bases—that is, they interact with those from whom they expect to derive the greatest individual benefit; (4) the social interaction occurs in the context of one or more social units, such as an ongoing relation, group, organization, community, or nation; (5) the immediate or local unit is salient to the people in it—that is, they recognize that they are interacting within a social unit; and (6) there are larger or more distant social entities (for example, communities, associations, corporations, nations) in which this proximal social unit is nested—for example, a department within a university, a division within an organization, or a community within a nation. Becoming aware of the local, proximal unit sets the stage for the larger unit within which it is nested to also become salient and a potential target for emotional attributions. Thus, whereas the micro foundation of order and commitment in local, immediate interactions is central, the result of micro processes may be shared ties among larger numbers of people who do not know or interact with each other.

In the remainder of this chapter, we emphasize three main components of the theory: the major assumptions that orient the analysis and broadly outline the argument; its central or most fundamental propositions about structure, emotions, and social commitments; and several implications of the theory's main ideas.

The Orienting Assumptions of the Theory

The line of our theoretical argument is that an individual's private, internal feelings from social interaction or exchange are inextricably bound up with social units or entities such as relations, groups, or organizations. The social units constitute the context within which the positive or negative emotions are experienced. The emotions felt by the individual help to make more salient the relational or group affiliations involved in the situation, and in that process relations and groups become "a reality" or object in the individual's range of vision.

There are six orienting assumptions of this theory, based on previous research. Summarizing them serves to communicate the overarching framework of our theory.

1. *Any social interaction involves a degree of jointness, which is a characteristic of any activity or task that people engage in with others.* Even very simple tasks, such as getting on a bus at a bus stop, involve an element of jointness. Each person in the line coordinates his or her behavior with that of others to avert interference, bumping, and potential rudeness. Social interaction involves subtle, mutual adjustments in a context where people can have an impact on each other's behavior or outcomes (Mead 1934; Kelley and Thibaut 1978). The degree of jointness can vary, however, and we aim to understand how and what effects this variation has on person-to-group ties.

2. *Social interactions foster individual emotions that fall along a positive or negative dimension.* The theory makes a sharp distinction between global emotions and specific emotions, an idea introduced in chapter 3. Global emotions are immediately and involuntarily felt as a result of interaction; specific emotions are associated with or attached to particular social objects (self, other, group). In our theory of social commitments, global emotions are the nonrational responses to external social conditions, whereas specific emotions have a rational component because they are based on how people cognitively process and interpret the global emotions. In this sense, we do not exclude the rational or render it epiphenomenal, as do some sociological theories of emotion (Shott 1979; Scheff 1990); nor do we exclude the nonrational, as do most economic accounts (see, for example, Williamson 1985; Elster 1986). The rational and nonrational are distinct and complementary, but also intertwined, in the theory of social commitments.

3. *Emotions are internal (self) reinforcements (rewards) or internal (self) punishments (costs).* These internal (self) reinforcements are distinct from extrinsic reinforcements (see Bandura 1997) and therefore not as readily controlled. Neuroscience research affirms, for example, that experiences of joy activate regions of the prefrontal cortex, which is also where thinking is believed to originate, whereas sadness deactivates these regions (Damasio et al. 2000). However, global emotions, being somewhat vague and diffuse, are difficult for people to fully understand or anticipate. There are strong reasons for believing that people tend to associate such feelings with events, other people, or situations (see Clore and Parrott 1994) and that this is how they come to

understand their own feelings. The importance of interpretation leads to the next two assumptions.

4. *People strive to experience positive emotions and to avoid negative emotions.* Chapter 3 discussed the common principle from psychology (Izard 1991) that emotions and emotional experiences are motivating. An implication is that people seek out positive emotional experiences and that, on this basis, they choose to enter or avoid certain situations, choose to interact with some and not others, and decide which of their group affiliations to continue and nurture. Feeling good is something people want to experience, and feeling bad is something they want to avoid. For instance, employees should be more motivated to stay with an organization and behave like good citizens if the work organization is a setting in which they are regularly made to feel good. This fourth assumption posits that emotions are goal states for individuals.[2]

5. *In response to the motivating effects of emotion, feelings produce cognitive and interpretive efforts to understand their sources or causes.* Emotions essentially direct people's attention to elements of the social situation that may account for those emotions. In other words, "cognitive work" is directed at figuring out why and when the individual experiences the feelings and when he or she might experience the same feelings in the future. The sequence assumed here—from emotion to cognition—receives support from recent work on the neuroscience of emotion (LeDoux 1996; Damasio 1999). When a stimulus enters the brain, neurological emotional correlates or responses tend to begin before the perceptual and cognitive processing of the stimulus is completed. This assumption, in combination with the fourth assumption, also captures the rational-cognitive component of emotion and affect.

6. *People interpret and explain their positive or negative emotions with reference to the social units within which they experience those emotions.* If events, tasks, or activities make a person feel good, he or she can explain these feelings by attributing them to another, to self, or to the group. Some research by psychologists indicates that people feeling positive affect engage in more global processing of information (big picture–oriented) that emphasizes broad, general features of the social situation, whereas those feeling negative affect engage in local processing (detail-oriented) focused on the "trees" (see Gasper and Clore 2002). This is generally consistent with the notion that people view overarching groups or organizations as the cause of their individual feelings. This tendency should be stronger if groups or organizations are perceived as stable, persistent features of the person's environment (see Weiner 1986).

To suggest how these assumptions apply to different situations, consider three illustrative questions:

1. *Why might a person frequent the same coffee shop morning after morning, despite having many other good alternatives?* Answer: the person feels good there (assumptions 2 and 3); he wants to have that experience every morning (assumption 4); he thinks the feelings are tied to the place (assumption 5), either because of the coffee shop's characteristics (ambience) or because of the other people there (assumption 6).
2. *Why might a person turn down a very attractive, professionally enhancing job opportunity?* Answer: she feels good about her current workplace (assumptions 2 and 3); she wants to ensure the continuation of those feelings (assumption 4); and she believes that those feelings are tied to her current employer (assumption 5), either because of the organization's treatment of her or because of her interactions with fellow employees (assumptions 1 and 6).
3. *Why might a person want to work on joint projects or efforts with the same coworkers time and time again?* Answer: working on joint projects with coworkers generates positive feelings (assumptions 1 and 2) that the person wants to experience again (assumption 4); and she believes that these experiences are tied to this particular group (assumption 5), either because of the people in it or because of its value or importance to the larger organization (assumption 6).

Across these examples, how people choose the targets—self, other, or social unit—for their emotional experiences is a crucial issue.

The example of a faculty meeting can illuminate further the problem at hand. We can compare an academic department's successful handling of a difficult issue or choice, in the context of strong differences of opinion among the faculty, with its unsuccessful handling of such a situation. Success would make the faculty as a whole feel uplifted or good if the success leads to inferences such as "we work well together," or "when we face strong differences, we can get beyond them." Failure, on the other hand, would make faculty members feel down or bad, by generating a sense that they cannot work well together or resolve issues in the face of ongoing interpersonal animosities or distrust. The positive or negative feelings generated by the meeting could be attributed to particular individuals or to the department as a social unit. Assumption 6 suggests that people associate their feelings with the social units that are implicated in interpretive accounts of the emotions experienced. This leads to a key question: under what conditions are individual emotions likely to be directed at or associated with a social unit?

Our answer emphasizes the nature of the joint activities or tasks being undertaken (see assumption 1). Joint activities or tasks can vary along numerous dimensions—for example, how clear or vague they are, how complex or simple, how specific or general, or how implicit or explicit. Of particular importance is the degree to which objective properties of the task or subjective definitions emphasize the joint, shared nature of the social activity. Fundamentally, what makes a task joint is that it takes two or more people to accomplish it, these people have to coordinate with one another in order to succeed, and they experience costs if they fail. Examples of joint tasks include work teams, business partnerships, homeowners' associations, social movement organizations, and even child-raising by two parents or partners. Still other examples are spending a social evening with friends, attending a sports event, coauthoring a paper with a colleague, or holding a department meeting to resolve a problem. There is jointness in virtually all of these examples, yet they are likely to vary in the degree to which the activities highlight joint, shared results versus individual behaviors and results. With this in mind, let us turn to the core propositions of the theory.

The Core Propositions of the Theory

The psychology of attribution processes (see chapter 3) raises some important questions for us: How are attributions of individual emotions to the social unit possible? If they occur, how much effect can they have, given people's strong tendencies to make attributions designed to serve their own interests, enhance their self-esteem, or generate approval from others? Attribution theory in psychology is concerned primarily with people's attributions of stable qualities or characteristics to persons (self or other), not to social units in the situation (relations, groups, organizations). Our focus is on attributions to these larger social units. If the tasks or activities around which people interact have a significant measure of jointness, it is reasonable to suspect that people may attribute their positive or negative feelings from success or failure to the relations, groups, organizations, or other social units that have brought them together to interact and that define and frame the tasks and activities they have undertaken. The theory of social commitments argues that answers to the questions with which we open this section can be found in the jointness of tasks and activities. Attribution theory and research has not addressed this issue.[3]

The basic idea of the theory is probably now becoming clear—namely, that people attribute their individually felt emotions to their relation or group, especially if the task is high in jointness. In the context of joint tasks or activities, people infer that their emotions are jointly produced, as are other results or effects of the task activity. Imagine a game of chess played either alone against a computer or face to face with another person. Winning gives the winner an "emotional buzz" in both cases, but according to our theory, an enjoyable, exciting contest in the interpersonal setting gives the loser an "emotional buzz" as well. The game with a computer-partner can generate a similar result (winning or losing and associated good or bad feelings), but the social interaction with another person in the chess game is a part of the pleasure each player experiences in playing the game. A plausible hypothesis is that, in a game of chess played with another person, each player is more likely to view his or her positive feelings about the game as a joint product of the two players' individual efforts and contributions. In the interpersonal setting, the chess game is a joint endeavor with another person that produces a collective result and leads the players to interpret their individual emotions in more collective terms.

The jointness of tasks can vary both objectively and subjectively. A work group may face tasks that have an inherent jointness. For instance, on an assembly line each job is intertwined with the prior and subsequent points on the line, and some work teams have a highly interdependent task structure. Yet the same task may be defined or framed by the organization (or its leaders) in either joint or individual terms, with an emphasis on either individual or collective responsibility. The use by some corporations of the term "associates" or "partners" to describe employees can be construed as an effort to convey joint or shared responsibility for organizational success across job categories. Child-rearing by two parents is a quintessentially joint task, but even here, parents may define it in more individual terms or in more collective terms, depending on how precisely and specifically they divide the components of the task and how stable this division becomes in the relationship. We contend that both the objective structural conditions of a task and the subjective definitions of it have important effects on the relational, group, or organizational affiliations of the actors.

The theory of social commitments identifies a key structural condition (objective) and a key cognitive condition (subjective) for social-unit attributions of emotional experiences:

Structural condition: The degree to which each individual's efforts or contributions to a joint task activity are separable (distinguishable) or nonseparable (indistinguishable).

Cognitive condition: The degree to which the joint task or activity generates a sense of shared responsibility.

The contrast of separable and nonseparable tasks is drawn from Oliver Williamson's (1985, 245–47) analysis of work structures. He views "relational teams" as a governance structure that is likely to emerge and to be effective when the contributions of different workers to the task cannot be identified or distinguished. This ostensibly generates a strong sense of common endeavor and solidarity among coworkers—that is, a sense of "we are all in this together." Thus, nonseparability should produce a stronger sense of shared responsibility for task results, and also for the emotions felt from the task activity.

Consider the example of role definitions in a work organization. These are structural conditions that bear on where people locate themselves on the individual-collective responsibility dimension. Discrete, specialized, independent roles draw attention to individual responsibility and thus should reduce the sense of shared responsibility. Here, expectations, measures of performance, and structures of accountability are specific, clear, and individual-based. Diffuse, overlapping, intertwined roles, on the other hand, may highlight jointness and shared responsibility, especially if expectations, measures of performance, and structures of accountability have salient group-based features. Thus, job definitions, job designs, and structures of accountability generate objective and subjective conditions of individual and collective responsibility. Job designs send important signals to employees about how the organization views their tasks relative to others in the organization.

In sum, our argument is that if the tasks or activities around which people interact generate a strong sense of shared responsibility, they are likely to interpret their individual feelings as jointly produced in concert with others, and therefore they are likely to attribute those feelings to salient social units—be they relations, groups, organizations, communities, or even nations. The result is stronger person-to-group commitments and patterns of behavior that reflect such affective ties. Four core propositions of the theory of social commitments capture the theoretical argument.

1. The greater the nonseparability of individuals' contributions to task success or failure, the stronger the perceptions of shared responsibility.
2. The stronger the perceptions of shared responsibility for success or failure at a joint task, the more inclined actors are to attribute the resulting emotions to social units (small groups, organizations, communities).

3. Social-unit attributions of positive emotions strengthen social commitments to the unit (P-G affective ties), whereas social-unit attributions of negative emotions weaken such social commitments.
4. People are more likely to stay with, invest in, and sacrifice for social units to which they have stronger social commitments.

These propositions are highly, and intentionally, abstract. The theory is designed to be a useful device for understanding the effects of any structural force in any social situation on social commitments. All that is required is that the structure produces variations in the degree to which individual efforts and contributions are nonseparable (objective) or the degree to which people perceive shared, collective responsibility with others in the situation (subjective). We argue that these are the most fundamental conditions under which one or more social units take on expressive value and the associated group affiliations or identities become ends in themselves, though they are not necessarily the *only* conditions. The next chapter uses the theory to analyze the effects of several of the structural foundations for groups on person-to-group ties.

Applications and Examples of the Theory
The four core propositions can be applied to organizational policies and practices that shape task, role, and interdependent structures. First, additive tasks (where group results are an aggregate of individual performances) should strengthen the sense of individual responsibility, whereas conjunctive tasks (where the group result is a multiplicative function of individual performances or behaviors) should strengthen the sense of shared responsibility. All other things being equal, groups with conjunctive tasks should generate stronger social commitments to the group than those with additive tasks. Second, as suggested by our earlier discussion of role differentiation, discrete, specialized, independent roles draw attention to individual responsibilities, whereas overlapping, collaborative roles highlight shared responsibilities. This has counterintuitive implications for the design of jobs. Job designs that promote shared responsibility should generate stronger social commitments to an organization than those that focus solely on individual responsibility.[4] In work organizations, the sense of shared responsibility is likely to be tied to formal systems of accountability. Systems of accountability that target individual performance, versus those that target group performance, should have differential consequences for social commitments. In each of these examples of applications of the theory, the "sense of shared responsibility" is the central explanatory principle, and the endogenous mechanisms are affective.

To illustrate concretely how it is that our theory of social commitments can produce commitment to a larger social unit, consider the following example. The second author, Shane Thye, is currently serving a three-year term on a twenty-four-person University Committee for Tenure and Promotion. The charge of this committee is to review and evaluate the file for every candidate who is applying for tenure and promotion to associate or full professor in the university. There is a tremendous amount of reading involved, the work is largely anonymous and uncompensated, and the committee meets very regularly to discuss and vote on candidate files. The members of this committee are from various academic departments around the university—for example, music, engineering, public health, biology—and share nothing but the larger institutional affiliation. The work is divided among three subcommittees, that is, each eight-person subcommittee is responsible for taking the lead on some of the candidate files. Though the work is distributed in this way, each person is expected to review each of the files independently and firmly reminded of a joint responsibility to do so.

There are a number of ways in which, from the perspective of our theory, the university has structured the committee so as to promote a strong person-to-unit commitment (in this case, to the committee). First, there is much objective task jointness built into the interaction. The twenty-four-person committee meets only at the faculty senate office and meets as a committee of the whole; each member is responsible, as mentioned, for reviewing each and every file. The committee is relatively flat in that all votes are counted equally, and the leaders of the group simply coordinate meetings and make sure the files are ready to be evaluated. Second, university leaders (the president, the provost, deans) periodically attend meetings to affirm the joint mission, stress collective accountability, and recognize the committee's joint work and accomplishments. Those in positions of power and status not only affirm the importance of the committee's work but legitimate the committee and express much gratitude (a specific positive emotion) for the service of its members. Third, the work occurs in a context that promotes positive global feelings. The university provides very high-quality food at each meeting (gourmet coffee, exotic cheeses, lush desserts) and periodically rewards the members with small token gifts (gift cards from Barnes & Noble, coffee mugs, and so on). In addition, committee members routinely joke about various aspects of their work and engage in much friendly banter.

The effect of these conditions—task jointness, a sense of shared responsibility, and positive emotions—produces a sense of "being in this together."

Further, the effects of this person-to-unit bond radiate outward to produce new kinds of prosocial behavior. Committee members, for instance, sometimes schedule lunch with one another and are more likely to serve as outside readers on MA and PhD committees when asked to do so. The overall effect is that by structuring the tasks in a manner consistent with our theory of social commitments, the university, knowingly or not, has produced positive feelings and a sense of pride among those serving on the committee and fostered strong person-to-unit bonds or commitment. The next section elaborates the role of task interdependence, as implied by this example, and proposes a classification scheme that distinguishes varieties of task interdependence.

Task Interdependencies and Shared Responsibility

Task interdependencies do not have simple, straightforward effects, given our theory. People may engage in a highly interdependent task but still be able to distinguish their individual contributions and tie these to the results of the task activity. The task interdependence should make the collective results of their individual behavior salient, as in a social dilemma, but this does not necessarily generate a comparably strong sense of shared responsibility, for which the intertwining of individual behaviors and contributions is necessary. It is conceivable that conditions of high task interdependence could involve either clear reward contingencies between the behavior of individuals—that is, individually focused activity and accountability—or jointly focused activities and collective responsibility. To address this issue, we ask how joint the activities themselves are, and how accountable individuals are for the collective results versus the group as a whole.

The connections between task interdependence and shared responsibility are elaborated by crossing two dimensions: whether the activity involved in the task behavior is primarily individual or joint, and whether accountability for the results of the activity is primarily individual or joint. Group or collective tasks may focus on or be framed as either individual activities or joint, shared activities. Similarly, systems of accountability may be directed at individual members of a group or at the collective results and the group as such. Activity and accountability also may be generated endogenously as people interact on a task, or they may be produced exogenously by policies, practices, or the explicit directives of a larger organization. We hypothesize that these dimensions have important effects on people's sense of shared responsibility. Table 4.1 distinguishes four prototypes of task interdependence

Table 4.1   Forms of Shared Responsibility

	Accountability	
Activity	Individual	Joint
Individual	Personal	Social dilemma
Joint	Production line	Team

Source: Authors' compilation.

based on the intersection between individual-joint activity and individual-joint accountability.

The nonseparability of task behavior and a sense of shared responsibility should be lowest in the upper-left quadrant and highest in the lower-right quadrant. The upper-left quadrant is exemplified by a regional sales office used by salespeople as a base of operations. Much of the work activity (selling) is done individually, and each salesperson is held accountable by the company for the total value of his or her sales performance. The salespeople may operate as a group in some respects—for example, coordinating their contacts with clients, or exchanging information that is useful to everyone—yet the framing and nature of the work task is primarily individual. The sales office may have goals or targets and be accountable for aggregate sales, yet the salespeople who contribute to the aggregate (office) sales are held accountable primarily as individuals. In the regional sales office, there is little jointness in either the activity of the salespeople or the method of accountability; both are individualized and personalized.

The lower-right quadrant of table 4.1 is exemplified by work settings in which teams are the principal units for generating desired results. A work team is defined as a group of employees who have complementary skills, are committed to working together to achieve common goals, and who are collectively responsible and held mutually accountable for results (see Katzenbach and Smith 1993; Hackman 2002). Teams are generally different from departments, working groups, and many task forces in that they entail collective results and responsibility for these results is shared (Katzenbach and Smith 1993). The contemporary movement from traditional hierarchical work structures to team-based work structures can be construed as a move from the upper-left quadrant to the lower-right quadrant of table 4.1. In the former, productive activity is individual-focused; in the latter, productive activity is group-focused. We consider these to be the pure forms at the extreme ends of a shared-responsibility dimension.

The two other quadrants represent mixed forms of task interdependence and shared responsibility. The combination of individually focused activities and jointly held accountability is exemplified by a social dilemma, which is a situation in which individual and collective interests are in tension and behaviors that are individually rational are collectively nonrational (Axelrod 1984). In such situations, individual activity essentially has an emergent, collective result, intended or unintended. With a commons problem unbridled, individualized activity draws on and depletes an existing collective resource (for example, overusing a common grazing area in a village), whereas, with a public good problem, free-riding leads some not to contribute in the expectation that others with an interest in maintaining the public good will provide sufficient contributions (such as volunteering to devote time or money to public radio). The commons and public good problems are two sides of the same coin (see Komorita and Parks 1996) because, across both, if people follow their individual interests, the result of their individual activity is a jointly damaging result to a collectively available resource (Axelrod 1984; Hechter 1987; Kollock 1998). For our purpose, the important point is that distinct and separate individual activity generates a joint, collective result. This places social dilemmas in the upper-left quadrant of table 4.1.

Turning to the lower-left quadrant—the combination of joint activity and individual accountability—a good example is an assembly line. The task activity of individuals on an assembly line is highly interconnected and sequentially dependent, since what each does affects the next person or function in the assembly process. Individual responsibilities are well defined, and if something goes amiss, it is usually possible to trace the problem to particular individuals. Thus, whereas the productive activity is jointly undertaken by individuals in an assembly line, accountability tends to be individualized. A measure of shared responsibility—with its attendant group-level effects—can be introduced into an assembly line by, for example, assigning larger chunks of the assembly-line tasks to distinct work groups or introducing group-based processes to reduce errors (for example, quality circles). Nevertheless, the basic task structure remains one in which the activities of individuals are joint, but the accountability is primarily at the individual level.[5]

To conclude, the activity and accountability dimensions elaborate the theory's analysis of shared responsibility. Each dimension has a long tradition in the social sciences, and by bringing them together, we can infer how different task conditions will bear on the sense of shared responsibility. We suggest that the sense of shared responsibility is therefore a function of the interconnections of the activities of individuals in the group and the structure of accountability. The confluence of joint activity and joint accountability should generate the strongest sense of shared responsibility and the strongest tendency to attribute individually felt emotions to social units. Moreover, changes in either the nature of the activities people engage in or the structure of accountability under which they undertake their activities should increase or decrease the sense of shared responsibility and, accordingly, change individuals' inclinations to attribute positive feelings from their activities to the larger organization.

Endogenous Mechanisms

Together, the four core propositions constitute a causal chain: task jointness → sense of shared responsibility → social unit attributions → social commitments. This chain fleshes out the conditions under which repeated social interactions are likely to generate emergent social orders through an emotional or affective process. Recall from the introduction of relational cohesion theory (see chapter 3) that repeated exchanges or interactions lead to more cohesion and commitment in relations, because positive feelings are generated by repeated exchange and these feelings, in turn, foster cohesion and commitment. A sense of shared responsibility is likely to accentuate these effects. More specifically, if a joint task, repeatedly undertaken, generates a sense of shared responsibility, this should increase not only the impact of repeated interaction or exchange on positive feelings but also the likelihood that these feelings will be attributed to the social unit. Thus, the role of shared responsibility in emergent orders can be portrayed as shown in figure 4.1.[6]

Figure 4.1   Shared Responsibility and Emergent Orders

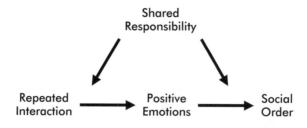

Source: Authors' compilation.

To conclude, four core propositions capture the main ideas of the theory about how and when a social structure generates stronger or weaker person-to-group social commitments. Central to these are the sense of shared responsibility for task activities and results and the social-unit attributions of individual emotion. The following section develops further implications of the theory.

ADDITIONAL IMPLICATIONS OF THE THEORY

Specific Emotions Directed at Self and Other

Individuals' self-serving attributions of their feelings could undermine the predictions of the theory. Social commitments to a group would be difficult to generate or sustain if people consistently credited themselves with the group's success or blamed others when the group failed at a task. With self-serving attributions, allocations of credit are essentially zero-sum—that is, the more credit is given to the other for success at a joint task, the less credit is given to oneself. By the same token, pride in self and gratitude toward the other is inversely related, because giving gratitude to the other diminishes the credit one can take and therefore the pride one can feel from group success at a task. An important implication of our theory of social commitments is that social-unit attributions mitigate or eliminate self-serving attributions and thereby set the stage for people to share credit for success or blame for failure.

Based on the theory, a sense of shared responsibility and related social-unit attributions generate a non-zero-sum relationship between emotions directed at self and those directed at others. Thus, success at a joint task, in the context of social-unit attributions, is likely to simultaneously generate feelings of both pride in self and gratitude toward the other. Giving gratitude to the other does not reduce the sense of pride in self, or vice versa. For this reason, where task conditions generate a strong sense of shared responsibility, person-to-group ties should strengthen person-to-person ties. In the case of positive emotions, the capacity for mutual gratitude and mutual pride to occur side by side is an important way in which shared responsibility accentuates the impact of P-G ties on P-P ties. Thus, social-unit attributions of emotion strengthen the link between P-G and P-P ties, enhancing both. There are important implications for social order here because, as can be recalled from chapter 2, Parsons (1951) viewed the strength of P-G and P-P ties as dual dimensions underlying social order. Shared responsibility and social-unit attributions of emotion interconnect more tightly these fundamental aspects of social order.

The case of task failure and resulting negative emotions is less straightforward than the case of positive emotions, but generally parallel. Here a sense of shared responsibility and social-unit attributions for task failure should promote feelings of mutual shame, whereas individual responsibility and self-serving attributions should generate mutual anger and internal dissension. Negative emotions directed at self (shame) and other (anger) are not positively related, as is the case for positive emotions directed at self (pride) and other (gratitude). Nevertheless, one can argue that the shared experience of shame for group failure sets the stage for a collaborative response to failure that affirms or strengthens P-G ties. For example, if members of a work team collaborate well with each other but produce a bad result (failing at the task), their capacity to learn and regroup from the failure may depend on whether they make social-unit attributions for the failure and the negative feelings they get from it. Social-unit attributions therefore are important to future productivity when ongoing work groups or teams fail at particular tasks. All other things being equal, perceiving a shared responsibility for group failure may have a positive effect on P-P ties.

Thus, we argue, shared responsibility and social-unit attributions will have a positive effect on P-G and P-P relations overall, regardless of the valence of the emotions felt from the task activity. These effects should be stronger for positive emotions from joint success than for negative emotions from joint failure. The implied hypothesis is this: given social-unit attributions of global emotions, person-to-group commitments generate common or shared specific emotions about self and other (mutual pride, mutual gratitude, mutual shame), and these, in turn, strengthen person-to-person ties; these effects are stronger in the case of task success and related positive feelings compared to task failure and related negative emotions.

Finally, these specific emotions can be applied to affective sentiments about the social unit or group. Assume that a group of homeowners face a social dilemma (a commons problem) regarding a shared parcel of land designed for picnics, sunbathing, and the like. If the common property is well maintained because each user does his or her part, the common property fosters pride at being a part of a successful community and gratitude toward the "community" as such. If the common area is not well maintained, the result may be shame or anger, again directed in part at the community itself. Other examples are feeling gratitude toward an organization that has treated you well and facilitated your career development and feeling shame because of actions of your nation, such as the torture of noncombatants at Abu Ghraib or violations of the Geneva Conventions under the George W. Bush presidency. Based on our theory, person-to-group commitments and the underlying sense of shared responsibility also lead people to develop more specific feelings about their groups or group affiliations, such as pride and gratitude.

The Spread of Emotions in Groups

It is well known that emotions tend to spread from person to person in social situations and also from situation to situation. Person-to-person emotional contagion occurs because people synchronize the behavioral manifestations of their feelings (smiling), and these exterior manifestations have feedback effects on their feelings states (Hatfield, Cacioppo, and Rapson 1993). If I smile at you because we have just accomplished a task together, you tend to smile back at me (a synchronization effect). Moreover, your smile unleashes a physiological change in you that enhances your emotional response (a feedback effect). Partly owing to such emotional contagion, interacting with a negative, pessimistic, depressed person tends to generate less pleasant feelings than interacting with a positive, upbeat, enthusiastic person (Hatfield, Cacioppo, and Rapson 1993).

Emotional contagion also occurs at the level of the group or social unit. Assume that you frequent a particular coffee shop each morning. If the staff are friendly and engage in humorous banter with customers and with each other, this probably generates a more "upbeat" emotional tone to the place and corresponding positive feelings among customers. If staff are dour, unfriendly, and unwilling to engage in small talk or banter with customers or with each other, a neutral, muted, or constrained emotional tone tends to prevail. Colloquially, people pick up the emotional "vibrations" of the place, and customers' behavior reflects in part this emotional tone. This is dramatically illustrated by the different emotional tones one encounters when attending a symphony versus a rock concert or a jazz club. Positive emotional responses in a symphony performance are muted, invisible, and constrained, whereas in a jazz club they are characterized by small, visible movements of the head or feet, and at a rock concert by large, exuberant, physical movements. These behavioral expressions of affect reflect emotion norms for these contexts (see chapter 3), but they also foster emotional contagion that further strengthens these feelings.

Emotional contagion has been empirically documented in recent research on affect and mood in work settings (Barsade 2002; Brief and Weiss 2002; George 1995, 1996; Kelly and Barsade 2001; Sy, Cote, and Saavedra 2005). It has been observed that there is more convergence of affect across individuals in work groups with stable memberships and high task interdependence (Bartel and Saavedra 2000). This group-level effect is consistent with our prior analysis of task interdependence and shared responsibility. In addition, research indicates that in work teams, emotional contagion among members generates prevailing affective states or emotional tones at the collective or group level, increasing cooperation and reducing conflict (Barsade 2002; Brief and Weiss 2002). Based on this work and our theory, we hypothesize that emotional contagion among members of a group is greater when task conditions generate a sense of shared responsibility.

However, emotions spread not only among people but also across unrelated situations or tasks. This is indicated by the extensive research of Alice Isen and her colleagues (see Isen 1987) on the trans-situational effects of positive affect. Isen shows that if individuals are in a state of positive affect, regardless of its source, they will interact more cooperatively with others who have nothing to do with their positive feelings. In other words, if person A is feeling good in situation B, but then enters situation C, that person will carry the emotion over to situation C, and this has an impact on how cooperatively he or she will interact with others in that new situation. Randall Collins's (2004) theory of interaction ritual chains makes a similar point. He argues that people derive emotional energy (uplift, confidence) from interactions in one setting and then carry them to other interactions with different people. Overall, positive or negative emotions may spread across situations or groups, in part because individuals with broad or dense network ties become "carriers" of affective tones or moods produced in and by a particular group. This helps to explain why leaders who exude excitement and enthusiasm can have widespread effects on the motivation and commitment of employees in an organization.

The theory of social commitments can incorporate ideas about the spread of emotions. First of all, given joint tasks and a sense of shared responsibility, emotions should readily spread across individuals in a group, because under such conditions people are more likely to carefully attend to each other's emotional expressions. Mimicry and synchronization should generate greater convergence of emotional expressions across time (see Hatfield, Cacioppo, and Rapson 1993). Once emotions spread in this manner, a group-level affective tone emerges and essentially becomes a property of the group. This, in turn,

Figure 4.2   Role of Emotional Contagion

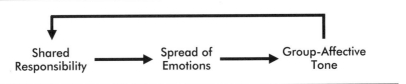

Shared Responsibility → Spread of Emotions → Group-Affective Tone

Source: Authors' compilation.

has feedback effects that enhance the sense of shared responsibility. Examples are groups with an upbeat, confident, optimistic atmosphere and those that appear "beaten down," lacking in confidence, and unmotivated. The implications of this argument are captured in figure 4.2.

Micro Social Units Nested in Macro Social Units

At any given moment, the local, more immediate groups tend to attract the lion's share of people's attention. Whether you are in your office finishing a task, in a meeting designed to solve a problem with coworkers, or at home planning a vacation with your family, the local relations and groups are likely to be very salient. Larger social units—your company, your town, your neighborhood, your nation—may be present in some sense, but generally these social units are left in the background. We have suggested in earlier chapters that one of the features of the world, as it appears to be changing, is that the daily micro experiences of people are more distant and removed from larger, overarching social units. This implies that larger, more distant macro units have receded even further into the background, thereby accentuating the micro-macro disconnect that underlies problems of commitment and social order.

Yet, on an objective level, it is hard to imagine a social context in which only the local setting or group is relevant and important. When people interact, it is invariably within two or more nested or overlapping groups or group affiliations. Interactions in neighborhoods occur in cities that are within states or provinces, which in turn are in nations. Interactions in academic departments are nested within colleges, which are nested within universities; companies are nested within corporations, functional divisions within companies, and so forth. Interacting with other people in nested groups is seemingly a universal human experience.

To address the issue of nested group commitments, Lawler (1992) developed a theory based on the following idea: people form stronger affective commitments to social units that they perceive as giving them a greater sense of control. A sense of control refers to self-efficacy, that is, the perception that one can have an impact on the surrounding world by anticipating and shaping events of import to self (White 1959; Deci 1975; Giddens 1984; Westcott 1988). People are known to experience positive feelings when situations give them a sense of control and negative feelings when they experience a lack of control (White 1959; Brehm 1966; Deci 1975; Kohn and Slomczynski 1990), and thus it is possible to build the micro-macro dimension of nested commitments into our theory. What is important to understand about organizational commitments is that people's sense of control is based in organizational structures and that self-efficacy is intertwined with collective efficacy.

This theory of nested commitments (Lawler 1992) argues that closer, more immediate or proximal units are generally the object of stronger affective attachments, for two interrelated reasons. First, local units generally have more visible, discernible, and persistent effects on people and therefore seem to be stronger sources of control and self-efficacy compared to more removed or distant units. Second, the local units shape how people define their relationships and allocate responsibility for results. Local units have a "social interaction advantage," being the units most directly experienced by people. Collins's (1981, 1989) theory of interaction ritual chains makes a strong and persuasive argument for the central importance of the immediate, local situation in understanding macro-level phenomena, which Collins contends are manifest in local situations. From our theory, social-unit attributions for experiences of self-efficacy and control are likely to be directed to the local, proximal social units, whereas experiences of a lack of control are likely to be attributed to the more distant or removed social units. Thus, in the context of nested groups, positive feelings from joint activity are likely to be attributed to the local (proximal) unit, whereas negative feelings are attributed to the larger and more distant social unit. Jonathan Turner (2008) uses an evolutionary framework to arrive at a similar point of view—namely, that people push negative feelings outward and direct positive feelings inward. This idea has important implications for decentralized organizations. We return to this in chapter 6, where we analyze nested commitments in large organizations. Chapter 9 then applies this notion to affective sentiments about political units (cities, regions, nations) at different levels, asking if and when people are more emotionally attached to their local units than to their nation.

CONCLUSIONS

The theory of social commitments suggests an emotional or affective mechanism through which larger problems of social order may be "solved" in an increasingly individualized and privatized social world. It is an argument based in micro-sociological conditions and processes: social commitments to a group are likely to emerge when people interact with others and work together on joint tasks or in joint activities repeatedly over time. A fundamental reason is that people are emotional-affective beings (see Damasio 1999) who experience and respond to their feelings, whether they want to or not. Just as individual performances yield positive feelings if successful and negative feelings if unsuccessful, joint tasks or performances also generate these feelings. The difference is that if people experience such feelings in the context of joint tasks, there is some chance that they will associate those feelings with shared group or organizational affiliations and develop affective ties to those groups as a result. Such affective group ties are not developed intentionally and purposefully; they emerge naturally in the course of social interactions with others around joint tasks or activities in nested groups.

The theory aims to understand and predict when such affective ties are likely to develop. There are two basic conditions under which people attribute their individual feelings to the group: when the task involves joint activities in which people's behaviors or contributions are difficult to distinguish and for which there is joint accountability; and when people perceive a shared respon-sibility for their joint or collective results, which includes the individual emotions they experience. When these conditions occur, people attribute their individual feelings to a group and become more affectively committed or attached to that group, and the group takes on expressive value to members. Thus, simply put, the common theme here is that people become more socially and affectively committed to the groups, organizations, and communities within which they repeatedly or regularly experience positive emotions or feelings, insofar as they attribute these emotions to the social unit.

This chapter suggests that three additional conditions are likely to strengthen or weaken the emotional effects of repeated interaction on social-unit attribu-tions and commitments. First, the effects are stronger if the sense of shared responsibility generates complementary emotions directed at self and others (both pride in self and gratitude toward others). These build stronger connec-tions between person-to-person ties and person-to-group ties and enhance the effects on social order (Parsons 1951). Second, the effects are stronger when people communicate or share their emotions with each other intentionally or unintentionally. This sharing of emotions produces a feedback cycle of shared responsibility that builds or sustains high levels of shared responsibility. Finally, the effects are enhanced when structures give people a strong sense of control and self-efficacy; these accentuate positive emotional responses and strengthen commitments to those groups that are perceived as the prime sources of that control. While this tends to be the local, immediate group, it also can be the larger, more distant one, as we discuss in later chapters.

Organizational policies or leader behaviors are common sources of the instrumental incentives that bring people together around joint tasks or activities. Once people are interacting, however, non-instrumental processes and ties tend to develop. Organizational policies and leaders can make such effects more or less likely, contingent on how they design and interconnect jobs, how they frame and define tasks, what structures of accountability they employ, and so forth. The central ideas of the theory can address a range of important questions: How and when do social networks become grouplike and promote collectively oriented behavior? How do people in organizations weigh or balance commitments to their local units (chapter, company, state) and to the larger organization within which these are nested (national association, corporation, nation)? How do the commitments produced by hierarchical and network forms of organization differ? How is social order generated and sustained at the micro level if local status structures reflect larger social inequalities? How are national sentiments or loyalties sustained in the face of globalizing economies and work settings or given apparent "denationalization" of some areas of life (Haas 2000)? Subsequent chapters address these questions. Each chapter is a new variation on the common themes laid out here.

CHAPTER 5

The Structural Foundations of Groups

This chapter uses the theory of social commitments to identify the structural conditions that give rise to groups and group-oriented behaviors. *Social structure* refers broadly to how individuals or groups relate to one another—specifically, the ties that are possible (structural opportunities) and the ties that are realized (actual relations). A group minimally involves actual ties to a social unit that people perceive as distinct and "out there" (Berger and Luckmann 1966; Tajfel and Turner 1986). The subjective, cognitive dimension is critical. Groups do not always form from a set of ties because people do not always perceive those ties or act on them.[1]

Networks, by definition, are not groups, but they can evolve into groups and become grouplike affiliations (Emerson 1972a, 1972b). This occurs if people come to see a network as a singular social unit and act with reference to that unit. If perceived as a group, people treat fellow participants in the network more favorably and orient their behavior to the network itself as a group entity (Lawler and Yoon 1998). From our theory of social commitments, it is conceivable that a network could foster interactions and positive emotions that, in turn, could render that network an object of commitment. The same can be said of particular social relations within a network.

Group formation involves the development of a person-to-group tie; thus, asking how and when networks take on group properties is a relevant application of our theory. We ask more generally: what are the structural ties or conditions that generate high levels of jointness and thereby promote a strong sense of shared responsibility, leading people to attribute their feelings to the group affiliation? Structures link people together, and it is important to understand when people so linked come to see themselves as members of a common group. This focus is consistent with the micro-emergence theme of this volume. Before people develop or act on person-to-group ties, the group itself needs to be salient to them. Structures can activate and make salient group affiliation by shaping the incentives and tasks that people interact around. Once activated in repeated social interactions, a group or group affiliation becomes "real" to people, and they act accordingly toward each other and toward the group itself.

Our approach to the structural foundations of groups is informed primarily by social exchange theory from sociology (Emerson 1981; Molm and Cook 1995; Molm 2006), but we use the concept of a minimal group from social identity theory (Tajfel and Turner 1986). Social identity theory and research sets the stage by empirically supporting the idea that groups exist in a minimal or tacit sense if and when people perceive a group affiliation between themselves and others, and that under these conditions they act in a group-oriented way (Tajfel and Turner 1986; Hogg 2004). This reflects a rudimentary person-to-group tie. Social exchange theory helps to identify and conceptualize the structural dimensions that may foster such minimal or tacit groups. Our theory in turn points to the mechanisms by which groups emerge when people interact repeatedly to solve joint tasks (for reviews, see Thye, Yoon, and Lawler 2002; Lawler and Thye 2006). In this way, our theorizing links social exchange ideas about social structure to social identity ideas about group formation.[2]

What facets of social structure are foundational to the development of group affiliations? This chapter identifies and analyzes three implied by the social exchange tradition: structures contain incentives for some ties to be actualized and others to be left dormant; structures shape the nature of the tasks that people interact around; and structures enable, create, constrain, or prohibit opportunities for people to interact and develop ties with others. We take structural incentives, tasks, and opportunities as fundamental bases for the emotions people derive from task interactions and their inclinations to associate those feelings with a group or group affiliation. These are the exogenous conditions under which groups become salient social objects of attachment through the shared responsibility and the emotional and affective mechanisms specified by our theory.[3]

All three of the structural dimensions involve ties that are possible and ties that are actualized. In a more global, individualized world, the range of possible ties expands astronomically because people have more options about the ties they can actually develop. The local, everyday world of people appears to have only distant connections to the larger, global world, but the example of small-world networks suggests that this is not necessarily the case. Ties nested within a global web of relations are not unusual, and these have important effects on the daily opportunities and constraints of people. Frigyes Karinthy was one of the first to advance the idea that, although we live in a geographically large and fragmented world, most of us may be linked or connected by a fairly short chain of acquaintances and thus, operationally, we live in a structurally "small world."

The small-world phenomenon is familiar to anyone who has seen the movie *Six Degrees of Separation.* To understand the nature of small worlds, consider the link between you and the U.S. president. You probably know someone who knows your state representative, perhaps a professor, judge, or county official. If that state representative then knows the president, there are three steps between you and the president. Total strangers are often surprised and pleased to find that they are connected by some mutual acquaintances. These connections can be thought of as structural opportunities that have yet to be realized.[4]

The idea that we actually live in a small world is fascinating because it poses an interesting puzzle: we live on a planet inhabited by 6.5 billion people, separated by oceans and continents, and yet the average distance between any two randomly selected people on the globe is only about six steps. While this is relatively easy to explain if we assume that the social ties of 6.5 billion people in the world are randomly dispersed, it is clear that social ties are anything but random. Our social ties tend to be fairly small and heavily influenced by geographical distance and homophily. We overwhelmingly tend to associate with those who are similar to ourselves in race, age, occupation, income, geographic location, and so on. The upshot is that real-world personal networks tend to be localized, highly clustered, and fundamentally small. The paradox is not that we can't find our way out of our small social worlds, but that we can. Given that our social networks tend to be small, how is it possible that only six steps separate any two people?

The answer is not obvious. Everyone in the world is more closely connected than small-world networks imply because every now and then people develop a "long" tie to someone more distant in the world. This could be a friend in Korea, a brother in Thailand, or a former roommate who works in the White House. These long-tie shortcuts have a seemingly random structure (Watts 2003) that shrinks the world by "bridging" otherwise distant individuals, but they still maintain the "clustered" small-world property of local networks. An individualization narrative about the social transformations of the age (see chapter 2) suggests that as our social worlds become more private and market-oriented, the small clusters that normally pattern lives tend to shrink or become looser. There is in fact some evidence that our local networks are shrinking; this is manifest in the finding that more Americans report having no one to talk to about personal matters (McPherson, Smith-Lovin, and Brashears 2006) and also in a general decline of social capital, conceived in terms of actualized network ties (Putnam 2000). Robert Putnam (2000) proposed the "bowling alone" metaphor to capture the state of social ties.

Research on Internet usage, however, suggests a less pessimistic conclusion: new technologies of communication are strengthening social capital, both by supplementing traditional face-to-face interactions and by promoting new ties that then lead to face-to-face interactions (see Katz and Rice 2002; Haythornthwaite and Wellman 2002). "Networked individualism" is an alternative metaphor proposed by Caroline Haythornthwaite and Barry Wellman (2002); it portrays the social world as increasingly composed of individualized networks that, among other things, interconnect local and distant ties. Overall, they argue, networks are replacing groups as primary social-unit affiliations, meaning that people are living more and more in individualized network communities rather than in groups with definable boundaries. We argue, in contrast, that group affiliations and person-to-group ties are prone to emerge implicitly or tacitly even under these sorts of conditions. The small-world idea suggests some subtle ways in which social structures generate a degree of social closeness, possible or actual, that is counterintuitive and more widespread than typically thought. Person-to-group ties may be an unrecognized product of this.

The sections of this chapter progressively flesh out the structural foundations of groups and group affiliations using theory and research from the social exchange and social network traditions of sociology (Emerson 1972b; Molm and Cook 1995; Willer 1999; Burt 1992). To deal with the incentive dimensions of social structure we analyze how interdependencies affect interactions and relations; to deal with the task dimensions we apply ideas about the forms of interaction or exchange; and to deal with the opportunity dimensions we analyze the network configurations within which people find partners to interact with. In each case, we ask how these structural dimensions affect the emotions that people experience and their tendency to attribute them to the group. Our purpose is to show how and why these structural dimensions lead people to think of themselves as members of a group in cognitive and behavioral terms and to connect their individual feelings to something larger—a shared group affiliation. When tacit or implicit group affiliations emerge in this way, they promote an enduring, stable social order.

THE SOCIAL EXCHANGE ORIENTATION

At the heart of social exchange theorizing is a fairly sharp distinction between interdependence (structure), transactions (exchange), and relationships (see Emerson 1972). Structural interdependence refers to a network of possible social ties within which people interact and exchange for things that they need or want. The interdependence is created by the goods that people need or desire and the availability of those goods in a network. Transactions are the actual exchanges (giving and receiving) that produce the flows of benefit between individuals and groups. Some transactions are explicitly contractual in that they involve explicit agreements, such as when customers buy coffee at a coffee shop. Other transactions are noncontractual, such as friendship and marriage relationships. Transactions involve different tasks that vary in the degree of jointness or shared responsibility for the results produced. Relationships develop from repeated transactions by the same people and constitute a social tie, which can vary in the degree to which it is instrumental (transactional) or expressive (relational). The sequence in figure 5.1 underlies and orients social exchange theory across a wide variety of research:

Figure 5.1   The Orienting Model from Exchange Theory

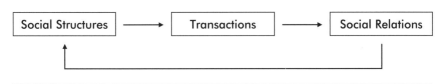

Source: Authors' compilation.

To elaborate, structures of interdependence determine who is likely to transact with whom, and relations of varying salience, strength, and value emerge from these transactions. Social relations, in turn, tend to change the structures within which future transactions take place; there is thus a cycle of feedback effects that help account for the regularity in transactions. These feedback effects also capture how social embeddedness emerges endogenously from economic transactions. Social embeddedness refers to the nesting of a local, immediate transaction in a larger network of relations. That social embeddedness emerges in networks and markets is now axiomatic in both economics and sociology. With this backdrop in mind, the following sections discuss three structural dimensions from the sociological literature on exchange: structures of dependence and interdependence (the incentive dimension, portrayed earlier), structural forms of the social exchange (the task dimension), and networks of possible ties (the opportunity dimension). We analyze how these bear on the tendency toward group formation, as conceived by social identity theory.

INCENTIVE STRUCTURES: THE ROLE OF INTERDEPENDENCE

Seminal research in social exchange theory has been devoted to theorizing the effects of interdependence in social exchange contexts. Early theorists such as Harold Kelley and John Thibaut (1978) distinguished three types of dependencies: reflexive control, fate control, and behavioral control. These refer, respectively, to the degree to which people's outcomes are determined by their own behavior (independence), the behavior of the other (dependence), or a combination of their own and the other's behavior (interdependence). Mutual fate control (dependence) establishes the foundation for trading resources or behaviors that do not produce new value to be divided but still involve contingencies. In contrast, mutual behavioral control (interdependence) promotes the negotiation of coordinated behaviors that have multiplicative effects on resources or exchange outcomes (Molm 1994). These forms of dependence are interwoven, and it is reasonable to hypothesize that the greater the degree of mutual behavioral control (interdependence) and the lower the degree of mutual reflexive control (independence), the more people perceive the results of their exchange—whether positive or negative—as produced jointly. Thus, these types of dependency have different propensities to produce shared emotions and perceptions that spark person-to-group ties.

The theory of relational cohesion (Lawler and Yoon 1993, 1996, 1998) elaborates on this idea. This theory argues that structural conditions of dependence—relative and total (mutual) dependencies—make exchanges between some actors more likely than others. Specifically, when mutual dependence is high (the exchange partners really need each other), people find one another more attractive relative to other potential exchange partners. When relative dependence is equal (people equally rather than unequally need each other), the exchange partners find it easier to reach agreement because neither has an a priori power advantage. The theory indicates that exchange frequencies across pairs of people in a network or group vary depending on these conditions of dependence (Lawler and Yoon 1996). The model in figure 5.2 captures the main ideas of relational cohesion theory.

The overall message is that exogenous structural power (dependence) conditions generate commitments to social relations indirectly through an endogenous process in which emotions are central—that is, an exchange-to-emotion-to-cohesion sequence. Repeated exchange fosters global positive emotions in the form of pleasure and satisfaction or interest and excitement. Positive emotions in turn produce cohesion, or the perception that the relation is a unifying force in the situation, because actors seek to interpret and understand the causes of their emotions, and in the process their exchange relations become more salient. The perception of cohesion in the relation captures the idea that the relation itself is a solidifying or unifying force or object, external to the people involved

Figure 5.2   The Theory of Relational Cohesion

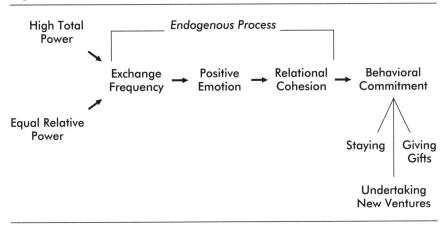

Source: Reprinted from *American Sociological Review* (Lawler and Yoon 1996).

(see, for example, Berger and Luckmann 1966). This idea can be extended to groups of three or more with a joint task (Lawler, Thye, and Yoon 2000).

The movement from individual emotions to perceiving the relation as a unifying force is movement toward an emergent person-to-group tie or a nascent group identity. For example, one can think of marriage or kinship ties as more or less cohesive and salient, depending on the feelings produced in interactions with wives or brothers. It is this sense of cohesion that produces various forms of commitment behavior, such as: (1) staying in the relation despite equal or better alternatives; (2) providing benefits or gifts unilaterally and without explicit expectations of reciprocity; and (3) undertaking new ventures in the context of a social dilemma in which there is risk or the potential for malfeasance (Lawler and Yoon 1996; Thye, Yoon, and Lawler 2002). Overall, the theory of relational cohesion explains how patterns of mutual interdependence unleash emotions that promote person-to-relation commitments.

The general message is that social order emerges to the extent that interdependent interactions produce positive emotions and make salient the unifying force of the social relation within these interactions. Based on the theoretical argument in chapter 4, the jointness involved in high mutual dependence or equal dependence establishes the conditions for individuals to attribute their own emotions not just to themselves or to the other person but also to the social relation that binds them. This is not uncommon. People often think about and are quite responsive to positive and negative feelings in interactions with children, spouses, coworkers, and so on. That we develop stronger or weaker emotional ties to these social relations in part as a result of the episodic feelings we experience in particular interactions with these others is an inherent feature of social life. The theory of relational cohesion explains how order or stability emerges at a relational level in such contexts and how the relation itself may become an expressive object.

TASK STRUCTURES: THE ROLE OF FORMS OF EXCHANGE

Returning to earlier examples, consider how exchange theory conceives the simple exchanges or tasks in a hair salon, morning coffee shop, and residential neighborhood. In both the hair salon and the coffee shop, the structure involves normative roles—customer and employee—that define their task, that is, what is expected of each. Customers must pay for a service (hair salon) or a product (coffee shop), and this exchange is contractual. In the hair salon, the patron's person-to-person relationship with the hair stylist is likely to be stronger than the patron's person-to-group relation to the salon. Over time some patrons may develop a relationship with the stylist and even exchange small things of value; tipping generously in return for somewhat flexible scheduling. In the coffee shop, there is also a contractual exchange (paying for coffee), but the social tie is primarily to the shop rather than to any of the constituent employees. In both the hair salon and coffee shop, the interactions involve a mix of contractual and relational elements, but the importance of person-to-person and person-to-group ties is different.

In the neighborhood, the ties are less clear or specified a priori. You may have a homeowners' association that exchanges community services to the neighborhood for a small membership fee. You may also develop friendship ties with neighbors who live close to you, in which case you exchange small favors with no strings attached across time. Physical proximity is an opportunity but also a constraint on who interacts with whom in the neighborhood: it makes possible some person-to-person ties but not others. The larger structure of the homeowners' association allows and may facilitate ties or emotions directed at the community or neighborhood as a whole. The overall implication is that some types of interaction foster person-to-person ties while others foster person-to-group ties. We analyze this by adapting ideas about different forms of exchange from social exchange theory (Molm and Cook 1995).

Social exchanges can take on a variety of structural forms; in the sociological literature, there are four basic forms. The first, negotiated exchange, involves an explicit trade of goods, services, or other benefits based on a negotiated or contractual arrangement—an employment contract, for example. Here the behaviors of giving and receiving are tightly connected and well defined. A second type, reciprocal exchange, entails a pattern of reciprocal assistance or advice across time. The behaviors of giving and receiving are loosely connected and not well defined—as with neighbors who exchange favors. A third form of exchange, productive exchange, occurs around a collective or group project: people give time, effort, or other resources to the group and receive something of value back from the group. Here people give to a group rather than to other people and receive benefits from that group. A homeowners' association is an example: members give resources to the association (fees, dues, time) and receive benefits (well-cared-for common areas) back from it. Finally, generalized exchange involves a string or chain of assistance or benefits in which, for example, person A helps person B, person B helps person C, and person C helps person A. Everybody receives the assistance they need, but from different people. Giving and receiving are separated because these activities are directed at different persons. Fitting this form is the act of stopping to help a stranded motorist with the hope in mind that someone will help you someday if needed. There is an emerging literature that compares and contrasts how these forms of exchange differ, suggesting that each may promote person-to-group ties of different strength (Emerson 1981; Molm 1994; Lawler 2001; Lawler et al. 2008).

To further illustrate how forms of interaction or social exchange differ, consider the alternative ways in which universities can address the task of meeting temporary teaching needs through cross-departmental resource flows. If a sociology department has a teaching need in statistics for a semester that only a faculty member from the statistics department can satisfy, any one of the four forms of exchange is a viable option. Through the negotiated form, the sociology department directly compensates the statistics department for the teaching done by a statistician in accord with an explicit contract that works out the salary and benefits between the two departments. In a reciprocal form of exchange, the statistics department would essentially provide a person to the sociology department as a favor, with no payment or strings attached. The statistics department may implicitly expect that if it has a teaching need in the future, perhaps in the social science methods area, it could be met by someone from the sociology department (Molm 1994).

Both the negotiated and reciprocal forms of exchange are task structures that would involve direct, dyadic interactions between the departments. Negotiated exchanges are more carefully monitored and contractual than reciprocal exchanges in that the accounting of who gives and gets what is more precise, neither exchange partner is prepared to give unilaterally to the other, and there is a joint problem that the partners solve through a contractual arrangement. In reciprocal exchange, the relational rather than the contractual component is essential because it involves looser accounting or tallying up of what each partner receives and there are fewer safeguards against being exploited. In negotiated exchange, the relations that emerge are built and sustained to solve joint problems when they occur. In reciprocal exchange, relations are built on the perceptions (such as trust) that people develop of each other in the course of reciprocal giving over time (Molm, Takawashi, and Peterson 2000; Molm 2003). In this sense, negotiated exchanges generate ties to the relation (the larger social unit), whereas reciprocal exchanges generate ties to other people. Because of this, the former has a somewhat greater capacity to produce group ties (Lawler 2001).

The other ways of solving the teaching problem would involve indirect ties to a larger formal or informal social unit, such as the college. A productive exchange might be undertaken by creating a pool of cross-listed courses that fulfill requirements in both departments. In productive exchange, there would be a single joint product (a pool of resources) from which individual departments benefit. Another option would be for this effort to expand across all departments in the college, with the college managing the pooled resources. Whatever the particular mechanism, inputs flow from department to group, and the benefits flow from group to department. The development of person-to-group ties here is clear and explicit.

In contrast, a generalized form of exchange would require at least three departments and would separate the givers and receivers, such that each department would give and receive help with its teaching needs from another department, but these exchanges would involve unilateral flows of assistance between different departments. This form of exchange could develop if college norms created expectations that departments would help each other with teaching needs as members of the same college out of obligation. An overarching monitor or authority, such as a dean, might be necessary to ensure that the norm is observed or to facilitate these arrangements. All things being equal, the group boundaries are more salient in the productive exchange than in the generalized exchange because productive exchanges are explicitly between individual actors (departments) and the group (college), whereas exchanges are interdepartmental in generalized exchange (see Lawler 2001). As such, productive exchange has a greater capacity to produce person-to-group ties, and consequently social order at the micro level.[5]

In sum, the theory of social commitments implies that these forms of social exchange or interaction have different propensities to produce stronger or weaker social commitments to social units (see also Lawler 2001). Productive exchange has the greatest capacity to produce person-to-unit ties to relations and groups or organizations, because productive exchange involves the greatest nonseparability of individual contributions to the group or collective task. It therefore should induce strong perceptions of joint responsibility and positive emotions for task success; in turn, individuals should attribute these perceptions and emotions to the overarching group. The very structure of productive exchange fosters person-to-group commitments through the emotions that are experienced in the context of the underlying social interaction.

Negotiated and reciprocal exchanges should foster direct person-to-person ties or relationships. These forms entail less task jointness than productive exchange and are less likely to lead people to attribute their feelings from task activity to the group. Person-to-group ties are weaker here. Negotiated exchange does involve more jointness than reciprocal exchange, because people come together to create a contractual agreement; however, it is also a cooler, more formal, and more impersonal kind of interaction. Reciprocal exchange is more interpersonal in nature, but it involves unilateral acts that are separated by time and carry the risk of exploitation, making trust crucial to social order. Such conditions should attenuate perceptions of shared responsibility and person-to-group commitments. Reciprocal exchange should be a stronger foundation for person-to-person ties than for person-to-group ties.

Finally, generalized exchange has the weakest potential for group formation and for the emergence of person-to-group ties from the actions and interactions of people within the structure. The giving behaviors are fragmented and disjointed, coupled with the fact that givers and receivers are distinct (A gives to B, B gives to C, and C gives to A); task jointness is thus very low. From our theory, generalized exchange produces weaker emotional responses, weaker perceptions of shared responsibility, and weaker commitments. To generate social order, generalized exchange requires an extant group with strong and enforceable norms of giving and cooperation.

With regard to the potential for endogenously generated order, our theory predicts the following ordering among the forms of interaction or exchange:

Productive > Negotiated > Reciprocal > Generalized

A recent study offers empirical support to this ordering of the forms of exchange (Lawler, Thye, and Yoon 2008). Specifically, the study compares these four forms of exchange along four dimensions that reflect the strength of micro-level social order in a three-person network: rates of exchange or giving valued benefits to another; positive emotions; perceptions of cohesion at the network level; and affective attachment to the network as a group. The results indicate that productive forms of exchange or interaction generate more exchange, more positive feelings, a greater sense of cohesion, and stronger affective attachment to the group (network); generalized exchange produces the least along all these dimensions; and negotiated and reciprocal forms of exchange are in between but not different from one another, as predicted earlier. Perceptions of shared responsibility mirrored these patterns. Overall, this study provides strong and consistent empirical support for our theory about the structure of exchange or interaction tasks.[6]

The next section examines network structures that may naturally produce positive emotions and affective ties to the network as a unit—in other words, network dimensions that generate group formation at the network level. We consider two primary dimensions: the network connections, that is, the connections between ties or relations in the network; and the network shape, or the configuration of enabled or allowed ties. Each of these dimensions bears on the structure of the interaction opportunities.

OPPORTUNITY STRUCTURES: THE ROLE OF NETWORKS

Networks provide opportunities for and sometimes constraint on all sorts of social and economic activity and relations. For example, the notion of social embeddedness has been used to understand the influence of social relations on economic transactions. Recent research shows that this affects pricing in corporate law practices. In classic economic theory, there is a market supply of legal providers and some environmental demand for legal services. The exchanges between a particular legal supplier and a particular consumer are presumably guided by the "invisible hand" of the neoclassical market, which affects who exchanges with whom and the price paid for services. In principle, the exchange structure here is not unlike a network wherein all legal suppliers presumably have access to all potential consumers. In economic theory, the ties between suppliers and consumers are "arm's-length" in that they are fragile and easily broken as incentives change (Uzzi 1996).

Nevertheless, social and behavioral scientists have found that many markets do not operate this way. Instead, when individuals or firms in a market interact repeatedly with one another, they develop what are called "embedded ties." This occurs when the parties come to develop relations with one another that are more socially and less economically based. Close, special, or exclusive ties arise from regular or frequent interaction between the parties involved in economic exchanges. Research reveals that parties in embedded relations provide each other with proprietary information that they would not disclose in arm's-length relations, and they also develop less complete contracts (which reduces transaction costs) because they perceive each other as trustworthy. Brian Uzzi (1996, 678–79), in ethnographic fieldwork, shows that "embedded ties entail joint problem-solving arrangements that enable actors to coordinate functions and work out problems on the fly." These arrangements provide more rapid and explicit feedback than do market-based mechanisms (see also Uzzi and Lancaster 2004). Of particular interest, embedded relations create transaction patterns that depart from those expected by classical economic theory. Socially embedded relations, it seems, have the capacity to fundamentally alter the market structures from which they develop.

The work on embedded social relations illustrates that networks of personal ties can alter economic activity in markets. This raises a broader question: what dimensions of social networks are likely to produce stronger social commitments? Asked differently, when and how are networks of self-interested agents transformed into more cohesive groups with an overarching group identity?[7] From our theory, networks that foster a high degree of task jointness, perceptions of shared responsibility, and positive emotional reactions are the most likely to generate group formation and commitment at the network level. Exchange theorists have identified several network properties that should affect these phenomena, and here we use these to understand which kinds of networks may promote person-to-unit transformations. Network connections and network shape capture central themes of social exchange approaches.

Network Connections

To illustrate the effects of network connections, consider a network of three mutual friends who come together periodically to play racquetball with one another. Imagine that on Tuesdays the game of choice is two-player racquetball, but on Fridays the club requires that three players compete in games of cutthroat (a game in which each point is determined by two players against the third). For Tuesday games this means that each player has at least two choices for a partner, but once any given pair decides to play, the third is excluded. Exchange theorists refer to these contingencies across relations as "exclusively connected relations" (Willer 1999).[8] Many social relations are like this, including monogamous marriages or partnerships and most employment relations. A decision to interact in one relation (to get married or to take a job) often limits or precludes relations with other potential partners. In contrast, consider the case where the three players must all interact to play cutthroat. When any two players agree to play on Friday, they need the third to also agree to play or no game can take place. Here a successful interaction requires that all others agree to play that evening. Exchange theorists refer to these groups as "inclusively connected dyads."[9] Many social relations are like this, such as running a bakery that requires the head chef to successfully exchange with different suppliers for eggs, milk, and flour to produce pastries. In inclusively connected relations, failure to acquire any single component jeopardizes the entire transaction because all of the ingredients are required to generate a product.

To apply the theory of social commitments to the example, we must acknowledge that there are important differences between exclusive and inclusive network ties. Exclusive relations might be easier to produce and maintain in some ways, because they would require only two individuals and would be more easily coordinated. Yet, because exclusive relations would necessarily "leave out" one of the three individuals, they would entail less task jointness, lower perceptions of shared responsibility, and the potential for the excluded party to experience negative emotion. In contrast, inclusive relations would involve higher task nonseparability, since all three parties are required to interact and collectively produce the experience of the game itself. Whereas inclusive relations would involve person-to-person ties, they would also make more salient a larger social unit—the group of players—that is distinct from dyadic ties. This raises the prospect that positive emotions would emerge and be directed at the group rather than the other individuals in it. If so, over time a group identity could develop from the interaction. For these reasons, inclusive networks should produce greater perceptions of shared responsibility and stronger positive emotions and thus should be more likely to foster strong person-to-group commitments.

Network Shape

When people think of social networks, they probably think of how extensive or intensive the ties are that people have to one another and what kind of overall pattern there is to these ties. Social scientists have done significant work on both topics, but the latter topic on network shape has interesting implications for our theorizing. The overall shape of the network affects who can and cannot exchange with whom. We took up the question of when and how networks of individual agents come to see themselves as belonging to a common group, sharing a common identity, experiencing positive emotion, and behaving in prosocial ways (Thye and Lawler 1999). We developed a concept of network cohesion that captures two network conditions: the proportion of relations within a network that are of equal power, and the degree of relational density in the network. Equal-power relations are those in which no person has an advantage based on the network shape—that is, all positions are identical. The main assertion is that exchange networks containing a high number of equal-power relations and many direct connections between people will unleash positive emotions that are attributed to the larger group at the *network level*. In other words, the shape of the network generates interactions and emotions that make the social unit more salient and create an overarching group identity. In terms of our theory, this suggests that individuals who are exchanging within highly connected networks that comprise many equal-power relations should be more likely to sense a common experience and a shared responsibility with the others as they interact and exchange with select partners.

To illustrate, compare the five networks shown in figure 5.3. Assume that each position in the network represents a person who can interact with any connected other, but only one other at a time; in other words, the network ties are exclusively connected. Power is determined by the potential for exclusion among network members (the opportunity structure) and measured by the relative winnings from negotiated exchanges between connected parties. The three-line contains the largest power differentiation because the central position can never be excluded and one of the peripheral persons must always be excluded; clearly, in such a network power is centralized. This is why popular teenagers who have many dating options with partners who have fewer options are powerful in friendship networks. The four-line network is called a "weak power" network because, although exclusion can occur (when the two central actors exchange with one another), it need not occur (when each central position exchanges with a peripheral). Such networks tend to produce slight power advantages that favor the more central positions. Overall, it is unlikely that either strong or weak power networks will generate a sense of shared responsibility at the network level or make the network a target for emotions.

In contrast, the triangle is an equal-power network because all positions are structurally identical. The network shape gives no position an a priori

Figure 5.3   Five Common Social Networks

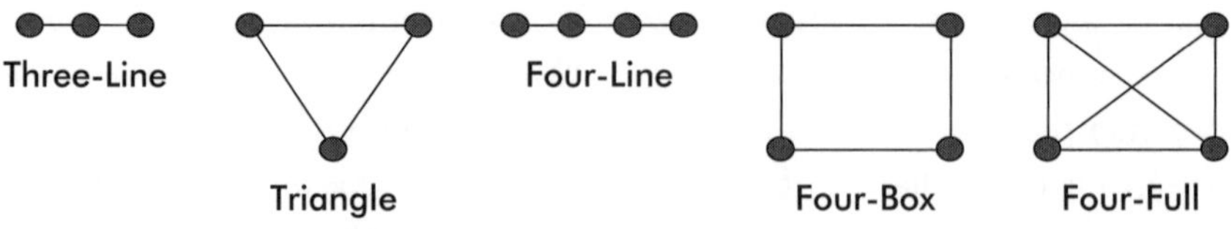

Three-Line   Triangle   Four-Line   Four-Box   Four-Full

Source: Authors' compilation.

advantage. Also, this network is more densely connected than the three-line, since each position is connected to every other position. The theory holds that because the triangle contains a high degree of equal-power relations, and many direct ties between actors, people are more likely to attribute positive emotions from dyadic exchange to their shared affiliation, the network, thereby giving it a group property. Thus, when repeated exchanges in dyads within a dense equal-power network produce positive feelings, people perceive the network as a group for which they share responsibility and to which they attribute their feelings. The result is stronger and more affective person-to-group commitments.

Just as the triangle is an equal-power network, so are the four-box and the four-full. Again, within each network all positions are structurally identical, so none has an advantage. The four-full is fully connected, like the triangle, in that every position can exchange with all others; the four-box is equal-power, but not all ties are possible, so it has less density than the triangle and the four-full. Like the triangle, however, these networks should unleash more positive emotions at the dyad level but also generate a sense of common experience and shared responsibility at the network level. Thus, people are likely to perceive the network as a group and to associate their individual feelings with that unit.

We tested these implications experimentally by examining how people exchange resources in equal versus unequal power networks, such as the triangle and three-line in figure 5.3 (Thye and Lawler 2004). The results supported the argument above. In networks with high network cohesion (such as the triangle), dyadic exchanges generate positive emotions, and these emotions generate group formation at the network level. The theory of social commitments interprets this as due to such networks promoting a sense of common experience and a corresponding sense of shared responsibility. The network shape or configuration affects when individuals come to see one another as members of a common group in identity terms. A general implication is that network (opportunity) structures contain the seeds of a collective order, because they yield interactions and emotions that can transform rational, self-interested individuals into collectively oriented members of a common group.

CONCLUSIONS

This chapter addresses the most fundamental foundations for the emergence of groups or group affiliations in the context of a network of self-interested agents who exchange valued resources. Group formation involves an emergent person-to-group tie. Structures are conceptualized, in network terms, as a set of ties between individuals that provide opportunities and constraints on social interaction. Networks manifest a number of structural properties that shape who is likely to interact with whom, the nature of that interaction, the degree to which the interaction is nonseparable, and the extent to which the network may become a group in cognitive and behavioral terms. Specifically, we analyze network incentive structures (based on relative interdependencies), task structures (based on the nature or form of social exchange), and opportunity structures (based on the pattern of ties in the network) that encourage group formation. The purpose is to use the theory presented in chapter 4 to identify structures that yield nascent (minimal) group formation and emergent person-to-group ties.

To review the main points, there are a number of network properties that determine if and when networks are likely to become groups in cognitive and behavioral terms. First, beginning with the incentive structure, the networks most likely to generate tacit or minimal groups are those in which people are equally dependent on one another for valued goods and highly interdependent or mutually dependent on one another. The latter condition provides strong incentives to work together or exchange, while the former makes it easier to reach agreement by mitigating issues of power, fairness, and trust. The theory of relational cohesion makes explicit how these two factors unleash an endogenous process wherein positive emotions and relational cohesion promote commitment.

Second, with regard to task structure, person-to-group ties are most likely when the task involves considerable jointness, because jointness leads those who experience positive feelings to attribute those feelings to something they share. Social exchange theorists have conceptualized four distinct forms of exchange task: productive, negotiated, reciprocal, and generalized. In productive exchange, in which individuals contribute to a group good and receive benefits from it, the focus of emotional attributions is likely to be at the group level, owing to its highly joint nature. Group formation is predicted to be strongest here. The other forms of exchange are more oriented to a particular exchange partner (in reciprocal and negotiated cases) and involve less jointness overall. Person-to-group ties can develop here but are not as likely as with productive forms of exchange. Finally, owing to the highly fragmented nature of giving and receiving, generalized exchange should have the weakest capacity to produce emergent person-to-group ties. Here it is not the task but exogenous group norms that generate ties to the group. Overall, the task structures that are most joint in nature should elicit the strongest sense of shared responsibility and, consequently, social commitments at the group level.

Finally, we considered how two kinds of opportunity structures bear on the capacity of a network to generate person-to-group ties: the connectedness of dyadic ties and the overall shape of the network. The former captures interdependencies across dyads, while the latter taps the capacity for individuals to interact frequently on equal terms with many connected others. Regarding connectedness, inclusively connected relations have higher group-generating capacities than exclusively connected relations, because in the former there is simply more incentive to act in concert as a group. In some ways this is similar to productive exchange in that people benefit maximally when all parties participate, and the collective good suffers if any single individual chooses not to participate. Regarding the network shape, we argue and find empirically that denser networks with more equal-power relations are most likely to evolve into groups through processes specified by our theory. Dense networks provide the opportunity to interact frequently with many others, while equal-power networks enable that joint interaction to occur without raising issues of inequity or injustice. In sum, the connectedness and shape of networks determine the potential of a network to promote emergent groups.

Social structures of various kinds have important effects on the emergence of person-to-group ties. One of the most interesting implications is that structures shape and pattern our lives in important ways, yet by and large these effects are invisible to most of those affected. We rarely think about friendly interactions with neighbors as "reciprocal exchanges," or about dating relations as being "exclusively connected." Yet structural foundations—the incentives to interact, the nature of the interaction task, and the range of opportunities—play a key role in the development of interpersonal and person-to-group ties. They do so in their capacity to bring people together around joint activity that produces positive emotion and perceptions of shared responsibility. We have shown how these structural foundations provide a pathway by which people socially construct person-to-group ties and commitments to larger units.

CHAPTER 6

Local Commitments in Organizations

Large organizations such as multinational corporations, labor unions, government agencies, and nationwide nonprofits have differentiated sub-units nested within them. These may be business units (companies) within a corporation, a local union within a state federation of labor unions, departments in a city government, or local chapters in a national volunteer organization. Nested sub-units pose well-known problems of coordination, fragmentation, and communication that broadly translate into a problem of order. This chapter addresses the commitment aspect of such problems and is organized around a theory of nested commitments (see Lawler 1992).

Nested sub-units pose problems of order in part because they are potential objects of attachment that compete with commitments to the larger organization. People may become more committed to their local sub-units than to the organization as a whole because of the immediacy and salience of local units to everyday experiences. Employees may be more committed to their local work unit, union members to their local, and volunteers to their local chapter of a national organization. Commitments to nested sub-units are an important part of the turf problems in complex organizations, often associated with decentralization. In this chapter, we analyze the conditions under which local units become stronger objects of attachment than the larger organizational unit.[1]

Jack Welch, an icon of corporate leadership and management, struggled with the problem of nested units at the outset of his tenure as CEO of General Electric. In response, he fashioned what was considered a new paradigm at the time: the idea of a "boundaryless organization" (Ashkenas et al. 1998). Among his first initiatives was a virtual declaration of war against turf battles between departments and divisions within the company. Welch spoke out forcefully about GE's bureaucracy having fostered balkanization and related inefficiencies. He believed strongly that the bureaucracy of GE had come to put an excessive emphasis on rules and erected invisible walls and organizational boxes between layers of management and organizational functions, as well as between customers, suppliers, and the firm. He set out to dismantle the existing bureaucracy and associated mind-set. In this effort, it was essential to confront and address the unit commitments of managers and employees in the organization.

Welch pared away layers of management from an original nine, delegating power to frontline employees at customer touch points so that they could make timely business decisions. Middle managers and seasoned employees who were more committed to their local work unit than the larger organization strongly resisted Welch's strategy (Welch and Byrne 2003) and insisted that GE was still a sound company that did not need a major overhaul (Tichy and Sherman 2001). Yet Welch persisted and implemented the "new paradigm" of a boundaryless organization, selling business units, tearing down turf boundaries between departments and divisions, and opening new partnerships with customers and suppliers. He created tighter lines of accountability between the corporate center and the sub-units while also delegating responsibility to the latter. Welch turned GE into a model in management circles, illustrating how to break through bureaucratic obstacles and overcome problems of fragmentation in large, complex, highly differentiated corporations (Tichy and Sherman 2001).[2]

Organizations combat problems of sub-unit commitment in a wide variety of ways, including symbolic measures. Organization-wide events, meetings, celebrations, newsletters, Web pages, and so forth, express the values, purpose, mission, and moral qualities of an organization. Token objects such as T-shirts, pens, cups, and glasses are symbolic reminders of an affiliation with or membership in the larger organization; organizational logos, slogans, and mottoes are reproduced widely; corporate philanthropy and civic participation are publicized for internal as well as external audiences. The assumption underlying these sorts of strategies is that fragmentation can be mitigated in part by making the larger organization more salient to members, highlighting its noble qualities, and rendering it a more valued identity. If people perceive and value their ties to the larger organizational unit, they ostensibly will respond with support when asked by organizational leaders to work even harder or in new ways on behalf of the larger organization, even to the detriment of their local unit. Nonetheless, the importance of sub-unit attachments and their capacity to weaken the influence of person-to-organization ties should not be underestimated, especially in a world of multinational corporations and nongovernmental organizations that spread employees and members over a multitude of social locations and boundaries.[3]

The problem of nested commitments is endemic in decentralized structures, though certainly not limited to them. How to balance local autonomy and central oversight or control is a perennial issue in virtually any large organization, from nation-states to corporations to unions to voluntary associations. Prevailing trends in how organizations structure collective efforts—whether in work organizations or voluntary associations—reveal considerable movement toward decentralized models. First of all, because hierarchy as the prime method for organizing work has waned (see chapter 7), the impact of an organization's hierarchy on daily work activity has become weaker and weaker (Baker and Cullen 1993; Ulrich and Lake 1990; Lawler and Galbraith 1994; Ackoff 1994). Efforts to delegate, empower, encourage participation and employee "buy-in," and tap diverse talents and expertise are all reshaping workplaces and other organizations. Command and control structures are "out." A second trend, noted in chapter 2, is that employees' ties to organizations have become more individualized and transactional. Contributing to this trend are the competitive pressures of a global economy, the growth of professional differentiation, and the decline of unions. Employment contracts involving lifetime employment are institutions of the past (Rousseau 1995; Arthur and Rousseau 1996; Morrison and Robinson 1997). Finally, there is increasing use of relatively small work groups and self-managed teams to coordinate roles and achieve tasks, thereby increasing individual and collective performance. Cross-functional collaborations are a key example. Together these trends imply that large, complex, differentiated organizations increasingly face significant problems of internal order owing to the nested commitments of members to local units or groups. Geographically disparate workforces and memberships accentuate the problems. We ask: What are the underlying sources of nested commitments? How can organizations manage or mitigate them? The answers implied by our theory are presented in the next section.

A THEORY OF NESTED COMMITMENTS

The theory of nested commitments, developed by Lawler (1992), puts forth principles that specify why people develop stronger commitments to local units and, by implication, how organizational structures mitigate tendencies that favor local groups over the larger organization. The theory interweaves three main ideas. First, social structures shape the degree to which people experience a sense of control or efficacy as they engage in activities within an organization. Some structures give people few feasible options about how to accomplish a task or work toward a goal, whereas others give people many good options from which they can choose (see also Lawler 1997). Second, people feel good when they experience a sense of control. That is, they experience pleasure, satisfaction, joy, happiness, elation, excitement, enthusiasm, and so forth. These emotions may be individualized or attributed to an organizational membership or affiliation. Third, people become more affectively committed to an organization that gives them a strong sense of control over their activities within the organization because they credit or attribute responsibility for their positive feelings to the organization. The result is a stronger affective component in person-to-organization commitments and a greater willingness to carefully attend to and sacrifice for the organization's welfare. A wide variety of theory and research is consistent with these three general ideas, though no research or theory to our knowledge has explicitly linked all three together (Giddens 1984; Kohn and Slomczynski 1990; Deci 1975; Westcott 1988).

Introducing the issue of people's sense of control or efficacy and using this issue to understand nested commitments extends our theory of social commitments. In chapter 4, we theorized the conditions under which local task interactions generate a sense of shared responsibility for collective results that then lead people to attribute their individual feelings to the group. This process can be applied to any group, whether local and immediate or larger and removed. This chapter goes a step further by arguing that task activities—individual or joint—also generate more or less sense of individual control and efficacy. This increase in an individual's sense of control, in turn, has two important effects: it strengthens his or her emotional responses (positive or negative) to the task activity; and it determines whether the person targets the local group or the larger group as the primary source or cause of his or her emotions. A new assumption is added here: at least two groups are salient—a local one nested within a more distant one. The implication is that we need to understand how people infer which social units are the sources of control. This is the main task of the theory of nested commitments.

A Sense of Control in Organizations

The term *sense of control* refers to the degree to which people perceive their actions to have effects on the world around them, that is, their efficacy, self-determination, freedom, or mastery over their environment (Deci 1975; Westcott 1988). In the theory, the main source of perceived control is the range of options or choices available to a person, given the structure of the organization. Structures have "enabling" and "constraining" dimensions (Giddens 1984). The more enabling and less constraining the structure, the greater the sense of control people tend to perceive and the stronger the positive emotions they feel from task activity. An example of enabling is when organizational units direct employees to undertake complex tasks without much supervision—for example, software engineers designing new software, or a corporate vice president of human resources developing a plan for a strategic change not mandated by the CEO. Organizational structures shape or determine the range of activity for addressing a task, but there are often gaps for which employees devise or choose among viable options. Even in highly constraining structures there are often areas of control and choice, and thus it is important to emphasize that perceptions of control are situational and involve a social comparison process.

Options and choices are also important because they generate a choice process involving "means/ends deliberation." Autonomy implies that a person deliberates about how to use that autonomy and about the choices to consider or make—that is, a person with autonomy goes through a "choice process" (Lawler 1992). Employees, of course, need the skills and resources to wisely exercise their discretion and take advantage of an enabling structure. The terms *efficacy* and *control* typically refer only to the outcome of an action or interaction episode, whereas the theory of nested commitments argues that deliberation itself can strengthen the generalized sense of control regardless of the outcome of a particular choice or activity (see Lawler 1992, 329–30). The very act of deliberation makes it clear to people that their work activity can make a difference, even though it may not in a particular instance. The theory therefore indicates that if employees in a work setting undertake tasks that can be accomplished in a variety of ways, and the organizational structure accords them substantial autonomy, greater organizational commitment will be promoted (for relevant research support, see Mathieu and Zajac 1990), providing that they have the necessary skills and resources. This in itself is not a new idea. What is new in the theory of nested commitments is a combined focus on the emotional effects of a sense of control and the attribution of those feelings to the organization. This focus also aligns the theory of nested commitments with our broader theory of social commitments. In brief, the theory argues that employees become more affectively committed to organizations with an "enabling structure," because such a structure gives them a sense of control and makes them feel good and they perceive the organization as responsible for these feelings. The obverse occurs when employees perceive constraining structures in the workplace as responsible for their negative feelings.

Giving employees a sense of control over their work is a long-held principle in the field of organizations (Tannenbaum 1968; Kanter 1977). This notion has inspired a variety of empowerment programs designed to derive motivational benefits from delegation and discretion (Lawler, Mohrman, and Ledford 1995; Smith 1997; Beer and Nohria 2000). In a study of randomly selected private firms in the U.S. manufacturing sector with more than fifty employees conducted by Paul Osterman (1994; see also Smith 1997), 35 percent of the firms surveyed reported having implemented at least two such empowerment programs. Moreover, a study by Eileen Appelbaum and Rosemary Batt (1994) of Fortune 1,000 firms found that 85 percent of the firms had implemented at least one empowerment program. Examples include quality circles, in which members on a shop floor participate in the design of products and services focused on improving quality; job enrichment programs, in which decisions are delegated to the rank-and-file employees (Myers 1970; Fink 1992); job enlargement programs, which assist employees in acquiring skills that will enable them to move beyond simple or routine tasks (Schoderbek and Reif 1969; Pruijt 1997); and self-managed work teams designed to encourage employees to manage and supervise their own areas of responsibility (Hackman 2002). Finally, project-oriented work strategies bring together people from different functional areas to accomplish a complex project from inception to completion. Such empowerment programs reflect a common goal—namely, to increase employees' sense of control by enlarging their choices in their work activities (Yoon 2001).

Our theory draws attention to and emphasizes the positive emotional effects of empowerment programs, suggesting that emotional responses determine whether such programs foster stronger non-instrumental, affective ties to the organization and therefore greater willingness to sacrifice on its behalf. Yet people may not associate the positive feelings generated by empowerment programs with the organization as a singular unit.

Attributing Feelings to the Organization

If the work a person does makes him or her feel good—that is, satisfied, rewarded, or self-enhanced—individuals can attribute their positive emotional responses to at least four sources: (1) themselves, owing to their own ambition, dedication, or talent; (2) others with whom they work, such as coworkers or partners; (3) a local, immediate group like a work group or department; or (4) a larger and more distant group, such as an organization. In chapter 4, we compared sources 1 and 2 with a group that could be either source 3 or 4. There we asserted that a sense of shared responsibility for the task results promotes attributions of individual feelings to a group. The theory of nested commitments provides a way to extend our analysis to conditions under which people attribute their feelings to local or distant units. For this purpose, there are two interrelated propositions put forth by the theory: a responsibility proposition and a distribution proposition.

The *responsibility proposition* is based in part on ideas from attribution theory in psychology, except that the focus is on attributions of emotions to a group affiliation (see chapter 4 for a related discussion of this point). The idea is that people make attributions about whom or what is responsible for their positive or negative feelings. They tend to make inferences and interpretations about where the emotions they feel come from. Attributions of responsibility may be internal and directed at oneself (for example, competence, talent, or the lack thereof) or external and directed at the situation (for example, luck, chance, constraint, or the lack of options or choice). Attributing feelings to a group is a special type of external attribution. The theory of nested commitments argues that employees develop explanations for the degree of autonomy and control they have to do their jobs, and these explanations involve attributions of credit or blame for perceived high or low control. The responsibility proposition is that people in a workplace attribute their individual feelings from work activity to the organization unit they see as responsible for the control and autonomy underlying those feelings. Positive feelings foster attributions of credit to those units and stronger affective attachments to them, whereas negative feelings foster attributions of blame and affective detachments from the responsible organizational unit. The implication is that successful empowerment programs generate stronger social commitments to the group or organizational unit that employees perceive as most responsible for these programs, and this may not be the larger organization, as explained next.

The *distribution proposition* addresses the question of how people target or allocate feelings to groups in a nested structure or hierarchy. What if a corporation initiates a corporate-wide empowerment program but allows particular sub-units, such as business units or divisions, to adapt it however they see fit? How the origins of the program are explained, how the program is framed, and how it is communicated at the corporate and sub-unit levels should bear on the effects of the program on employee commitments. If employees perceive the corporation as a prime source of empowerment, they are likely to attribute their positive feelings from such programs to the corporation itself. If employees perceive the local company as a prime source of the program, they are likely to attribute their feelings about it to the local company. Thus, an empowerment program may have unifying effects on the corporation as a whole if the corporation is perceived as having primary responsibility for it, but the program may enhance fragmentation among sub-units and between those units and the corporate center if the local unit is perceived as having primary responsibility for the program.

People can conceivably use two alternative "rules" or principles in assigning responsibility for positive or negative emotional events or experiences in an organization (Lawler 1992). One is the *proximal rule:* people tend to allocate more credit and less blame to local, immediate groups than to larger, more distant groups. Local groups are the immediate context for social interaction with others around joint tasks, and also the place where people interpret signals and communications from more distant, overarching organizations. All else being equal, the prediction is that people will use the proximal rule for allocating feelings, especially in decentralized organizations. The alternative is the *distal rule:* people give more credit and less blame to larger, more encompassing organizations. This rule may dominate in smaller, less differentiated organizations, but it may also prevail in large organizations with a strong and visible center. The changes that Jack Welch initiated at GE probably generated more use of the distal rule as people interpreted the prime sources of positive experiences and feelings in the workplace. In sum, use of the distal rule targets and creates more affective commitment to the larger unit, whereas use of the proximal rule targets and creates more affective commitment to the relevant local unit.

The use of the proximal rule or the distal rule reflects both the salience of the larger and nested units and the efficacy, individual or collective, that they provide to employees. The theory of nested commitments predicts that people are more likely to adopt the proximal rule, because local nested units are more salient and more immediately relevant and they involve frequent interaction with fellow employees who share the local affiliation. Shared, consensual interpretations of organizational events, both local and larger, are often crystallized at the local level, and this tends to favor the local group in the case of positive experiences and feelings. Decentralized organizations may generate greater fragmentation than is optimal, in part because the local unit is more salient as a source of individual and collective efficacy. In contrast, the larger organization may be perceived as a source of constraining bureaucratic rules and procedures. Universities are a good example: they are known to be highly decentralized, and the commitment of faculty to their local units—departments, colleges, or institutes—often seems stronger than their commitment to the larger university.[4]

There is an important difference, however, between positive experiences and feelings, on the one hand, and negative experiences and feelings, on the other. The main hypothesis of the theory of nested commitments is that people use the proximal rule to interpret and understand positive experiences and feelings, whereas they use the distal rule to understand and interpret negative experiences and feelings (see Lawler 1992). In other words, people attribute positive experiences to the local units or groups in which they participate daily and from which they can derive other satisfactions and rewards—for example, fellowship, advice, and assistance. In contrast, they push the causes of negative experiences outward to groups external to and more distant from their immediate unit (for a similar analysis of positive versus negative feelings, see Turner 2007). How often do we hear expressions of frustration, fear, or anger about programs or policies promulgated from more distant and central social units? For instance: "Here we go again," "Those people at the top don't understand or appreciate what we do or the problems we face," "What were they thinking?" and "Why don't they ask our opinion before doing these sorts of things?" The larger organization is an easy target for negative events and experiences because it is removed and distant from the local, everyday situation people face and within which they interact with others. Thus, the problem of organizational unity, posed by the theory of nested commitments, involves particular interpretations of enabling and constraining conditions—being more inclined to credit the local sub-unit for positive events or experiences and being more inclined to blame the larger organization for negative events or experiences.

Organizational practitioners are not unaware of the potential for stronger-than-optimal sub-unit commitments among employees. One can interpret common organizational interventions designed to deal with sub-unit fragmentation as a response to the patterns implied by the proximal rule. One class of interventions involves the development and design of cross-boundary work units, such as global teams, cross-subsidiary teams, cross-functional teams, or project teams whose activities span and bridge the sub-units nested within the larger organization (Ashkenas et al. 1998; Marquardt and Horvath 2001; Evans, Pucik, and Barsoux 2002). For example, Heineken built a global team called the European Production Task Force whose members represent each subsidiary and meet face to face to strengthen the company's production facilities across Europe. Another example is 3M, which utilizes companywide project teams with members from functional departments nested in each product and regional division.

Boundary-crossing interventions are structural interventions that, among other things, promote greater jointness and shared responsibility through collaborative interactions. Cultural interventions are framing efforts that are designed to keep the larger corporate entity salient—for example, by defining it with reference to a common vision and set of core values (Collins and Porras 1997; Pohlman, Gardiner, and Heffes 2000). With hundreds of operating units all over the world, companies such as Philips, Procter & Gamble, Unilever, and Matsushita have developed elaborate ways of infusing task activities with a distinctive corporate culture. The upshot is that structural and cultural interventions manipulate the jointness of tasks and sense of shared responsibility at the organizational level and thereby make the use of the distal rule more likely.

To conclude this part of the discussion, the theory of nested commitments points to a fundamental problem of order facing large, multinational organizations, in which power and control are necessarily decentralized. To the degree that employees' interactions are local, they tend to credit the local organizational units for positive experiences (opportunity, autonomy, and choice) and positive feelings (satisfying work, the joy of getting things done) and to blame the larger, more distant organizational unit for negative experiences (constraints and bureaucratic obstacles) and negative feelings (dissatisfying work, frustrations over difficulties in getting things done). Autonomy and empowerment therefore may strengthen ties to local sub-units more than to the larger organization. Organizations can reverse this pattern if they structure cross-sub-unit collaborations from which employees derive emotional satisfaction, maintain the salience of the larger unit as a source of autonomy, and successfully cast the larger organization as a collective endeavor for which all members share responsibility.

Thus, an important task for large, complex, highly differentiated organizations is to make the larger unit salient to members but also portray it as an object that promotes both individual and collective efficacy, locally and beyond. This appears to be a challenging task, especially given the effects of economic globalization on employee-employer relations. There are prevailing narratives about employment relations that shed further light on this challenge and suggest additional ways in which organizations can deal with it.

Narratives About Employment Relations

The early part of this book conceived employment relations as manifesting the tension between common and prevailing interpretations of life in the twenty-first century—the individualization narrative—and an alternative interpretation that is in closer sync with what is currently known about the human species—the social-relational narrative. Changes in employment relations are central to these broad interpretations, and in fact, nowhere is the transformation toward more transactional ties more apparent or more consensual than it is in descriptions of the contemporary work world. Changes in employment relations refer to the more transactional and short-term orientations to the employee-employer relations from both sides, but also to fundamental changes in the concept or meaning of a career. This section describes some implications of changing employment relations and sets the stage for an analysis of what forms of commitment are most likely to develop among different employees within organizations.

The "changing employment contract" was an early manifestation of the shift toward an individualization narrative about the world (Rousseau 1995; Arthur and Rousseau 1996; Morrison and Robinson 1997). In the 1980s and 1990s, private employers faced increasingly competitive markets and public employers faced persistent efforts to reduce budgets. Efficiencies in both public and private spheres, through strategic-level planning, rationalization of virtually all activities and procedures, and careful scrutiny of staffing levels, became a high priority. Many corporations articulated the view that "people are the most important asset," yet at the same time they were not hesitant to lay off long-term employees. Employment relations became decidedly transactional, because of cost pressures, efficiency concerns, and accountability to the public or shareholders. During the 1990s, a series of large layoffs by major corporations (Beer and Nohria 2000) and concomitant increases in the stock prices of firms that laid off workers sent an important signal to employees, management, and shareholders. In this context, the traditional employment contracts that implied a lifetime of employment in exchange for the loyalty and commitment of employees had come under considerable stress. Taking on new meaning, "employment at will" came to describe a mutual choice by employer and employee repeatedly and continuously made.

In its place, a new workplace narrative emerged—employability. This narrative involves a commitment of employers to contribute to the careers of employees by providing training, education, and experiences that enhance their employability in the labor market. Making employees more employable ostensibly is a win-win situation for both employees and employers. Under this new employment contract, employees maintain their employment only as long as they contribute sufficient value to the firm and their employment continues to be cost-effective; firms in turn provide opportunities for employees to increase their skills and talents, making them more marketable. Responsibility is placed on the employees to take advantage of these opportunities and carefully manage their own career without assuming they will enjoy a long-term association with a given organization (Rousseau 1995; Eby, Butts, and Lockwood 2003). If the employer enhances the human capital of its employees, those employees contribute more to the corporation, but they also more easily find other employment if they are terminated, taking pressure off the corporation to provide expensive severance packages. A plausible explanation for the spread of the policy of employability across corporations is that this policy addressed the significant commitment problem generated by more transactional, market-based ties between employees and employers.[5]

Another trend emerged along with the rise of the new employment contract—namely, the idea of a "boundaryless career" (Rousseau 1995; Arthur and Rousseau 1996). Under the traditional contract involving the prospect of lifetime employment, careers often could be developed fully within the same organization. A boundaryless career, by contrast, assumes that employees will move from firm to firm, developing their skills along the way and enhancing their ability to work in a variety of organizations or specific roles or jobs. Boundaryless careers are judged not solely by movement up the hierarchy in a given organization but also by the market value of one's human capital. Employees are thus encouraged to maximize their benefits in and through labor markets, just as corporations maximize profits in product markets. Larger social trends toward individualization and the use of market logic all are interwoven with such changes in the workplace. These work trends are concrete and real to people in their daily experiences at work. The idea of boundaryless careers promotes strong commitments to individual careers and weak commitments to organizations.

Overall, the confluence of employability contracts and boundaryless careers generates a significant problem of commitment that is manifested in high exit or turnover rates among valued employees in organizations (Barney and Wright 1998; Lepak and Snell 1999). People are more inclined to leave their firm when opportunities to upgrade their career materialize, and those with the most marketable talents and skills are the most likely to leave. At the same time, boundaryless careers and transactional ties to a larger organization create a context within which one would expect commitments to be focused on the local unit, because marketability is likely to be most enhanced by opportunities, experiences, and social ties at the local level. In this sense, it is reasonable to infer that the new forms of employment relation and related trends reduced the perceived value of larger organizations while in some respects increasing that of local units.

How have organizations responded to these sorts of commitment problems? There is a significant body of research on human resources practices in organizations that clarifies the conditions under which people develop commitments to an organization (Pfeffer 1994; Becker and Gerhart 1996). Common practices include gain-sharing, profit-sharing, group productivity incentives, job rotation, formal training, employee ownership, formal dispute resolution, and cross-functional projects. Each practice in some way addresses the commitment problems faced by organizations today and those conceived by the theory of nested commitments. Consider a few examples.

Gain-sharing is a bonus incentive system designed to improve productivity by involving employees in companywide activities. The gains achieved in terms of employee contributions are calculated by predetermined metrics for increased productivity that are shared between the company and the employees. Profit-sharing is similar to a gain-sharing program, in that it is designed to boost individual employees' participation in company performance, but it is more closely connected to the company's overall performance as measured by increased revenue and reduced costs. Group productivity incentives are designed to enhance the ties of departments, teams, and divisions to the larger organization by evaluating and rewarding their relative contributions to the company. Employee ownership gives employees an ownership stake in the company through stocks or stock options as part of the company benefits plan. This practice was originally directed at retaining key employees, but in many organizations it has evolved to include a broader range of employee categories. The goal is to have a workforce of employee-owners who view themselves as business partners with their company and are committed to it beyond their commitment to their local work unit. All of these human resource measures are directed at aligning the interests of employees with the interests of the organization.

These human resource practices seem likely to foster instrumental commitments, but the question is whether these will generate affective commitments. Such programs could enhance positive emotions from work activity in a particular organization, but it is not altogether clear that people would attribute their feelings to the organization as such (that is, adopt the distal rule). If human resource practices make the organization salient as a source of positive feelings, the theory of nested commitments answers in the affirmative. The theory of social commitment suggests further that people are more likely to use the distal rule for emotions felt during participation in programs that not only align employee interests to the organization but also promote a sense of task jointness and shared responsibility at the organizational level. This implies a different way to view and evaluate the effectiveness of human resource practices.

Some firms directly promote affective commitments by focusing on the relational orientations and attitudes of employees rather than human resource practices oriented toward individuals, such as training, compensation, and evaluation. These firms treat employee attitudes and the employee-employer relationship as firm-specific assets that cannot be traded on an open market and are important to mobilizing employees' efforts on behalf of the company (Adler and Kwon 2002). Southwest Airlines is an example of such a company, as illustrated by the following statement of company philosophy from its CEO, Herb Kelleher:

> We can train people to do things where skills are concerned. But there is one capability we do not have and that is to change a person's attitude. So, we prefer

an unskilled person with a good attitude rather than a highly skilled person with a bad attitude. We take people who come out of highly structured, hierarchical, dictatorial corporate environments if they have the attitude potential. We are interested in people who externalize, who focus on other people, who are really motivated to help other people. We are not interested in navel gazers, regardless of how lint free their navels are (Quick 1992, 51).

The message that Kelleher sends here is that human resource practices that rely on incentives such as wages and compensation or stock options may generate commitments to the larger organization beyond the local unit, but such commitments are purely instrumental. Instrumental commitments tend to be sustained only if organizations constantly "feed" employees with material rewards, which is impossible for most organizations. Kelleher's message dovetails with a fundamental point of our theory of social commitments.

To summarize, employability contracts and boundaryless careers have detached employees from their organizations and shifted their commitments to their individual careers. Various human resource practices designed to handle the issue of commitment may work, but these are most likely to generate instrumental commitments rather than affective or affectively based normative commitments. The key question, then, becomes what might account for employees who show affective and normative commitments beyond instrumental ones. We propose that part of the answer lies in the fact that in any organization there is considerable variation in the strength and form of employee-to-organization ties across different categories of employee. These differences can be attributed to differences in the emotional rewards and sense of shared responsibility associated with employee roles in the organization. The next section offers a framework for understanding how distinct forms of commitment may develop among distinct categories of employee.

EMPLOYEE ROLES AND SOCIAL COMMITMENT

Structural roles involve formal and informal expectations about behavior and performance—that is, obligations and responsibilities (Biddle 1986). In work organizations, roles have an explicit formal dimension that is manifest in job designs, job descriptions, employee evaluation systems, and the like, but they also have an informal dimension derived from the history and traditions of how people in given roles fulfill their responsibilities. Roles also are embedded in networks of ties to other roles, and these interdependencies have formal and informal effects. Structural roles typically send important signals to role occupants about their ties to the mission, goals, and success of the larger organization. For example, in a corporation it is hard to imagine that the vice president for finance (or CFO) would not be defined as having a central role and strong stake in the performance or success of the organization, whereas an administrative assistant at best has an implicit and more distant tie to the organization. The role activities of an administrative assistant are localized and oriented to the needs of the people in a sub-unit. Many other roles, such as that of a human resource director, a plant manager, or a computer technician, would seem to fall somewhere between these extremes of the vice president for finance and an administrative assistant. Structural roles vary in the centrality and scope of the activities associated with the role.

The main idea developed in this section is that the centrality and scope of structural roles determine (1) whether roles are likely to generate commitments to the larger (distal) units rather than the local (proximal) units, and (2) the forms of commitment that people in those roles are likely to develop. To flesh out this point, we cross-classify the centrality of the activities associated with a role (high versus low) and the scope or breadth of impact of those activities (broad versus narrow). The finance vice president is high in centrality and broad in scope, whereas the administrative assistant is low in centrality and narrow in scope. Centrality and scope are based both on the structural location of the role in the organization and on the subjective definitions of the role that prevail in that organization. The role of finance vice president can vary in centrality and scope across organizations; in fact, its definition can be somewhat contentious in mission-driven nonprofit organizations, such as a university. Our general point is this: structural roles that are high in centrality and scope produce a strong and direct tie between the role occupant and the organization as such, whereas roles low in centrality and narrow in scope generate a weak, removed, and indirect tie between the role occupant and the organization. The implications for commitment are summarized in table 6.1.

Beginning in the upper-left quadrant, occupying highly central roles with broad scope are those core employees who guide and implement the strategic directions of the organization. From the management literature, employees falling into this category are construed as the DNA of an organization (Byham, Smith, and Paese 2003). The organization carefully attends to and manages their careers; they have a strong stake in the success of the organization, and they are deeply immersed in the mission, vision, and values of the organization.

Table 6.1   Structural Roles and Commitment to Organizations

	Scope	
Centrality	Broad	Narrow
High	Affective	Instrumental
	Distal rule	Proximal rule
Low	Normative	Instrumental
	Distal rule	Proximal rule

Source: Authors' compilation.

Their organizational membership is likely to be an important source of identity, and those who share this identity tend to develop clannish, family-like ties to the organization (Ouchi 1980). Affective ties to the organization are likely to be strong in these roles. Furthermore, these are the employees who are most likely to reveal affectively based normative commitments to the organization. Their own interests and values are interwoven with those of the organization.

Turning to the upper-right quadrant, the prototype here is the professional or technical employee. These roles tend to be high in centrality but narrow in scope, given the degree of specialization they involve. Examples are software designers in a computer firm, research and development staff in an engineering firm, and accountants at a bank. Such employees are integral to the strategic tasks and success of the organization, and they generate economic value for a firm, yet their connection to the firm is primarily instrumental because the firm is mainly a venue within which to develop their professional careers. They are more committed to their profession than to their organization and may readily leave an organization if given a better offer that is consistent with their career. Given their professional commitments, they also are likely to attribute positive events and experiences proximally (locally), since their local technical unit is populated by specialists like themselves. Overall, roles that are high in centrality but low in scope of impact may contribute significantly to an organization's performance, but occupants of such roles tend to maintain some distance from the larger organization and form the closest ties to local units with professional colleagues.

Those employees in the organization who do routine but necessary support tasks engage in activities that are low in centrality but broad in scope. Low centrality stems from the routine nature of tasks and high scope stems from the generalized impact of support activities or operations. Take parking, transportation, travel, and compliance as examples. None of these functions is central to the organization, but the organization cannot operate effectively if snow is not removed from the parking lots, if travel reimbursements take a long time and involve many errors, if the electricity goes off and on during the day, and so forth. The difference between these roles and professional and technical roles is the widespread impact of these routine activities across the organization sub-units and functions. For these employees, the organization itself is more salient on a day-to-day basis, since their job activities are directed at the day-to-day operations of the organization as a whole. Thus, they are likely to form stronger ties to the organization than to sub-units. Their ties to the organization tend to be normative, and these tend to have an instrumental rather than an affective basis.

Finally, some structural roles have low centrality in the organization as well as a narrow scope of impact. Examples are support staff and employees who occupy the lower levels of the job and salary hierarchy, including most contingent and temporary employees. In these roles, ties to the organization are grounded in high levels of dependence on the organization owing to a relative lack of opportunity or obstacles to exit; such ties are largely instrumental. Stronger ties are likely to develop to the local units, within which their role activities are performed, than to the larger organization. At the sub-unit level, the ties may become affective for long-term employees to the degree that they perceive themselves and people like them as being treated fairly and with dignity. Fair treatment provides them with information about whether or not they are accepted as deserving members of the group (Tyler 1989).

To conclude, some organizational roles, almost by definition, imply minimal ties to the organization, while others imply strong ties. As table 6.1 shows, we suggest that this has an effect on both the forms of commitment that people in those roles develop to the organization and on their propensity to attribute positive experiences and feelings to the larger organization (distal rule) or the local sub-unit (proximal rule). Relational ties are more likely among employees who occupy structural roles that are high in organizational centrality and have broad impact on the organization, whereas transactional ties are most likely among those in roles whose centrality or scope is low.

CONCLUSIONS

The theory of nested commitments (Lawler 1992) addresses a fundamental problem of social order in organizations: how and when people develop stronger ties to sub-units than to the larger unit or organization. Centralization tends to mitigate the nested commitment problems, whereas decentralization accentuates them.[6] In more decentralized organizations, the theory suggests that people form the strongest affective commitments to their local organizational sub-units because they tend to perceive these as a source of control and efficacy. They credit their local unit for good things about their job or member activities and they blame the larger organization for the bad things about their job or member activities. The implication is that large, complex organizations have a nested commitment problem that may reduce their capacity to mobilize and organize support from those in local sub-units for larger organizational goals and strategies. Organizations can and do overcome this problem through structural and cultural interventions and with effective leadership.

A task for organizations, therefore, is to make the larger organization salient as a source of control and efficacy at the local level, and thus an enabling rather than purely constraining force at work. According to our theory, affective commitments to the broader organization should increase if people experience positive emotions, a sense of control, and a sense of shared responsibility in carrying out their task activities and if they attribute these conditions in part to the structure, culture, or leadership of the organization. Organizations play an active role in boosting affective commitments when roles and responsibilities are designed for employees, when employee programs and policies are developed and implemented, and when organization-wide communications and gatherings are organized. At the level of the individual role or position, the commitments of people tend to vary with the centrality of their role in the organization and the scope of impact it has on the organization's activities. More central roles with broader scope are the most likely to foster a greater sense of shared responsibility that in turn leads to affective commitments to the organization. These also are the roles likely to generate the greatest sense of control and to make the organization as such more salient.

We have emphasized work organizations in this chapter, but it is important to note that the principles herein apply to virtually any type of organization. Membership organizations and nonprofits, such as AARP, Habitat for Humanity, and Sierra Club, are as subject to these processes as corporations, unions, and governments. For example, in federated groups with active chapters and regular activities at the local level (for example, the Sierra Club and Habitat for Humanity), one would expect ties to the local unit to be stronger than to the larger national association. The jointness of the relevant activities, the positive feelings they generate, and the sense of shared responsibility tend to be locally generated and focused. From the theory of nested commitments, voluntary organizations with local chapters or units face the same fundamental commitment problems as multinational corporations, especially when they attempt to mobilize action across local units. No organizations are immune. The problems of commitment in organizations are difficult to resolve permanently because people tend to attribute positive events and experiences to their local, proximal groups and negative events and experiences to larger, more distant groups.

CHAPTER 7

Commitments in Hierarchy and Network
Forms of Organization

A central purpose of this volume is to understand how and when transactional ties are transformed into relational ties. The minimal requirement for this to occur is that people engage in repeated transactions with the same others. The relational ties that emerge from repeated transactions, however, can involve different organizational forms. Hierarchies and networks are fundamental organizing structures for repeated transactions, and importantly, they are distinct from markets (see, for example, Swedberg 2003). Hierarchies, networks, and markets have been construed as the most basic "forms of governance" in economics and sociology (Williamson 1985; Powell 1990). This chapter uses the theory of social commitments to examine the commitment implications of these fundamental forms of organization.

Transactions take place in all sorts of markets: labor markets, stock markets, flea markets, consumer markets, industrial markets, digital markets, and many others. Whatever the context of economic transactions, markets play an organizing role by creating opportunities and incentives for buyers and sellers of goods and services to find each other and conclude exchanges. Buyers and sellers, both individual and collective, aim to maximize individual self-interest, and the "invisible hand" of the market organizes and shapes the transactions mainly through pricing mechanisms. The market generates a range of opportunities and constraints within which people and organizations navigate in pursuit of their self-interests. There is no role for affect or group commitments in markets.

With standard neoclassical assumptions about markets, there are no a priori reasons to believe that market transactions would generate relational ties or person-to-unit commitments. In a perfect market, all information is open to every transaction participant. Alternative buyers and sellers move freely about among prospective partners and thus need not rely on specific persons or social relations. Consummated transactions have little impact on future transactions because social ties are episodic and one-shot. Relationships that endure beyond the completion of a given transaction are irrelevant or nonexistent because, in a perfect market, competitive, fully informed bidding processes lead to new price agreements between buyers and sellers. This is based on the profit maximization assumption. Overall, the pricing mechanism brings order and predictability to the market without enduring social ties or relations. Relation-oriented transactions expose people to the risks of inefficient outcomes or opportunity costs. Affective ties represent a type of market friction.

There are important traditions within both economics and sociology that introduce into or posit nonmarket dimensions for transactions in a market (Rauch and Casella 2001). What is sometimes termed the "new institutional economics" has directed attention to the role of transaction costs and the use of hierarchy to minimize such costs (Williamson 1975, 1981, 1991) and also to deal with market failures (Nelson 2005). Network theories in sociology have directed attention to the social embeddedness of market transactions, that is, to the ongoing relations within which repeated transactions often occur (Granovetter 1985; Eccles and Crane 1987; Powell 1990; Uzzi 1997; Nee and Swedberg 2005). Research has shown that transaction costs "distort" markets, and socially embedded transactions often entail nonmarket prices designed to nurture or build an ongoing relational tie (Uzzi and Lancaster 2004). From neoclassical economics, such phenomena are market frictions or market failures that are temporary and have mainly short-term effects; the same can be said of any emotions generated by transactions. Markets ostensibly override these relational forces in the longer run. The implication is that emotional by-products are either nonexistent or unimportant in the longer term.

In this chapter, we focus on the comparison of hierarchy and network forms of organizing transactions, in particular the implications these have for person-to-group ties. There is an enormous body of research on such topics, and our purpose is not to comprehensively review it. The chapter overviews the classic work comparing hierarchies and networks as alternative forms of governance, which identifies the basic conditions under which hierarchies and networks organize transactions more efficiently than do markets. Hierarchy and network approaches offer structural explanations for how economic activity is organized in nonmarket terms, yet they neglect to account for how people themselves may inadvertently develop social commitments as they engage in transactions repeatedly across time. If, as we have suggested in prior chapters, emotions are by-products of repeated interactions, our theory has something to say about the nature or strength of the commitments that people are likely to develop within these forms of organization. In carrying out our analysis, we first compare markets and hierarchies and then turn to networks as a form of organization.

THE ORGANIZING EFFECTS OF ECONOMIC TRANSACTIONS

Adam Smith first declared that the market pricing system is the most fundamental mechanism regulating economic transactions. Since Smith's time, neoclassical economists have focused their attention on formalizing this principle and refining it to be more accurate. In a neoclassical market world, every transaction is discrete and independent. Market frictions are events or conditions that interfere with the discrete and independent transactions that rational individuals pursue under a market's pricing system. They are an important source of uncertainty for buyers and sellers. Perfect markets exist only as an idealization, because market frictions are ubiquitous in most real markets. Hierarchies and networks are built in part on market frictions and essentially place market transactions in the context of relational ties, thereby reducing uncertainties.

Flea markets provide an interesting example of market frictions. Nobody knows exactly how many flea markets exist in the United States, but there are many. A flea market guide (www.fleamarketguide.com) estimates that more than four thousand flea markets operate in Kansas and Texas alone, and the number is growing. They come in all shapes and sizes and entail a wide array of goods, including used toys, Asian rugs, Indian pottery, authentic dinosaur bones, vintage collectibles, large pieces of furniture, and so on. There are weekly, monthly, and seasonal markets. Most are open on weekends. Some are free, while others charge ten dollars or more for admission.

The Rose Ball Flea Market is among the largest in North America. It opens at 9:00 AM for most people, but hundreds line up the night before with flashlights to wait for a special 6:00 AM entry, which costs an additional five dollars.

Once through the entrance, most people move quickly to vendors or sellers. Some come to look for a specific item, as at ordinary markets, but many people are "treasure-hunting"—looking to discover something on the spur of the moment. Moreover, unlike those who patronize modern marketplaces such as Wal-Mart and other department stores, flea market shoppers often show zeal for the sentimental value of items, not just their exchange value. Many seem to enjoy the process of negotiating, not so much for the sake of getting the lowest price as for the sport of it. The overall atmosphere is more like a carnival than a rational neoclassical market. People who frequent flea markets often know which sellers they are looking for, and regular shoppers develop loyalty to certain vendors with whom they have repeated transactions. Information is often incomplete, uncertainties over quality are considerable, and goods are not homogenous, all of which suggests organizing principles other than those of a neoclassical market. In flea markets, repeated transactions with the same vendor, the experience of positive feelings, and customer loyalty are part of what attracts shoppers.

Satisfactory transactions do not necessarily correspond with the best price in a market shaped by repeated transactions among the same buyers and sellers. Commitments that lead the same parties to repeatedly transact across time reduce uncertainties about the quality of products and enable the actors to spend less time than they would otherwise agreeing on a price (see Kollock 1994); these commitments also include an emotional component. Buyers and sellers may chat about other things, greet each other with broad, knowing smiles, and so forth. The uncertainty reduction and emotional effects of repeated transactions are crucial mechanisms for understanding how market conditions evolve into and are shaped by hierarchy or network forms of organization. In the following sections, we examine the nature of hierarchy and network forms of organization and then look at the implications these have for person-to-organization commitments.

From Markets to Hierarchy

Ronald Coase (1988) was the first to draw attention to transaction costs as a factor in understanding market failures. He stated that, "in order to carry out a market transaction it is necessary to discover who it is that one wishes to deal with, to inform people that one wishes to deal and on what terms, to conduct negotiations leading up to a bargain, to draw up the contract, to undertake the inspection needed to make sure that the terms of the contract are being observed and so on" (Coase 1988, 114). Market transactions thus entail transaction costs.

Oliver Williamson (1975, 1981, 1991) developed transaction costs theory in economics based on the premise that markets are the best form of transaction governance only when transaction costs are zero (Williamson 1981; Jones, Hesterly, and Borgatti 1997). He argues that as transaction costs grow in a free market because of increasing uncertainties and opportunistic behavior, hierarchies can organize transactions more efficiently than markets. In hierarchies, efficiency-minded agents abandon opportunistic motives by voluntarily committing themselves to the authority of management. In Williamson's approach, hierarchies reduce transaction costs by internalizing transactions to specific partners in the context of an established vertical (hierarchical) relationship.

Part of what sets Williamson's approach apart from neoclassical economics is that he adds to production costs the transaction costs that firms incur in completing transactions in free markets. Firms maximize profits by minimizing total costs—the sum of production and transaction costs—and thus they adopt the governance structure that is best for minimizing their transaction costs. Under hierarchy, the most powerful actor puts buyers, suppliers, or sellers under its direct control by vertically integrating them and thereby regulating upcoming transactions. This controls or reduces the uncertainties of the market. For such reasons, hierarchy develops not only between manufacturers and suppliers but also between firms and prospective employees who are selling their human capital on the labor market.

To illustrate, assume that a firm operates through a process comprising input, throughput, and output. From the focal firm's perspective, interest in hierarchical control increases when, despite sufficient demand, it cannot deliver products or services in a timely manner to customers because of understaffing or inconsistent materials supply at the input stage, or perhaps because its distribution partners act out of self-interest against the focal firm's welfare, pushing up transaction costs. If the firm faces growing uncertainty that it cannot control, it will try to restore control and impose order by internalizing transactions within its organizational boundary—that is, by vertically integrating the sources of uncertainty. Backward integration solves the issue of uncertainty created by suppliers at the input stage, whereas forward integration solves the uncertainty issue caused by distribution channels.

Williamson (1981) makes two important assumptions about people that are central to his argument about hierarchy. The first is that people have limited cognitive capacities to assimilate, recall, or access the information necessary to assess available alternatives. Second, people are opportunistic—that is, they are wholly self-interested and take full advantage of opportunities to generate payoffs for themselves regardless of the effects of their behavior on others or the group; moreover, they do this with guile. These assumptions are fundamental reasons why uncertainties can seldom if ever be fully resolved by a market. They also capture an important part of the foundation for Williamson's general hypothesis—namely, that hierarchies are generally more efficient ways to organize repeated transactions than are markets. The question is: under what conditions?

Williamson specifies three fundamental conditions that have an impact on whether hierarchies are better than markets: frequency, uncertainty, and asset-specificity. These are essentially moderators of hierarchy-to-efficiency effects. Each also is a point at which our theory of social commitments adds something. With regard to frequency, Williamson argues that market governance is more efficient for onetime transactions, whereas hierarchy works best for recurring transactions. Consider a firm's decision to either buy consulting services from an outside vendor or create an in-house unit and hire full-time consultants. If the firm needs consulting services only once every ten years, it will probably decide to buy consulting services under a contractual agreement with a professional consulting unit on the outside consulting market. However, if the firm needs consulting services regularly, it will tend toward hierarchical governance, creating an internal consulting unit and appointing an internal manager to control the consulting unit. Once the firm has created a governance structure that involves repeated transactions, the firm and the consulting unit will be subject to the principles of our theory. Levels of task jointness between the two may promote shared responsibility, emotion attributions, and nested commitments. Hierarchy therefore sets the stage for the development of social commitments to the degree that it establishes the requisite levels of task jointness and a sense of shared responsibility. However, this is problematic under hierarchical governance, as we explain later.

Next consider the role of uncertainty. Uncertainty is a function of the degree to which the contingencies associated with a transaction can be predicted in advance or as the transaction is being carried out. Uncertainty does not matter for a spot market transaction, which involves many sellers and buyers, because the uncertain result becomes apparent quickly if not immediately. In this case, market governance is the most efficient. Suppose, however, that despite sufficient demand from many buyers, opportunism on the part of suppliers makes it difficult for manufacturers to find reliable sources of the materials they need for the timely output of their products. In this case, the manufacturers generally prefer to regulate transactions via hierarchy, either by incorporating suppliers into the organization and subjecting them to organizational controls or by establishing a private contract with specific suppliers to ensure a stable supply of materials. Overall, uncertainty in transactions increases the likelihood that repeated transactions will foster other social processes that could lead to affective ties and commitment.

Finally, consider the impact of asset-specificity. Asset-specificity occurs when investments made for certain kinds of repeated transactions have particular value there but less or very little value in the context of other kinds of relations. Said differently, such assets provide no benefit or advantage beyond a particular context or relation. To illustrate, learning to speak English is a non-specific asset that has substantial payoff across many kinds of transactions, as there are many English-speaking countries in the world. Learning to speak Inuit, by contrast, is a more specific asset that helps with plying specific trades in the Arctic, but practically nowhere else. Transactions exhibiting high asset-specificity tend to generate hierarchy, because the parties save transaction costs by internalizing the transaction in the organizational boundary and coordinating their relationship under a common authority. Applying our theory, an emotional or affective commitment becomes possible if and when asset-specificity is high, because the instrumental benefits of the relation are specific to that particular relation and nontransferable to others.

The combined effects of frequency, uncertainty, and asset-specificity lead partners into relational contracts (Williamson 1985). A relational contract safeguards an exchange relationship to ensure the credibility of the transactions in future exchanges and aligns the incentive structures for both parties. Relational contracts should set in motion an incipient commitment process, but commitment developed through relational contracting (between manufacturers, distributors, and suppliers) is likely to be purely instrumental. From a transaction cost framework, as a firm integrates suppliers or distributors vertically, its management team tends to rely more on authority and sanctions that strengthen the instrumental component of person-to-organization ties. Larger firms generally hire additional staff and managers to control the functions integrated into an internal unit or subsidiary of the firm. Such growth often creates internal issues related to order, and thus a vertically organized firm tends to establish stronger hierarchy and control to maintain unity and coherence within the organization. Hierarchy adds force to bureaucracy by setting up clear lines of individual responsibility, detailed reporting relationships, and formal decisionmaking procedures through a command-and-control structure.[1]

The iron cage of bureaucracy tightens as hierarchical forms of organization grow (Weber 1918/1968). Management's visible hand within an organization essentially replaces the "invisible hand" of the market. Once vertically integrated, all parties are subject to employment relationships and remain in such vertical relations insofar as the firm generates sufficient instrumental incentives. Such tight vertical control removes task jointness among work units and reduces the sense of shared responsibility between management and employees, thereby dampening social commitments at the organizational level. Instrumental commitments are the dominant form of person-to-unit ties with hierarchical forms of governance. Normative commitments also may develop, but these tend to be instrumentally based rather than affectively based.

The Network Form of Organization

Williamson sees market and hierarchy forms of organization as the ends of a continuum of organizational governance, and he locates many hybrid forms at intermediate locations on this continuum (Williamson 1991). Market and hierarchy forms of organization predominate, while hybrid forms are rarer; the continuum has a "thick in the tails" property (Williamson 1985). The contrast of market and hierarchy, however, has been the object of substantial criticism from network theorists in sociology, who emphasize the social and structural embedding of economic transactions (Dore 1983; Granovetter 1985; Eccles and Crane 1987; Powell 1990; Uzzi 1997). Here networks are put forth as a third form of governance structure different from both markets and hierarchies.

Walter Powell (1990) points out that network governance was common even before Adam Smith's effort to formulate market principles. George Richardson (1972) caricatured Williamson's view as one that depicts a firm as being like an island of planned coordination in a sea of market relations, with its organizational boundary as a fortress. The modern firm is no longer an isolated castle, if it ever was. In line with this argument, anthropologists and sociologists suggest that markets are products of social and cultural construction—specifically, that economic transactions in markets are intricately and thoroughly nested or embedded in social and cultural contexts (Agnew 1986; Granovetter 1985).

The network argument is that networks are a more efficient way to regulate transactions than markets, especially in an age that puts a premium on speed, flexibility, agility, and innovation. A network is a cluster of independent parties whose transactions are coordinated by long-term contracts and collaboration rather than through a formal authority or a market-pricing system. In ever-changing environments, firms cannot survive unless they can capture key environmental trends and make quick decisions, many of which involve forming new ties or using old ones in new ways. Powell (1990) argues that network governance helps firms build diverse channels linking them with other entities that can bring mutual benefits, especially in the context of rapid, unpredictable industry or environmental changes. Network-based organization ostensibly is more conducive than other forms of organization to promoting cooperation and coordination along these channels. If an entity cannot satisfy the unpredictable needs of customers, it must find others who possess the required knowledge, skills, and information with whom to build a network. There is considerable evidence in the literature that a network form of organization is more effective than hierarchy or market forms at creating and acquiring new knowledge (Powell 1990; Uzzi 1997; Hamel 1991; Podolny and Page 1998).

Brian Uzzi (1997) argues—and shows—that network forms of organization generate a more fine-grained exchange of information than market or hierarchy forms of organization. Parties even exchange "private" information in networks because of the longer-term ties. He cites a manufacturer that made a strategic decision to move its production facilities offshore in order to improve profitability. Despite the dissolution of their relationships, the company told its suppliers well in advance so that they would have sufficient time to prepare and adjust. Because of end-of-game effects (Axelrod 1984; Murnighan 1994), this announcement could have made the manufacturer vulnerable to opportunistic behavior on the part of suppliers. However, the CEO of the manufacturer visited the suppliers to explain the decision, thus giving the suppliers time to prepare, and the suppliers reciprocated by promising to supply high-quality materials as long as the manufacturer's current plant remained in operation. Participants in the relationships cooperated with each other even when the end of the relation was imminent and despite the prospects for opportunism.

Powell (1990) and others (Jones, Hesterly, and Borgatti 1997; Podolny and Page 1998) summarize the conditions under which networks offer advantages over market or hierarchy forms of organization. Our theory is consistent with these in important respects. First, network-based organization is more efficient when the parties exchange intangibles such as knowledge and technology, the value of which are hard to measure in monetary terms. Second, networks operate most efficiently when parties engage in long-term and recurrent transactions.

Third, networks are efficient especially when participants do not see each other as separate entities, as they would in a market, but rather as interdependent entities. Contrary to command-and-control hierarchies, in network relationships participants maintain an autonomous identity as knowledge producers or brokers, using their own unique domains of skills and knowledge. Fourth, networks are particularly effective for transactions that involve flexible and lateral channels of communication, open-ended contracts, and mutual obligations. Transactions carried out within networks are more collaborative, balanced, interdependent, easily repeated, long-term, trust-based, and learning-oriented than those in hierarchies and markets. In the terms of our theory, these conditions imply that network forms of organization, compared to hierarchy, provide more opportunity for individuals to solve joint problems through collaboration and thus to develop the sense of shared responsibility necessary for social commitments.

Many network studies examine the circumstances under which actors choose networks as a governance framework for their transactions. However, relatively little work considers the processes or micro-level mechanisms through which network participants construct social commitments that involve person-to-group ties more resilient than instrumental ones (for exceptions, see Lawler and Yoon 1998; Lawler, Thye, and Yoon 2006). Some of the inherent features or conditions of network forms of organization suggest that people will develop social commitments to the network as a social unit. These conditions include structural interdependencies, joint tasks from which people receive benefits, and positive emotions that people may experience when they navigate the network terrain in a profitable way. In the next section, we elaborate further how the theory of social commitments addresses network forms of organization.

SOCIAL COMMITMENTS AND NETWORK ORGANIZATIONS

The theory of social commitments indicates that structural power, rooted in network configurations or dependence relations, can facilitate the transformation of instrumental relations into expressive relations. Social commitments should be strongest when mutual power and dependence is high and when power and dependence are distributed equally across participants in a network, because these conditions heighten the actual or perceived jointness of the tasks that people engage in. From the theory, task structures that make individual contributions to collective outcomes more indistinguishable (the nonseparability condition) and also promote a sense of shared responsibility lead people to attribute feelings to something larger—a social unit.

The role of task nonseparability and shared responsibility for macro-level governance structures can be approached by contrasting simple dependence and interdependence (see Kelley and Thibaut 1978; Molm 1994). We suggest that network participants perceive greater task jointness and more shared responsibility when their network relations evolve from ties of dependence to ties of mutual interdependence. Dependence relations exist when each person values outcomes that are contingent on and controlled by the actions of another. Interdependent relations, by contrast, occur when the outcomes for each party depend on some combination of behaviors enacted by both oneself and the other. The people in an interdependent relation exercise control jointly, as in the coauthoring of a book by several authors. Strictly speaking, dependence relations are more like market transactions in exchange networks: each person maintains an independent identity and tries to enter into an exchange for resources it would otherwise not control. Interdependent relations in a network, on the other hand, reflect a grouplike tie because all people in the network collaborate to produce jointly desired outcomes, essentially by pooling individually unique assets or resources.

Applying this idea to network forms of organization, social commitments should become stronger when relations of simple dependence evolve into relations of interdependence. Examples include strategic alliances among corporations in a network involving minority ownership and joint ventures. Japanese keiretsu use minority ownership to create collaborative network ties that increase interdependence with respect to the resources and skills necessary to develop new joint business opportunities. Japanese automobile companies use keiretsu to manage input linkages with suppliers (Aoki 1988); in fact, Toyota owns a minority stake of up to 49 percent in most of its supplier companies, and this minority ownership helps Toyota work jointly with suppliers to improve product quality and reliability. Manufacturing keiretsu are often associated with a financial keiretsu managed by a large bank group. For example, Fuji Bank manages the Fuyo keiretsu (Jones 2000); the board of directors of Fuji Bank is composed of representatives from most large corporate group members, such as an electronic company (Hitachi), a brewing company (Sapporo), an automobile company (Nissan), an optics company (Canon), and so forth. Such business groups are network organizations that operate as units and are recognized as such by those inside and outside of the unit. Our theory identifies conditions under which those units become important objects of commitment and attachment for the people within them.

The social embeddedness of transactions is another source of interdependence and task jointness among network members. In recent years, the role of embeddedness in generating joint tasks and collective outcomes among network organizations is implied by diverse studies of organizational networks, including interfirm networks (Granovetter 1985), industrial districts (Leung 1993), marketing channels (Moorman, Zaltman, and Deshpande 1992), entrepreneurship (Larson 1992), lending relationships (Podolny 1994), and organizational adaptation (Uzzi 1996). Some of this work emphasizes structural embeddedness, which refers to the impact of the network configuration itself on economic activity, and some focuses on social embeddedness, which refers to the impact of shared cognitive symbols, politics, and cultural context on economic activity (Uzzi 1996). In these terms, structural embeddedness increases the degree of interdependence at the network level, while social embeddedness increases interdependence especially at the dyadic level. It is common knowledge that, in most craft-industry networks, for example, greater structural embeddedness makes the jointness of tasks salient and promotes social embeddedness among actors in the network. The textile-based industrial districts in southwest Germany (Sabel et al. 1987; Brusco 1982) and north-central Italy are famous for the well-established social infrastructure infused throughout entire networks. Comprising small and midsized manufacturers of knitwear, clothes, ceramic tiles, motorcycles, shoes, and woodworking machine tools, these networks share a socially embedded pool of human and physical resources.

Embedded social infrastructures operate like collective goods through which network participants become more highly interdependent and engage in more joint activities. It is much easier in these networks to locate human resources, mobilize financial resources, and gather needed business information. The networks may maintain research institutes, vocational training centers, and consulting firms as well as marketing agencies, hospitals, and schools. With such infrastructure in place, network participants become more interdependent and engage more routinely and regularly in joint task activities. Thus, based on our theory, networks with stronger structural and social embeddedness have greater potential for producing social commitments to overarching social units among their participants and stronger ties between the local immediate relations or sub-units (micro) and the larger network relations (macro).

Our theory indicates further that inequality of dependence in networks dampens the structural potential for social commitment because it raises issues of shared responsibility. This is implied by the widespread failures of corporate alliances and joint ventures. The Boston Consulting Group published a research report on the failure of network-based alliances between airline companies (Podolny and Page 1998). According to the report, of the 401 alliances that were in force as of 1995, fewer than 40 percent of domestic alliances and fewer than 30 percent of international alliances had been successful. Another study of joint ventures (Savona 1992) reports that joint ventures last fewer than three and a half years on average, and only one-third of them are successful. Importantly, unequal dependence and the problem of producing and sustaining a sense of shared responsibility among actors was an implicit, if not explicit, factor in most explanations for the widespread failure of such alliances. If firms use organizational power and politics to gain the upper hand in new ventures or alliances, jointness and shared responsibility suffer. Imbalances of power and the resulting lack of shared responsibility tend to surface in many such transactions. Thus, it is reasonable to argue that, as the power distribution in a network becomes more equal, problems of shared responsibility diminish and the network has greater structural potential for promoting social commitments at the collective or network level.

In sum, network forms of organization are likely to produce stronger person-to-group social commitments relative to hierarchical forms of organization because of their capacity to foster joint tasks that produce shared responsibility. In hierarchical organizations, repetitive transactions lead to weaker social commitments or to purely instrumental commitments, whereas in network forms of organization, the mutuality of ties is a source of self and collective efficacy as well as of positive feelings; the organization as a singular unit is thus a more likely target for positive feelings and affective commitment. However, networks face an important problem not present for hierarchical organizational forms: they lack the clear social boundaries present for a hierarchy. As a result, the social unit may not be as salient as an entity and the nested commitments hypothesis could operate, meaning that affective commitments are directed at particular ties within the network, not the network itself. To overcome this tendency, people in networks need to be made aware of the force of the network in their local ties; for example, that their opportunities to benefit stem from the network itself. Network boundaries have to become salient endogenously and be affirmed by the social ties and regular interactions they encompass.

Network forms of organization also are consciously generated for certain purposes. This is illustrated by what some organizational scholars have termed *quasi-network firms,* such as those found in the film industry. When Steven Spielberg and George Lucas make films, they establish a quasi-firm bringing together a group of diverse professionals—such as producers, scriptwriters, set designers, and film editors—who function in multilayered networks to accomplish a joint task. These are socially constructed film production units with boundaries, but they exist only for the duration of the project. Our theory suggests how and why such network-based organizations may generate stronger social commitments than one would expect from their temporary nature. The success of these quasi-network firms also could make more salient and important the larger networks from which they are put together.

CONCLUSIONS

This chapter examines the commitment implications of three fundamental forms of organizing social and economic activity: markets, hierarchies, and networks. While each form generates social order on its own terms, the stability and resilience of these orders vary to the degree that they also generate different forms of commitment. We argue that these different forms of organization determine the structural opportunities and constraints within which people construct ties to each other and, by implication, to the organization. The most general conclusion is that network forms of organization are most likely to produce affective commitments to the organization, that is, create social units of expressive value; hierarchical forms tend to produce instrumental commitments, or normative commitments that are instrumental; and markets are unlikely to produce person-to-unit ties at all, though they are a context in which relational ties between particular actors often flourish.

Markets work most efficiently for organizing transactions when there are many buyers and sellers who have the requisite information for making efficient transactions. In a complete or perfect market, a pricing system should be the only element that affects transactions; nothing else should stand in the way. People carry out transactions in markets in an emotion-neutral way and settle contractual conflicts through negotiation, arbitration, or litigation. Within markets, affect and commitment between people are forms of market friction or stickiness that reduce efficiency. When markets work efficiently, economic actors develop no commitments to partners or to overarching social units.

At the opposite pole of the spectrum lies hierarchy. Within hierarchies, a buyer can effectively establish an order by vertically integrating sellers and incorporating them into a unified vertical structure in which authority can be brought to bear. The hierarchical form of organization predominates especially when transactions are uncertain, asset-specific, and likely to recur. Hierarchy assumes that people have limited cognitive ability and behave opportunistically in pursuit of individual gains. A buyer acting as a manager with authority controls activities after vertical incorporation or integration. Relations under hierarchy thus form the basis for instrumental commitment, and these relations are sustainable insofar as they are beneficial or profitable. Inequalities of power and dependence are obstacles to social commitment in hierarchies.

In network-based organizations, order and stability depend primarily on the flow of information, knowledge, skills, and other resources across people and firms. For example, it is often said that innovation in an information age requires that firms (and the individuals in them) adapt quickly and flexibly, and networks make this more feasible than hierarchies. Network forms of organization promote collaborations and ties across extant social boundaries, and as such, they have greater capacity to generate the sort of conditions and effects of relevance to our theory of social commitments—joint tasks, a sense of shared responsibility, and positive feelings from successful collaborations. Network forms of organization are the most likely to generate commitments with a significant affective component.

Broadly, we conclude that, among the three forms of organization, networks provide the most promising ground on which to build social commitments. Markets are a key force driving and promoting the individualization of modern lives. Hierarchies produce instrumental commitments by reducing flexibility and thereby making it difficult to adapt to rapidly changing environments. Networks, in contrast, call upon the social skills and capacities of people to collaborate on joint tasks and generate a sense of shared responsibility, which leads them to attribute positive emotional experiences to the collective unit.

CHAPTER 8

Social Inequality and Order at the Micro Level

In 2006 the U.S. Post Office announced that it was going to break up the 10021 zip code that historically had been assigned to the Upper East Side of Manhattan, New York. Some parts of the Upper East Side would retain the 10021 zip code, while other parts would be assigned a new zip code. This announcement was met with protests, both individual and collective, by residents of the Upper East Side. Some residents refused to stop using the 10021 zip code. Upon first glance, this response is surprising. Why would people become so attached to a particular zip code? Why would a change produce such a strong response? One answer is that the 10021 zip code had become symbolic of the status of those living in this Manhattan neighborhood and therefore an object of value in and of itself. The Upper East Side of Manhattan is associated with persons of substantial wealth and power in business, government, and the arts, and the status of such groups had rubbed off on their zip code. This case illustrates how subtle and pervasive the effects of status inequality are, and how nominal objects can take on status value if associated with people of power and prestige.

Trivial or small differences among people or minor distinguishing aspects of their groups, neighborhoods, or regions can become very important because such differences have implications for their status. *Status* is defined as actors' relative standing in prestige, honor, or competence (Berger, Cohen, and

Zelditch 1972); it is an evaluation of generalized worth or value that carries implications for perceptions of competency. People respond to virtually anything that bears on their own or others' perceptions of their worth, competence, or performance, and it does not matter whether these perceptions are accurate or not. Thus, if the 10021 zip code signified honor, worth, status, or competence, then it ostensibly strengthened the "status value" of living on the Upper East Side of Manhattan (Thye 2000a, 2000b; Thye, Willer, and Markovsky 2006). To lose the zip code was to lose a bit of the prestige or status value associated with it.

Status advantages yield real, tangible benefits but also are self-affirming, emotionally arousing, and intrinsically satisfying. People sometimes fight for status—to acquire it, preserve it, or enhance it. Yet casual observation suggests that challenges to one's status in many situations are the exception rather than the rule. Status structures are more often assumed or taken for granted—that is, they are social frameworks within which people operate and which they do not consciously attempt to change. The work setting is a good example of a highly status-differentiated context in which, on a daily basis, collaboration, cooperation, and compliance are the rule and status conflicts or contests the exception. People perceive differences in worth or competence that are relevant to the work situation; they tend to share these beliefs and to act on them in concert, which affirms or reproduces the status structures.

Those in lower-status positions, however, tend to be less happy, to experience more negative emotions (sadness, depression), and to perceive greater injustice than those higher in the status structure. Such effects have been observed in laboratory studies of status and emotion (see Ridgeway and Johnson 1990; Willer, Lovaglia, and Markovsky 1997; Lovaglia and Houser 1996), as well as in national and international surveys that find positive correlations of general well-being (reports of "life satisfaction") with indicators of status such as income ranking and educational level. Similar associations have been observed for individual income and health outcomes (Mullahy, Robert, and Wolfe 2004). In light of a range of negative outcomes for those with low status, we ask whether status inequality may attenuate or provide barriers for the commitment process. In terms of our theory, this could occur in two ways: by reducing the jointness of the task if high-status people are seen as directing the interaction, or by reducing the positive feelings from success at the joint task. Thus, whereas status structures have the capacity to produce stable and orderly interactions over time, they may simultaneously under-mine the strength of social commitments that lower-status people develop to the groups or organizations within which they are status-disadvantaged. This issue is the primary focus of this chapter. We first discuss status and social order in general terms, and then we summarize a particularly relevant labo-ratory experiment on status inequality. Finally, we theorize in some detail how social order at the micro level may be generated and sustained in spite of significant status inequalities.

STATUS AND THE PROBLEM OF ORDER

In classic sociological theory, social inequality has a dual character in that it promotes both social order and social conflict. One class of theories—termed conflict theories—asserts that inequalities generate order by providing some actors with the capacity to influence, control, or dominate others (Weber 1918/1968; Dahrendorf 1959). The order-producing effects of inequality primarily involve coercion and power, and the use of power by authorities is legitimized by collectively validated ideas and beliefs. Coercion and suppression are necessary for order because people from different groups have conflicting interests, and legitimacy is necessary to give that order a normative justification. Yet social order remains tenuous or problematic because underlying conflicts of interest remain. Another class of theories argues that inequalities generate order by differentiating and coordinating tasks on behalf of collective goals (Durkheim 1893/1964; Collins 1975). Here complementary goals and inter-dependencies among people or their positions are the structural bases for social order, and the resulting orders are more stable than presumed by conflict theories.

These two themes are interwoven in micro-sociological literatures on power and status (Willer and Anderson 1981; Emerson 1972b; Molm 1987; Lawler 1992). From social exchange theory, interdependencies are a source of power and conflict as well as order and cohesion. The main program of research in micro-sociology that analyzes the causes and consequences of status is the expectation states program (Berger, Fisek, and Freese 1977; Berger and Webster 2006). This theory explains how status structures organize social interac-tion by generating differential status or competency evaluations for self and other, and how these translate into observable differences in deference and influence. In both theoretical traditions, people are assumed to be involved in a joint task and to be motivated to do as well as possible at that task. The main ideas from these traditions facilitate a more thorough and deeper understanding of how macro-level inequalities are manifested and reproduced in the local, immediate situations where people interact. The argument is that status processes in local interaction settings "bring to life" and mirror the social inequalities that exist at the macro level. An important question is how status differences affect the commitment process theorized in chapter 4.

We start with a key assumption: the evaluations that underlie status are collectively held and perceived as consensual within or across groups. Individuals may not believe or agree with the differential evaluations underlying status, but the evaluations have "social validity" in that they are perceived as generally held beliefs in the group or population. In this sense, status evaluations are an ever-ready framework or cultural "tool kit" that people can bring to or invoke in their interactions with other people in almost any situation. The strength and persistence of status evaluations stem, in part, from the fact that people often take what they believe others believe about "social worth" as a given, and they tend to act consistently with these beliefs (Ridgeway and Correll 2006). Status structures therefore involve beliefs perceived to be consensual and out there. These consensual status beliefs associate worth or esteem with categories or positions and are the ultimate foundation of the status structures that differentiate people and create repetitive patterns of deference and influence.

Status structures are resilient, but they can and do change, especially if legitimately challenged (see, for example, Ridgeway and Correll 2006). Status structures can be altered because they so strongly depend on *perceived* differences in worth, honor, or competence, which those lower in a structure have incentives to challenge. This malleability is probably one reason why those with high status can become attached to objectively trivial and unimportant by-products or correlates of status, such as zip codes, designer apparel, expensive watches, and the like. Purely symbolic dimensions of status affirm or magnify the status divide reflected in more objective indicators of status (such as education or intelligence), and thus symbolic dimensions of status become integral to how status is defined by self and others. For this reason alone, status challenges tend to produce strong reactions and are characterized as illegitimate from those whose status would be reduced.

Most research on social inequality, whether by economists, sociologists, or political scientists, is at the macro level and tends to focus more on large groups (for a comprehensive review, see Neckerman 2004). A key issue is to understand how differences in occupation, education, race-ethnicity, where people live, how and where their children are educated, health and general well-being, political participation, civic engagement, and income contribute to social inequality (Neckerman 2004). Missing from this large body of macro work is a sustained attention to the micro-interaction mechanisms through which fundamental differences in life chances and life experiences play out in people's everyday lives (Berger and Webster 2006; Ridgeway 1991; Thye 2000b). We subscribe to the view that it is in local, micro-level social interactions that status-related perceptions (expectations) and behaviors (deference) are reproduced and sustained (see especially Berger, Ridgeway, and Zelditch 2002). Expanding educational opportunities and reducing income differences may reduce extant social inequalities only insofar as these change the status beliefs associated with social positions, that is, consensual perceptions about worth and competence. Understanding the micro dimensions or manifestations of macro social inequalities is important for these reasons.

The individualization narrative suggests that, with widespread access to new modes of communication and opportunities that essentially flatten the world, we should be observing an overall decline in social inequality. By equalizing access to knowledge resources and equalizing opportunities to develop network ties, the structural foundation of extant status inequalities should erode to some degree. If a greater proportion of people across the world have access to the same pool of information, to common stores of knowledge, and to common experiences, shouldn't differences among them be a function of "what they do" more than of "who they are" or "where they come from"? Status differences should more closely mirror or reflect performance in markets that govern access to and use of knowledge and network resources.

Evidence to date does not support these inferences about the social transformations that are under way. For example, in the United States, the gains from economic growth over the last twenty-five years have been very substantial at the higher income levels, modest at the middle levels of income, and nonexistent at the lower levels. Income inequality between those in the top and bottom quintiles of the income divide has grown significantly (Frank 2007). In fact, in the early years of the twenty-first century, inequalities of wealth (income plus other assets) in the United States have returned to magnitudes found in the 1920s, which reflected the high point of the twentieth century. Overall, the evidence on changes in global inequality is mixed, but it seems clear that the current transformations are not promoting dramatic or necessarily even reliable trends toward less social inequality (Firebaugh and

Goesling 2004). The commitment problems associated with social inequality are likely to be as relevant as ever.

The current trends make it likely that persons of different backgrounds (such as different education, race, and ethnicity) interact more often at work. However, the effects of differential backgrounds may be to import macro-cultural patterns of inequality and deference into specific workplace settings (for a review of diversity in work teams, see Mannix and Neale 2005). This is likely to occur if the background characteristics arouse generalized cultural beliefs about competence and worth. This chapter takes up this issue, drawing heavily on work in the expectation states tradition to address status (Berger and Webster 2006) and work in the social exchange tradition to address power (Molm 2003, 2006; Willer 1999). We then use the theory of social commitments to indicate how and when affective ties to a group may develop even in the context of local inequalities of power and status that reflect larger patterns of social inequality. To move toward this goal, the next section presents an overview of data from a laboratory study that dramatically illustrates the resilience of status and power inequalities at the micro level and pinpoints the phenomenon we aim to explain in subsequent sections.

EMPIRICAL FINDINGS ON STATUS AND EMOTIONS

Here we report the results from an experiment that integrated standard, well-established procedures from both research on exchange networks (Markovsky, Willer, and Patton 1988) and research on status processes (Berger and Webster 2006). The overall goal was to determine how status differences affect the use of power and the emotions felt as individuals negotiate. In particular, this experiment brought pairs of subjects who were undergraduates at the University of South Carolina together in a small-groups laboratory to engage in a negotiation task (see Thye and Witkowski 2003; Thye, Willer, and Markovsky 2006; Thye, Lawler, and Yoon 2008). Their task was to divide a pool of resources—thirty poker chips—repeatedly across sixty episodes of negotiation, which they did by making a demand for some portion of the pool on each round. Their goal in these negotiations was to maximize their own resources or profits, and their pay for the experiment was based entirely on the individual profits they accumulated in the study. If they did not agree on a division, each received zero points for that episode. In each episode, they could divide the pool of thirty points in any way, from one and twenty-nine, or twenty-nine and one, to fifteen and fifteen; these negotiations took place via computers (see Thye, Lovaglia, and Markovsky 1997). On each round, both subjects simultaneously entered a demand on the profit pool. If the sum of the two demands was less than thirty, each got what he or she requested, and the next round began. If the sum of the requests was more than thirty (for example, when each subject requested sixteen), each earned nothing.

It is important to emphasize that neither party had an alternative partner or another source of payoffs. This means that, structurally, they were an equal-power dyad in which neither had an advantage due to the network shape. On this basis alone, one would expect them to divide the thirty points equally (fifteen and fifteen). For inequality of outcomes to develop, one person would have to demand and receive more of the fixed pool (thirty), and the other would have to capitulate to this demand and accept less. Social exchange theory and research on power predicts that people in this situation will divide the pool equally, and that this pattern should become more pronounced over time as they learn more about the task and also about each other in the task situation (Emerson 1972b; Willer 1999; Thye 2000b). Some initial inequalities could occur, but they should not last. In the context of prior work on exchange (Molm and Cook 1995; Willer 1999), this is a simple and straightforward situation that, in and of itself, is not of much theoretical interest.

The interest comes from the fact that the experiment manipulated another dimension: the status difference between the subjects. The status manipulation made use of demographic characteristics known to have status implications and effects both in and outside of the laboratory: race and gender. The pairs of subjects differed on both of these characteristics. Gender and race stereotypes in American culture contain status beliefs—that is, generalized evaluations of worth and competence, which could conceivably be brought to and have an impact in the local situation (the small-groups laboratory). Substantial research already documents that people in small groups who are engaged in joint tasks are likely to infer differential performance expectations for males versus females and for whites versus blacks, even when race and gender are totally irrelevant for performance or competence at the particular task (Wagner and Berger 1997; Ridgeway and Erikson 2000). Thus, all other things being equal, status research suggests that white males will receive a greater share of the fixed pie from the negotiations than African American females (see Thye 2000b; Thye, Willer, and Markovsky 2006), even though these status characteristics have no demonstrable tie to the negotiation task.

The experiment compared three conditions, all of which involved negotiations between a white male and an African American female. In all conditions, the experimenter was a white female, but that matters little, since the experimenter had minimal contact with the subjects. To minimize her impact the experimenter simply escorted the subjects to separate rooms and administered written instructions. In condition A, subjects were informed of the race and gender of their partner; in condition B, they were not informed of their race and gender differences with their partner; and in condition C (a control), they were misinformed and told that they were working with someone of the identical race and gender. To do this, the experimenter showed subjects a description sheet that contained their own demographic information (age, year in school, race, gender, major) and that of their partner, as well as a digital photo of themselves and the ostensible partner appropriate for each condition. Subjects were randomly assigned to one of these distinct conditions. To further make salient the race and gender differences, subjects took a bogus "meaning insight test" and were given feedback indicating that the white male scored higher than the African American female. This is a standard procedure used to create status differences (see, for example, Berger, Fisek, and Freese 1977; Wagner and Berger 1997).

The experiment measured the degree of social inequality manifested in the negotiated outcomes; important for our theory, it also measured the emotional reactions of the subjects who worked to jointly produce agreements. Inequality was measured for the last ten (of sixty) rounds of negotiation, and emotions were measured on a post-questionnaire that asked subjects to report their feelings about the negotiations along the following bipolar adjectives: displeased-pleased, unhappy-happy, not satisfied-satisfied, not joyful-joyful, and discontented-contented. These items compose an index of "pleasure/satisfaction" that has been used in previous research and shown to be a precursor to relational cohesion (Lawler and Yoon 1993, 1996; Lawler, Thye, and Yoon 2000). The question is: does inequality emerge from this joint task, and if so, how does it affect emotional reactions? The main results were as follows:

1. There were large differences in payoffs from negotiation favoring white males over African American females. Across the two status-differentiated conditions (A and B), the former received 75 percent of the fixed pool, and the latter 25 percent. Thus, it is clear that race and gender combined to produce powerful inequalities in this local situation (the experiment).

2. There were no significant differences in pleasure and satisfaction between the higher- and lower-status persons. Those disadvantaged by the negotiated outcomes (African American females) did not report more negative feelings about the negotiations than those who were advantaged (white males). In fact, responses to the pleasure and satisfaction index were on the positive side of the emotion measurement scale. This lack of emotional difference is contrary to a number of prior laboratory studies of power in the absence of status differences (Lawler and Yoon 1993; Willer, Lovaglia, and Markovsky 1997).

3. Yet there were significantly lower rates of agreement relative to past dyadic studies (exchange frequency). Subjects came to agreement on 70 percent of the negotiation rounds despite the fact that the procedures of the experiment made it clear that non-agreement produced zero payoffs. This pattern suggests that reaching agreement was problematic for the participants and, by implication, that many of those with lower status did not simply roll over and capitulate.

4. More frequent exchanges produced more positive emotion (pleasure and satisfaction and more interest and excitement) independent of and controlling for payoff inequalities. This finding is consistent with relational cohesion theory (Lawler and Yoon 1996). The implication is that people who exchange more frequently build a more cohesive relationship.

Overall, the results pose an interesting paradox (Thye, Lawler, and Yoon 2008). The combined effects of race and gender produce a highly unequal allocation of a fixed pie that favors white males. Yet both the advantaged and disadvantaged persons express similar and positive feelings about the results of the negotiated exchanges. A plausible explanation is implied by the fourth finding—namely, that emotions here are based on how frequently they "solve" the negotiation or exchange problem, not the utility from what they actually earn.[1] Time and again it has been found that frequent exchange under such circumstances generates a sense of cohesion and a commitment to the relationship (Lawler and Yoon 1993, 1996, 1998; Lawler, Thye, and Yoon 2000, 2006). In this experiment, the emotional reactions and relational implications of the exchange may be more important to lower-status people in this situation than their relative outcomes. Chapters 3 and 4 identify theoretical reasons for positing such an interpretation and also provide some supporting evidence. However, these chapters do not discuss the conditions under which repeated interaction or exchange has cohesive effects in highly stratified or unequal relations. That we observed this in this experiment suggests an emotional foundation for social commitment among persons of unequal status. The remainder of this chapter is devoted to further theorizing this issue in the context of our theory of social commitments and existing research.

EXPLAINING ORDER IN THE CONTEXT OF STATUS STRATIFICATION

This section integrates key ideas from expectation states theory, social exchange theory, and our theory of social commitments. We argue that status differences and social exchange unleash dual, interwoven processes that can account for enduring social inequality. The line of argument developed in the following pages contains four main points. First, status beliefs (differential evaluations of competence and worth) in the larger culture tend to be activated in local situations, thereby generating initial inequalities (Ridgeway 1991; Berger, Ridgeway, and Zelditch 2002). Second, structures of power and interdependence generate patterns of repeated interaction or exchange, directed at individual or collective task goals. These tend to reproduce initial inequalities, but they also build more cohesive relationships (Emerson 1972b; Thye 2000b; Lawler 2001). Third, status beliefs are validated by the repeated inequalities in the local situation, and over time these "perceptions of what most others believe and act on" are internalized by lower- and higher-status persons, thereby becoming "perceptions of what they themselves believe" (Berger et al. 1998). Fourth, while reproducing inequalities, repeated interactions also produce stronger person-to-unit affective ties to the degree that the tasks people undertake are joint tasks that generate a sense of shared responsibility (Lawler 2001; Lawler, Thye, and Yoon 2008). The tendency to internalize and accept status evaluations is stronger under these conditions, as specified by the theory of social commitments.

Status Processes

Status beliefs contain inferences of generalized worth and competence that connect the local (micro) to the larger (macro) group context. Such beliefs develop either on the basis of actual performance or on the basis of potentially irrelevant factors such as status cues. Status beliefs tend to legitimize inequality in the local context, but they also give larger meaning to and affirm the cultural beliefs manifest in the larger macro group context (Berger, Ridgeway, and Zelditch 2002). Status beliefs provide a readymade menu of principles, scripts, or biases that may be activated in a given situation, and when activated, they forge a connection between stratification at the macro and local levels. Some important questions arise: How and when are status beliefs likely to be activated? How and when do they have legitimacy? To set the stage for answers to these questions, we provide a brief overview of the main concepts and assumptions of expectation states theory.

Expectation states theory (Berger, Cohen, and Zelditch 1972) is founded on the idea that when people interact to accomplish a joint task, they develop performance expectations for themselves and others based on observable characteristics and behavior. Those perceived as most competent on the task will be given more opportunity to suggest ideas or contribute to task success, their contributions will be perceived as better than those of others, they will be evaluated more positively, and they will have more relative influence in the interaction with others. Even in a setting where no status differentiation is present at the outset (Bales 1953), status stratification is likely to emerge endogenously because people will interpret and give meaning to observed differences in behavior, appearance, and demeanor and infer performance expectations from these cues. These patterns are especially prominent if the task is a cooperative one and if group members are collectively oriented, that is, they believe it is necessary to take each others' ideas into account. Thus, social inequalities—giving more influence and weight to those who are likely to be better at the task—are likely when people have a joint task and collective goals. Ironically, the task jointness that brings people together has the capacity to stratify and fragment them as well.

One branch of the expectation states program, termed status characteristics theory, takes up the issue of how and when culturally based status beliefs about social characteristics or categories shape performance expectations in local situations. A diffuse status characteristic is any characteristic that signals general and specific competence because of the cultural value attached to some states but not others. For instance, being male carries more status value than being female in many cultures. Other status characteristics include race, gender, education, occupation, and age. In general, status characteristics become activated in a group to the extent that they differentiate members of the group (gender in a group of men and women) or are directly related to the task at hand (a doctor in a group administering first aid).

Once activated, status characteristics can have many effects, but here we focus on two that bear on the nature of joint interaction. First is the spread of status value from a person to his or her resources or possessions (Thye 2000b).

This occurs when the resources or possessions of high-status individuals become symbolic reflections or indicators of status (see Thye, Willer, and Markovsky 2006; Ridgeway 1991). Such a spread of status value is illustrated by the subjective value of the 10021 zip code in Manhattan. People who live on the Upper East Side of Manhattan may be treated preferentially by city officials, cabbies, restaurants, repairmen, and post office employees because the status of the people in that area has spread to the area itself. In specific situations, the zip code may be a visible indicator or marker that activates high status and generates deference.

To further illustrate this phenomenon, note that items owned by high-status persons, such as former presidents or star athletes, take on very high-status value for which people are willing to pay large amounts of money. A given item is likely to be worth more if it is associated with a high-status person, which itself can foster unequal exchange. An objectively unequal exchange may not appear unequal to a lower-status party who is exchanging resources of less status value for those of greater status value. People who pay exorbitant prices for a pair of Lebron James's shoes do not perceive inequality, nor do they resent the retailer who sells the shoes (Thye, Willer, and Markovsky 2006). Similarly, people who make low wages in organizations with highly paid executives may assume that the contributions of the latter are worth more than their own. The key point is that the spread of status value diminishes the degree of perceived inequality, especially for lower-status individuals, when exchanges are objectively unequal. This implies that lower-status people do not necessarily experience negative emotions from unequal outcomes.

A second way in which activated status beliefs can affect joint interaction is through a referential structure (Berger, Ridgeway, and Zelditch 2002). A referential structure refers to cultural beliefs about the association between a status characteristic, such as gender or race, and goal objects, such as rewards or payoffs (Wagner and Berger 1997). On the one hand, status characteristics tend to activate referential structures that shape performance expectations and produce unequal reward distributions in local situations. On the other hand, this process also can work in reverse—that is, differential reward allocations can activate an ability referential structure. When this happens, people make post hoc inferences that those who get more are more able, competent, and deserving (Berger et al. 1985). For example, knowing only that a particular doctor makes half a million dollars annually may lead one to presume that the doctor is quite skilled.

In both of these ways, cultural definitions or beliefs about "what is" (the referential structure that associates a status characteristic with reward allocations) become "what is expected" in the local social interaction. Applying this idea of a referential structure to the experiment described earlier, being African American and female is associated with receiving lower rewards in society more generally, and in fact African American women received less in the negotiated payoff allocations. A plausible argument is that the experiment activated referential beliefs about the association between the particular status characteristics and reward allocations and that people in the experiment acted in accord with the referential structure. However, this does not explain why lower-status people felt as positive as they did about the negotiations. For this, we turn to Morris Zelditch and Henry Walker's theory of legitimacy (1984; see also Zelditch 2006).

Legitimating Inequality

The two phenomena just described—the spread of status value and referential structure—legitimize social inequalities by tying inequalities to taken-for-granted beliefs, norms, and principles. Zelditch and Walker (1984) theorize two dimensions of legitimacy: validity and propriety. Validity is the collective-level dimension of legitimacy, and propriety is the individual-level dimension. A status structure is valid if people treat the norms, beliefs, and procedures as taken for granted and matters of fact. Validity implies that people accept the status structure and associated referential beliefs and values as reflecting "the way things are done," but not necessarily that they personally believe this should be the case. The stereotypes and expectations associated with status characteristics, such as gender and race, often reveal the taken-for-granted-ness implied by validity. The validity dimension helps to explain the resilience of social inequality and the tacit acceptance people accord it.

Propriety refers to a person's own evaluation of a status structure or the beliefs and expectations that underlie and justify it (see Dornbusch and Scott 1975). Is it proper, correct, or just to differentiate people along a particular dimension? Impropriety, of course, is a source of resistance or challenges to status structures and an important source of social change. Zelditch and Walker (1984) argue that validity and propriety are distinct dimensions, in part because it is quite common for people to act on status values and referential structures that they do not themselves share (validity) or to act consistent with "the way things work" because this is expected, despite having strong personal reservations. Nevertheless, validity often gives rise to propriety as people cognitively adjust or accommodate their own beliefs to those that appear to be validated (for examples and evidence, see Walker and Zelditch 1993 and Ridgeway and Correll 2006).

Our theory of social commitments implies that repeated interactions or exchanges among people, in socially validated status structures, lead them to perceive those status structures as proper. In the experiment described here, validity-to-propriety effects may have occurred as people repeatedly experienced unequal payoff allocations in the context of a referential structure that associated race and gender status characteristics with differential rewards and outcomes in the larger society. It does not require many repetitions of a pattern to generate an emergent order and external reality for people (Berger and Luckmann 1966). It is plausible that, in our experiment, the activation of a referential structure for gender and race accorded validity to the inequalities and that the repetition of these over time made these inequalities seem proper for the participants. This validity-to-propriety effect could account for the fact that both higher- and lower-status people reported positive feelings about the negotiations. Yet status or legitimacy theories do not really specify how this occurs. We turn to social exchange theory for this purpose.

Social Exchange Processes

Status structures in groups involve dependencies and interdependencies among members, but these are generally peripheral to theories in the expectation states tradition. Instead, the focus is on situations in which people are collectively oriented and have a joint task and the opportunity to influence each other's decisions on the task. Social exchange theory, however, takes structures of jointness or interdependence as central and assumes a mixed motive orientation in which people have reasons to act in concert with others but also to act alone or in competition. In exchange theory, patterns of dependence or interdependence determine the allocation of rewards and the degree of order and commitment in relations (Emerson 1972b; Molm and Cook 1995; Willer 1999). The experimental evidence presented here is of special interest because unequal allocations of reward mirrored larger status beliefs about race and gender rather than the patterns of dependence that entailed equal power.

Relational cohesion theory helps to account for this. It explicitly addresses the emotional responses to social exchange under different structures of dependence and interdependence. Inequalities of power dependence reduce, while high mutual dependence increases, the frequency of exchange among a given pair of actors, which in turn fosters more positive emotions. Positive feelings from repeated exchange promote stronger relations (cohesion) and transform an instrumental relation into an expressive one (see Lawler and Yoon 1993, 1996; Thye, Yoon, and Lawler 2002). The results of a significant number of experiments support these predictions, while also affirming that such effects are mediated by positive feelings from successfully solving an exchange task with the same partner (for relevant reviews, see Thye, Yoon, and Lawler 2002; Lawler and Thye 2006). Mutual dependencies promote relational cohesion because the repeated exchanges make people "feel good" (experience pleasure or satisfaction), and inequalities of power dependence reduce relational cohesion by making people feel bad, in part because they have more trouble reaching agreements. In the experiment described here, both people are highly and equally dependent on each other, suggesting the ideal conditions for relational cohesion to emerge, status differences notwithstanding. Because more frequent exchange did indeed generate more positive feelings in those with low and high status or power, the results of the experiment suggest a relational cohesion interpretation.

The theory of social commitments, however, adds an important dimension to a relational cohesion account—namely, the jointness of the task and the sense of shared responsibility this induces. If high- and low-status persons are involved in a highly joint task, this should generate stronger perceptions of shared responsibility for task results. Further, if the sense of shared responsibility for these results is greater, positive feelings from exchange are likely to be attributed to or associated with the group or unit affiliation (see chapter 4). The implication is that lower-status individuals become more oriented to establishing a relation that fosters success at the joint task and pay less attention to their lowered distribution of rewards or payoffs (Thye, Lawler, and Yoon 2008). The same process may explain why and how both the low- and high-status persons become committed to the relation, but they may do so for somewhat different reasons: for the high-status person the instrumental and relational aspects of the exchange converge, whereas for the low-status person the instrumental and relational diverge. Thus, people accept and act in accord with social inequality, even if they are disadvantaged, to the degree that they develop affective ties to the social unit—in this case, the relation.

Real-world examples of the role of shared responsibility abound. Almost invariably, leaders of top organizations stress to internal audiences the collective nature of the endeavor and the importance of each person's contribution to that endeavor. Corporate-wide meetings or communications often contain a "we are family" theme. Some corporations, such as Starbucks and Wal-Mart, choose terms other than "employee" to describe the members of their work-force, referring to them instead as "partners" or "associates." In other cases, corporations are associated with worthy social goals through philanthropic contributions and sponsorship of local community events. Our theory sug-gests that the success of policies and communications about "being in this together" are contingent on the degree to which these efforts produce a sense of shared responsibility across positions, hierarchical levels, functions, and departments. Under these conditions, it is most likely that positive experiences in the workplace will form the basis for positive sentiments about the organi-zation as such. Thus, the theory of social commitments points to one way in which people build and sustain strong person-to-group ties, even in the face of significant social inequalities.

CONCLUSIONS

Our explanation for social order in the context of status inequality involves a convergence of status and social exchange processes. Because status character-istics have cultural content, being based in fundamental beliefs about worth and competence, they tend to be activated in local task situations. Once acti-vated, they produce interaction and reward inequalities that affirm and (with repetition) legitimize those status inequalities. At the same time, the repetition of social exchanges leads to cohesive relations based on the experience of suc-cess at a joint task. This occurs especially if the task gives lower- and higher-status individuals a sense of shared responsibility for the results. To conclude, we present a theoretical model that integrates the main themes of the chapter.

The convergence of status and exchange processes involves four steps. First, there are existing status differences—that is, people in the local situation are different along characteristics that are evaluated in the larger social unit. These may be social demographic categories, such as race, gender, and age; they may be categories associated with specific achievements, such as education and occupation; or they may be group or organizational memberships. Regardless of the particular source, the situation makes the categories salient enough to spread status value (making the goods held by high-status individuals seem more valuable) and activates a referential structure that links the characteris-tics to evaluations and expectations. The referential structure is a mechanism by which the cultural beliefs of a larger social unit are imported into and brought to bear on a local situation, while the spread of status value makes the resources of the high-status person take on more value than those of the low-status person. In a real-world setting, there are innumerable cues and subtle behaviors that activate status characteristics, and in fact it is difficult to prevent them from becoming activated (see Berger et al. 1985). We posit that referential structures and the spread of status value together generate the initial differences in payoffs in the exchange.

Second, if people are highly interdependent and engage in a joint task involving an exchange of resources, they perceive a shared responsibility for successful exchanges. Recall that in our experiment even the worst payoff from a negotiated exchange is better than no agreement at all. People are highly dependent on each other because payoffs or benefits from the joint task cannot be obtained alone or in other available relationships. This interdependence exerts a structural push for status-differentiated persons to interact in an effort to accomplish the joint task and to successfully generate benefits at the collective level. Thus, whereas status conditions promote unequal divisions of the payoff, exchange conditions promote successful exchanges.

Third, initial social inequalities therefore emerge, and payoff differences from exchange correspond to status differences and are in accord with the status value of the good and associated referential structures. Owing to structural interdependencies, these social inequalities are experienced repeatedly over time, thereby making this pattern a "reality" for those involved. This repetition of a pattern that is consistent with the referential structure validates (legitimizes) the inequalities of status and reward for people in the situation.

Finally, three consequences flow from the fact that inequalities are experienced repeatedly but in the context of success at the exchange task (reaching agreements): (1) people feel good about being able to accomplish exchanges and develop a cohesive relationship, that is, a relation perceived as coming together rather than coming apart; (2) given the inherent jointness of an exchange task, people have a sense of shared responsibility for success or failure at that task, which in turn leads them to attribute positive feelings from success in part to the larger social unit in which the referential structure is embedded; and (3) people come to see the inequality as appropriate or proper, meaning that there are validity-to-propriety effects, and self-evaluations are consistent with larger status beliefs about what differentiates them in the local situation. For such reasons, it is not uncommon for low-status, low-wage persons in an organization to accord significant expressive value to their membership in the organization. The relational aspect of the situation can trump the transactional aspect for people lower in a status hierarchy.

To conclude, the argument is complicated but it can be reduced to a relatively simple message: inequalities are legitimized through status processes, while valued relations and person-to-unit ties are generated through social exchange processes; when these processes converge, status structures generate order and stability in social interactions between lower- and higher-status persons. Status structures activate referential beliefs and the spread of status value that justify status and reward differences in local, micro contexts. If inequalities occur repeatedly, it becomes socially validated (legitimate) as a standard practice for that situation, which in turn reaffirms status beliefs about competence and worth. The repeated exchanges of low- and high-status persons, however, also build cohesive relations and strengthen ties to the larger units in which they are nested, especially if the interactions entail joint tasks that foster a sense of shared responsibility. In this sense, social exchange is a process that enhances the legitimacy of social inequality by generating social commitments to larger, macro units, beyond strengthening the local relations of higher- and lower-status persons.

Ours is a micro-sociological approach to social inequality that is based on two long-standing theoretical traditions: expectation states theory (Berger, Cohen, and Zelditch 1972) and social exchange theory (Homans 1950; Emerson 1972; Willer 1999). The former has the advantage of providing a general explanation for how and when macro-based cultural beliefs are brought to and enacted in local social situations, whereas the latter has the advantage of explaining how and when structures of dependence or interdependence generate emergent relational ties among people pursuing individual instrumental goals. This chapter integrates central themes of these theoretical traditions to understand how and when micro-level social orders emerge in the shadow of larger social inequalities.

CHAPTER 9

Nationalist Sentiments in Modern States

Is the nation-state in decline? In a world of highly interdependent nations, do nation-states lose autonomy and power? Given increasingly open and free international markets, are there growing constraints on the capacity of states to provide their citizens with valued services and protections (see Rodrik 1997)? Is the nation-state's decentralization or devolution of services and functions to sub-units (provinces, states, cities) making those sub-units more salient and important to people than the central, overarching state (Ferejohn and Weingast 1997; Rodden 2006)? In the context of globalization and its correlates, are the attachments of people to their nation eroding? Such questions are in the forefront of debates about how major social transformations are affecting the nation-state as an institution (Rodrik 1997; Scharpf 2000; Haas 2000; Fukuyama 2004; Calhoun 2007). Our theory of social commitments can shed light on a particular dimension of the problems facing the modern state—namely, its capacity to generate and sustain nationalist sentiments. Nationalist sentiments are affective feelings about the state (person-to-group) that are likely to be manifested in loyalty, patriotism, and commitment.[1] This chapter suggests why nation-states may remain important sources of social commitment, despite the pressures of a global economy and international interdependencies on state capacity.

Nations or states can be construed as the largest and most powerful social units of which people are members. They are historically a source of highly valued individual benefits, protections, and opportunities and therefore have instrumental value to people. They also are meaningful social or group identities that shape how people define themselves and others, and they can thus have non-instrumental (expressive) value as well. Our theory indicates that if people form non-instrumental, expressive ties to their state, they are more prepared to orient their behavior to the nation-state and to make individual sacrifices on its behalf. They may overlook declines in state services and protections because of their loyalty and commitment to the state. However, there are good reasons for suspecting that person-to-state ties are increasingly problematic in a highly interdependent, global world. This is a subject of considerable debate among sociologists, economists, and political scientists (see Rodrik 1997; Scharpf 2000; Greenfeld and Eastwood 2005).

Scholars have offered widely disparate views of how the globalization of the world is affecting the nation-state as an institution (compare, for example, Haas 2000; Rodrik 1997; Laitin 2007; Calhoun 2007). Some argue that globalization reduces the capacity of states to exert internal control over their economies, to control their external political environments, and to sustain the attachments of their citizenry (see, for example, Haas 2000). Others argue that states are the foundation for liberal democratic institutions and remain important, overarching sources of identity that bridge other social differences and shape definitions of community (Greenfeld 1992; Calhoun 2007; Laitin 2007). Still others suggest that while states do indeed face significant internal and external pressures as a result of globalization, they reveal a capacity to adapt by changing taxation policies, increasing public expenditures, and formulating new administrative and legal regulations (Rodrik 1997; Scharpf 2000; Ganghof 2000). Our emphasis on affective sentiments about national affiliations is aligned with the second view, but we use ideas from all three perspectives.

This chapter draws on an array of theory and research on states, nationalism, and state formation in order to apply our theory to the question: how are person-to-nation affective ties sustained in modern states? We elaborate two general implications of the theory of social commitments. The first is that nation-states sustain nationalist sentiments to the degree that they generate a sense of shared, collective responsibility for the affairs of the state and foster positive emotional experiences that people associate with their national identity. Nation-states should generate weaker instrumental commitments if they are losing their autonomy and power on the world stage and if they have less capacity to meet the social and economic needs of their citizens (Rodrik 1997;

Haas 2000; Ferejohn and Weingast 1997), yet affective ties or commitments to the nation may remain strong. Our theory suggests how. The second implication is that people tend to form stronger affective ties with local political units, such as cities and regional entities (provinces, states), than to more distant or removed units, such as the nation-state. This tendency to develop stronger commitments to local sub-units should be accentuated if nation-states are becoming weaker and less effective institutions because of the global economy or because of the internal decentralization or privatization of central state functions and services. Under such conditions, the nested commitments principle of our theory predicts stronger attachments to local political units—cities and provinces—than to the overarching nation-state (see chapter 6). This implies that "federalism" may have negative effects on commitments to the state.[2]

The chapter is organized into four sections. First we compare the main lines of argument about whether modern nation-states are declining as important sources of benefit and identity. We then identify two theoretical dimensions for understanding when person-to-state nationalist sentiments are likely to become stronger or weaker. In the succeeding discussion, we use data from the International Social Survey Program (ISSP) on national identity to examine the nested commitments hypothesis—specifically, whether people tend to feel closer to their local units than to their state. Finally, we develop a theoretical model that suggests in general terms how nationalist sentiments are sustained in modern states, drawing on our own theory as well as select political and sociological theories of nationalism.

ARE STATES IN DECLINE?

States organize and regulate national economies, provide basic protections to a population within a territory, support universal educational programs, provide systems of health care, and offer social services of various forms. In this context, it is striking that many scholars argue that the power of the state is declining as the twenty-first century takes shape. The globalization of economic activity, the growth of international organizations, widespread abuses of state power by public officials, unmet expectations or demands from citizens, the decentralization or privatization of state functions or services, and high levels of cross-state interdependencies all ostensibly constrain autonomous state actions and limit the capacity of states to mobilize collective action (see, for example, Haas 2000; Fukuyama 2004; Stiglitz 2006). As exemplars, consider some fairly provocative arguments about the decline of states from Francis Fukuyama

(2004) and Ernst Haas (2000). Focusing on declines in the institutional capacity of states both from within and outside, Fukuyama (2004, 119) says:

> For well over a generation, the trend in world politics has been to weaken stateness. The trend came about for both normative and economic reasons. Many states in the twentieth century were too powerful: They tyrannized populations and committed aggression against neighbors. Those that were not dictatorships nonetheless impeded economic growth and accumulated a variety of dysfunctions and inefficiencies due to excessive state scope. The trend therefore has been to cut back the size of state sectors and to turn over to the market or to civil society functions that have been improperly appropriated. At the same time, the growth of the global economy has tended to erode the autonomy of sovereign nation-states by increasing the mobility of information, capital, and, to a lesser extent, labor.

Ernst Haas (2000, 450), in the conclusion to his two-volume work on nationalism, links this decline of state capacity with erosion of the state as an object of attachment or commitment for citizens:

> Most nation-states are increasingly turbulent. The older ones seem unable to govern as they once did; they cannot solve outstanding problems with finality. Their self-confidence about solving national problems nationally is gone. . . . The happily integrated nation-state of the early twentieth-century West is no longer with us. . . .
>
> The nation-state, under conditions of turbulence, ceases being humankind's terminal community. People learn to play different roles in different contexts, profess different loyalties, and form different attachments for different purposes. Modernity implies the ability, instrumentally, to fragment one's self to suit the main purposes at hand. Global capitalism contributes to this ability. . . .
>
> This fragmentation has the odd effect of both causing turbulent politics at the national level and inducing intense multilateral cooperation at the international level. Territory as the sovereign definer of identity and welfare erodes.

These are complementary arguments about the decline of the state. Fukuyama (2004) draws particular attention to the tendency of states in the twentieth century to accumulate, concentrate, and misuse power, whereas Haas (2000) draws particular attention to the decline of the state as a subjective object of attachment and source of identity.[3] Our theory of social commitments connects these complementary notions. Citizens are less committed to their nation-state in part because nation-states are less important or central sources of benefit and have difficulty mobilizing collective efforts and actions from which people may experience positive emotions and feelings.

A number of other scholars make strong arguments for the continued importance of the state (Greenfeld and Eastwood 2005; Calhoun 2007; Laitin 2007). For example, Craig Calhoun (2007, 171) concludes a recent work on nationalism in the modern nation-state as follows:

> Globalization has not put an end to nationalism—not to nationalist conflicts nor to the role of nationalist categories in organizing ordinary people's sense of belonging in the world. Indeed, globalization fuels resurgence in nationalism among people who feel threatened or anxious as much as it drives efforts to transcend nationalism in new structures of political-legal organization or thinking about transnational connections. Nationalism still matters, still troubles many of us, but still organizes something considerable in who we are.

The nation-state is the principal unit within a "world of nation-states" and in fact is legitimized by international bodies. Moreover, it is a basis for intergroup perceptions. For such reasons, nation-states remain important sources of identity, and under some conditions they override or counteract divisions among other group identities—for example, those based on ethnicity, region, or religion—in a population (Laitin 2007). Overall, arguments for the importance of nation-state identities in the modern world tend to stress the symbolic, expressive character of such identities and the ways in which these identities connect the local interactions and experiences of people with macro cultural and structural conditions (see Greenfeld 1992, 18–19).[4] Liah Greenfeld (1992) shows that the contemporary idea of a "nation" originated in a semantic shift in its meaning in sixteenth-century England to denote "a people" or, by implication, a community in which each member shares its defining properties. The identity dimension was therefore fundamental to modern forms of nationalism from the beginning.

The third position on the state-decline thesis is that there are no straight-forward effects of globalization on the viability of the nation-state as an institution. This position is based on empirical tests of specific hypotheses derived from the state-decline thesis with cross-national survey data (see

Scharpf and Schmidt 2000).[5] Typical hypotheses, for example, hold that increasing international competition and the threat of exit by multinational corporations should exert downward pressure on rates of taxation and public expenditures as a percentage of GDP. Steffen Ganghof (2000) assessed these hypotheses among eighteen OECD nations for the 1970 to 1996 period. Contrary to the state-decline thesis, he found general stability in rates of taxation and public expenditures as a percentage of GDP. There was some evidence of a reduction in corporate taxation, but states responded to corporate tax reductions by broadening tax bases and using administrative and legal mechanisms to increase the costs of exit by capital (Ganghof 2000). In another study, Dani Rodrik (1998) tested the impact of a key dimension of globalization—increasing open trade (defined as the share of trade in GDP)— on the size of government (as measured by government expenditures as a percentage of GDP). Finding a positive rather than negative relationship between free trade and the size of government, he attributes this to governmental actions and policies designed to reduce the risks of the economic volatility associated with more open trade. Studies such as these document the adaptability of the modern nation-state. When globalization threatens state resource flows or capacity, modern states tend to adapt their tax, budgetary, and trade policies in ways that preserve or, in some cases, increase the power of the central state. We conclude that, while there is mixed evidence on some issues, the available evidence from the last couple of decades of the twentieth century does not support the state-decline hypothesis.[6]

Our theory reframes the issue of state decline as a problem of commitment and national identity. We need to consider whether the forms of commitment to the state are changing and also whether people are becoming more committed to their local units than to the state. States may effectively adapt to increasing economic competition (and threats of exit by corporate entities), as suggested in the work of Fritz Wilhelm Scharpf (2000) and Steffen Ganghof (2000), but in the process person-to-state ties may become more instrumental and less affective. Globalization may not reduce the viability of states, but it still could make the primary ties of people more instrumental, especially if globalization also has individualizing effects. Thus, the strength of commitments to the state may be weaker than is apparent on the surface, as well as more vulnerable to change. Nationalist sentiments may counter such tendencies and be a more important source of social order under such conditions. The first step in our analysis is to clarify the interrelationships of states, nations, and nationalism.

NATIONS, STATES, AND NATIONALISM

Anthony Smith (2001), along with most political scientists and sociologists, makes sharp distinctions between a state and a nation (Gellner 1983; Anderson 2006; Tilly 1990; Greenfeld 1992; Hutchinson and Smith 1994). A state involves sovereignty over a defined territory and institutional structures that exercise authority and control over activities within that territory (Smith 2001). A nation is fundamentally a community that includes a socially recognized name (identity), a shared heritage or history, and a recognized public culture (Smith 2001). States may develop such community properties over time, and nations may develop a measure of independence and self-determination without becoming states (Guibernau 1999; Smith 2001; Alter 1994). Nations can exist without states (Guibernau 1999), and the causal and temporal order of states and nations is subject to different interpretations and some controversy (Greenfeld and Eastwood 2005). The prevailing view is that modern states have been major sources of nationalism for more than two hundred years (see Gellner 1983; Hechter 2000; and Anderson 2006), which raises a question for us: how do states promote nationalist sentiments?[7]

Weber (1918/1968) defined "nationalism" as involving communal, affective sentiments that are manifested in or directed toward the state. States, on the one hand, are a condition for the development of nationalist sentiments, and nationalism, on the other hand, is a transformative force that turned emerging states of the eighteenth and nineteenth centuries into "national states" (Smith 2001). Nations are cultural units that bind together actors with similar histories, ethnicities, languages, or religious beliefs (Alter 1994), whereas states are political units that bind actors through common instrumental goals (Weber 1918; Gellner 1983; Smith 2001). Nations involve communal ties (Gemeinschaft) based on subjective feeling, while states involve noncommunal ties (Gesellschaft) based on individual or collective interests (Weber 1968). States are organized to generate collective or joint goods that actors cannot produce in other, extant, or alternative groupings (Hechter 2000), to monopolize the means of force or coercion within a territory (Tilly 1990), or to generate a unifying order among diverse or differentiated populations (Gellner 1983). It is reasonable, therefore, to posit that states establish a stronger foundation for collective action than nations, whereas nations establish a stronger foundation for a salient group (national) identity than states.

Nationalism can be construed as an ideology that forges the necessary link between state and nation (see Greenfeld 1992; Smith 2001). Yet the ideology or beliefs surrounding nationalist sentiments may have little substantive content. Smith (2001) argues that the "ideology" of nationalism gives salience or prominence to the nation and its welfare, but tends to involve ideas or beliefs of little substance or content. Eric Hobsbawm (1990, 176) echoes this view, saying of nationalism: "Its very vagueness and lack of programmatic content gives it a potentially universal support within its own community." Thus, nationalism is little more than a vague notion that the state, a political unit, also constitutes the nation, a communal unit, with distinctive symbols, practices, and patterns of behavior (Greenfeld 1992; Anderson 2006). Conceiving of nationalism as an affective sentiment or feeling about a state, as we do, recognizes this minimal ideational content. We argue that nationalism is an emotional and affective phenomenon at its core.

To conclude, our theory suggests that states and nations generate different forms of commitment or person-to-unit ties. States in principle should be effective at producing instrumental forms of commitment, based on coercion and reward power, but in themselves they have less capacity to generate affective forms of commitment. Nations, as cultural units, have greater capacity to produce affective commitments because of the communal, identity-affirming ties between person and nation, but less capacity to generate instrumental commitments than states, because alone they lack the structures of bureaucratic control available to states. The legitimacy of "nations without states" tends to be contested, whereas states in a world of states are taken for granted, mutually recognized, and internationally legitimated organizational forms. The point is that states are primarily instrumental groupings, whereas nations are primarily expressive groupings. Since a central purpose of this volume is to understand in general terms how and when instrumental ties become expressive, our theory has implications for the conditions under which states or state structures generate stronger or weaker nationalist sentiments. The next section suggests two fundamental dimensions of state structure that should bear on the strength of nationalist sentiments.

DIMENSIONS OF STATE STRUCTURE

Francis Fukuyama (2004) uses two primary dimensions of state structure to analyze the plight of the modern nation-state: the scope of the functions assumed by the state, and the strength of the state's impact within whatever functions are assumed. *Scope* refers to the range of human activity regulated, monitored, or penetrated by the social-political institutions of the state, and state *strength* refers to the impact of the state structures that do exist on people within the state. Highly centralized states tend to have relatively broad institutional scope but relatively weak institutional strength, whereas highly decentralized states (for example, federations) tend to have more limited institutional scope but higher institutional strength. States in the modern era could expand or decline along either or both of these dimensions. Fukuyama suggests that globalization has negative effects on state scope, but not necessarily on state strength within a given scope. Scope and strength are useful dimensions for theorizing how states balance freedom, opportunity, and decentralizing forces with control, constraint, and centralizing forces, a classic issue in sociological theorizing (see Giddens 1984).

We reinterpret scope and strength in terms relevant to the theory of social commitments. State scope should be manifest in the salience or immediacy of the state in the lives of citizens. State strength should be manifest in the degree to which structures of the state are a source of collective efficacy. Recall from chapters 4 and 5 that the salience of a social unit is a condition for "group formation," or the activation of an existing group identity, and collective efficacy is a counterpart to shared responsibility. Both are grounded in structural interdependencies, joint activities, and collective outcomes. Thus, insofar as the state is salient to citizens and perceived by them as an instrument of collective efficacy, nationalist sentiments should develop and be sustained. Recasting Fukuyama's (2004) dimensions of state structure, we suggest the theoretical model of how state structures affect nationalist sentiments—and therefore social commitments to the state—shown in figure 9.1.

Figure 9.1   Role of Salience and Efficacy in Nationalist Sentiments

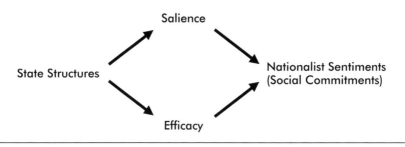

Source: Authors' compilation.

Salience is an "attention mechanism" that reminds people of the "presence" and "relevance" of a social unit—in this case, the state. A minimum threshold of salience is probably required for nationalist sentiments, because the state unit has to be salient as a social object "out there" before people can attribute their feelings to it. Collective efficacy, in turn, presupposes joint activities that generate goods that people can only produce with others in the state— for example, security, protection, or social welfare. From our theory, repeated experiences of collective efficacy by the state as a singular unit strengthen nationalist sentiments as long as citizens perceive a shared responsibility for the collective (nation-state) results and experience positive feelings as a result of the collective efforts. Yet, because nations are such large, differentiated, distant organizations with many sub-units, positive feelings may be directed at local, more immediate social units, such as neighborhoods, communities, towns, or regions, rather than at the state as such. Nested commitment effects could be an unintended identity by-product of federalist state structures in which central functions are devolved to political sub-units within the state (Rodden 2006). The next section offers a global test of the nested commitments hypothesis, using data from two international surveys that measure how close citizens feel to their nation-state versus local sub-units within it.

INTERNATIONAL DATA ON NESTED POLITICAL UNITS

The key assumption of the theory of nested commitments is that people invariably interact in multiple social units, some nested within others. They rise in the morning and find themselves in a neighborhood within a city or town, and that town is nested in a county, province, or other regional unit. People seldom, if ever, act or interact within only one social unit. The proximal hypothesis of nested commitments theory indicates that, all other things being equal, people tend to become more committed to local units because those units give them a greater immediate sense of control and freedom, whereas larger, overarching groups tend to be blamed for constraints and perceived as sources of constraint. If this principle applies to the state, then the distal, removed nature of people's tie to their state will reduce its salience in daily interactions or activities, and perhaps also its perceived efficacy. Because nation-states seem to be under increasing economic and political pressures from globalization, and "new federalism" policies (Ferejohn and Weingast 1997) are promoting the devolution of central state controls to more local units, the proximal hypothesis appears even more plausible than otherwise. People may increasingly feel closer to local or regional groupings than to their nation-state.

Despite these objective structural conditions, there also are good reasons for believing that the nation-state may not be so distant on a subjective level in people's daily lives. If you pick up a morning newspaper, the front page is likely to highlight at least some national news; if you turn on the television, the national news is prominent, if not the first story covered; if you travel by air, you place yourself directly under a national framework of federal aviation rules and policies. If you drive any distance, you are likely to spend time on an interstate highway or on other highways funded in part by federal funds. The food you eat for breakfast or the medications you take are ostensibly safe because they have passed through federal testing and standards programs—for example, those of the Food and Drug Administration (FDA). Thus, on a regular if not daily basis, the state as a unit is implicated in or penetrates the experience of most people. Although the scope of its penetration appears broad, its impact may be subtle and taken for granted, such that the subjective salience of the state is relatively low. There are two contradictory hypotheses: (1) people tend to feel closer to a local unit than to their state, ostensibly because the state is distant and low in salience, or (2) people feel closer to their state than to the more local unit, ostensibly because the state is salient in local settings and interactions. Recent international surveys have relevant data.

An assessment is possible using surveys sponsored by the International Social Survey Program (ISSP) on national identity in 1995 and 2003. The surveys included questions about how close respondents felt to their countries and to other social units, such as their town or city. These questions represent a reasonable indicator of a social (affective) commitment to state or nation. The 1995 survey sampled citizens in twenty-three countries, primarily European or with historic ties to European nations, and the 2003 survey included thirty-three countries, with expanded coverage of Latin American and Asian regions. The questions on "feelings of closeness" differed slightly across the two surveys. The 1995 survey asked respondents, "How close do you feel to X?" where X was one of four objects or units: neighborhood; town/city; county/region/state; or country. The 2003 study had the same questions but instructed respondents that "feel close to" should be interpreted as "emotionally attached to" or "identifying with." Thus, the explicitness of the tie to affective commitment is stronger in the 2003 survey. The 2003 survey also dropped the neighborhood unit while retaining the other three more clearly political units. We compared the percentage who felt "very close" to their country versus the other units in each survey, as well as the means for closeness.[8]

Table 9.1 shows the percentage of respondents who were "very close" to the four possible units across twenty-three countries in the 1995 survey, and table 9.2 contains the results for thirty-three countries in the 2003 survey. There is a fairly consistent pattern for the citizens to feel closer to their

Table 9.1   Respondents Who Were Very Close to Different Social Units, by Country, 1995

	Neighborhood	Town/City	County/Province	Country
Australia	13.2%	19.0%	23.0%	61.0%
Austria	49.6	44.0	47.5	56.1
Bulgaria	55.0	62.1	57.7	72.1
Canada	22.2	19.4	24.5	34.6
Czech Republic	36.4	38.5	21.7	47.5
Germany (West)	26.0	19.5	16.3	24.2
Germany (East)	25.1	22.6	21.1	27.7
Hungary	53.3	58.8	59.0	79.6
Ireland	40.9	33.6	36.6	53.8
Italy	30.1	39.6	35.2	42.9
Japan	41.8	37.1	41.0	60.2
Latvia	28.3	39.7	45.9	41.3
Netherlands	20.0	15.1	9.5	28.3
New Zealand	16.3	19.8	19.5	55.5
Norway	12.4	18.4	25.3	51.7
Philippines	27.8	15.1	16.2	21.9
Poland	26.4	49.7	21.4	54.6
Russia	29.5	31.8	24.6	41.7
Slovakia	43.7	36.7	21.9	41.6
Slovenia	32.6	32.6	29.2	49.3
Spain	43.7	47.7	45.9	42.7
Sweden	18.4	14.9	16.9	32.9
United Kingdom	18.4	12.8	12.0	24.0
United States	14.9	13.1	14.2	35.4

Source: Authors' compilation based on International Social Survey Program 1995.

Table 9.2   Respondents Who Were Very Close to Different Social Units, by Country, 2003

	Town/City	County/Province	Country
Australia	25.1%	21.7%	51.0%
Austria	57.7	56.3	59.8
Bulgaria	55.9	48.1	66.1
Canada	25.5	30.2	47.3
Chile	50.9	48.2	58.0
Czech Republic	48.0	33.7	39.1
Denmark	30.8	16.7	56.1
Finland	28.1	12.7	48.4
France	33.1	35.3	57.0
Germany (West)	33.8	21.7	25.5
Germany (East)	37.1	25.4	24.0
Hungary	55.8	53.2	75.0
Ireland	41.6	42.6	53.7
Israel—Jewish	45.9	32.2	79.9
Israel—Arab	64.5	60.5	25.7
Japan	38.7	33.8	48.9
Latvia	28.3	16.6	27.8
New Zealand	27.6	22.0	61.7
Norway	22.7	23.2	43.1
Poland	33.4	18.5	45.2
Portugal	44.0	45.6	51.5
Philippines	33.7	32.1	35.7
Russia	29.2	16.5	26.4
Slovakia	44.9	25.3	39.5
Slovenia	47.9	36.6	46.7
South Africa	63.4	51.2	60.8
South Korea	31.7	20.1	40.4
Spain	51.0	49.3	44.0
Sweden	24.1	19.7	41.2
Switzerland	36.0	28.3	40.9
Taiwan	35.6	27.2	32.1
United Kingdom	32.4	27.4	33.7
United States	22.8	23.7	52.4
Uruguay	49.9	31.0	56.4
Venezuela	53.3	47.2	58.7

Source: Authors' compilation based on International Social Survey Program 2003.

country than to their neighborhood, town/city, or regional political unit. Using a 5 percent difference as the criterion, 74 percent of countries in the 1995 survey (seventeen of twenty-three) and 70 percent of countries in the 2003 survey (twenty-three of thirty-three) revealed at least a 5 percent difference between the percentage of citizens who felt closer to their country than to any of the other units. This suggests that, among these particular social and political units, the state is relatively salient and strong on a subjective level. The mean values for closeness across all countries reveal a similar overall pattern—that is, people reported greater closeness to their country.[9] Thus, in the aggregate, people in most of the countries reported stronger emotional attachments to their country than to the several sub-units nested within them.

Pushing the analysis one more step, we asked whether there was a decline in the percentage of respondents who felt "very close" to their nation between 1995 and 2003. This is only an eight-year period, but it was an eventful period worldwide. During this time the economic expansion and dot-com boom of the 1990s came and went; globalization of the world economy grew dramatically; and the terrorist attacks of September 11, 2001 significantly changed the international environment. With such changes in mind, we compared the percentage of citizens—only in the twenty-one countries that were included in both surveys—who felt very close to their country in 1995 and 2003; again, we used 5 percent as the difference criterion. In six countries, there was an increase in closeness to country by 5 percent or more; in six others, there was a decline by 5 percent or more; and in nine, there was no change. The means for closeness to country were virtually identical in 1995 and 2003: 1.78 in 1995 and 1.77 in 2003. Thus, there is no indication of either a decline or an increase in how close people felt to their nation between 1995 and 2003.[10]

In sum, these data from 1995 and 2003 surveys of national identity provide suggestive information on the relative commitments of citizens to their nations across a range of countries and a global test of whether the nested commitments hypothesis applies to nationalist sentiments.[11] There are three implications:

1. States appear to remain important objects of commitment for citizens in spite of globalization and its by-products. Across the vast majority of countries surveyed, people reported being closer to their nation-state than to their neighborhood, their town or city, or their county, province, or region.

2. There is no evidence of a decline in the state as an object of affective commitment between 1995 and 2003, a period during which such a decline might have been reasonably expected, given the social transformations associated with globalization and internationalization.

3. The proximal hypothesis from the theory of nested commitments does not apply to states as social units.

The salience and subjective strength of the state vis-à-vis neighborhoods and towns is noteworthy, and in light of the major social transformations under way, it warrants further discussion and explanation. The next section develops a highly general explanation for the subjective salience and strength of the modern state by using our theory to elaborate the pathways to nationalist sentiments in figure 9.1. To accomplish this, we relate the principles of our theory of social commitments to some key ideas about the emergence of modern states developed by political scientists and sociologists.

EXPLAINING NATIONALIST SENTIMENTS

Explanations of nationalism from work on state formation focus on changing macro-level social, economic, and political conditions, especially those that emerged in the Enlightenment period of Europe. During this time states concentrated secular power in monarchical or republican forms of government, created legitimating (secular) ideologies, organized state-based economies, and unleashed expansionist military campaigns on behalf of trade or territorial interests (Tilly 1990; Greenfeld 1992; Smith 2001; Anderson 2006). In the process, the state became a "national state," that is, a political-cultural social unit (Gellner 1983). Most explanations for nationalism are historically based and directed at the eighteenth and nineteenth centuries (see, for example, Gellner 1983; Hobsbawm 1990; Tilly 1990; Smith 2001; Haas 2000; Anderson 2006). The two most central explanations are modernization (Gellner 1983) and conflict (Hobsbawm 1990), but more recently a rational-choice theory of nationalism has gained a foothold (Hechter 2000). With the exception of rational-choice theory, these explanations are not designed to address whether or how modern states generate and sustain nationalist sentiments, yet there are important implications in this literature that are useful to our generalizing purposes. By extrapolating ideas from this literature, we show how the theory of social commitments helps identify the general conditions under which states today may sustain nationalist sentiments, despite downward pressures on state capacity and salience. This section focuses on three theoretical traditions or streams in the extant literature on how states emerged: modernization, conflict, and rational choice.

Modernization theory is the dominant tradition from political science. Here nationalism is portrayed as a unifying ideological response to the industrialization of the eighteenth and nineteenth centuries. Ernest Gellner (1983) offers the classic version of this approach. He argues that, as modern states formed, nationalism became an important source of social order, owing to three interrelated conditions: cultural convergences that bridged subgroups, such as ethnicity and region; centralized educational systems; and direct, unmediated ties between individual citizens and their state. Centralized educational systems shaped and transmitted an overarching set of beliefs about the state to a diverse citizenry and led citizens to perceive a direct, personal tie between themselves and the state. Importantly, Gellner suggests that nationalism was important to the social order of the state in part because it created a direct tie between citizens and their state. This person-to-state (P-G) tie made the state a salient group identity, while the central educational system transmitted beliefs about its efficacy as a collective endeavor. Thus, at the heart of Gellner's argument are ideas that dovetail with the theory of social commitments. Applying our theory, a centralized educational system is likely to enhance the sense of shared responsibility for the state across a population and strengthen the positive feelings from joint activities promoted or organized by the state.

In another version of modernization, Benedict Anderson (1991, 2006) suggests some other conditions that promote person-to-state ties. Nationalism to Anderson is an "imagined community," because states are too large for all members to know who all the other members are, much less to really know them. Imagined communities are human creations or social constructions. They strengthen social order and foster the loyalty of citizens by defining the state as a horizontal communal affiliation that bridges or transcends the diverse set of nested-group affiliations and widespread social inequalities subsumed within a state. Historically, nationalism conceived the state as an equal-power affiliation. The state was a new form of fraternity, made possible by the capacity of people to "reimagine" their communal ties in broader and more horizontal terms.

As modern states emerged, new forms and expanded opportunities for social interaction were crucial to the reimagining of human communities, and the rise of "print capitalism" was especially important (Anderson 1991, 2006).[12]

New means of communication and widespread dialogue about the state spread nationalist discourses and narratives, transmitted historical myths, and defined communal (nationalist) aspirations. Print capitalism in Anderson (2006) has a role similar to centralized educational systems in Gellner (1983). Expanded communications allowed citizens to reflect on the nature of the state, kept the state salient as a social object of relevance to their lives, and facilitated debate about the state as a source of collective efficacy. A general implication is that nationalist sentiments emerge in networks of social interaction, making Anderson's underlying argument parallel to our own about how people at the micro level develop person-to-unit social commitments.

Modernization theories about nationalism suggest some ideas about how and why modern states maintain subjective salience and efficacy. First, centralized educational frameworks or systems sustain and transmit nationalist ideas, narratives, and sentiments. Educational systems are not subject to internationalization or globalization in the same way as economic systems or corporations. Second, developments in computer technology, such as the Internet, are a contemporary counterpart to the rise of print capitalism in the eighteenth and nineteenth centuries. Just as newsletters, pamphlets, and the like expanded communications in earlier times, emailing, blogging, teleconferencing, posting comments, creating Web pages, and so forth, are expanding communications today. Internet means of communication can increase the salience of the state as a social unit (witness the use of the Internet in political campaigns), but they can also be the source of new forms of association and group identity that transcend state boundaries. Overall, modernization approaches point to macro conditions that promote person-to-state affective ties (nationalist sentiments), and our theory suggests the micro-level mechanisms through which these may operate.

Conflict theories of state formation attribute nationalism to conflicts of interest within or between states. Charles Tilly (1990) argues that accumulations of coercive (military) power by modern states, especially in eighteenth- and nineteenth-century Europe, occurred as states contended with each other. Interstate conflicts led to large armies organized by the state and composed of citizens across strata and divisions within the state. States incorporated military functions as core elements of the state's centralized administrative apparatus, thereby enhancing the capacity of the state to control internal events. Thus, wars generated the formation of states because they concentrated power in the state as a singular unit (Tilly 1990). In contrast, Eric Hobsbawm (1990) emphasizes internal conflicts; he argues that nationalism entailed an "invented tradition" that manufactured state legitimacy and supported elite interests. As the modern state formed, national symbols were created, such as flags, monuments, and anthems, and large public events celebrated the communal (national) affiliation and helped to create and sustain nationalist sentiments. Nationalism promoted social order in the context of external threats and internal joint activities.

Conflict approaches draw attention to two conditions under which nationalist sentiments are a source of social order. First, nationalist sentiments that are tied to intergroup conflicts should make the national identity (ingroup affiliation) even more salient and produce greater ingroup cohesion (Tajfel and Turner 1986). In dealing with interstate conflicts, state authorities invoke and define the nation as a common, horizontal tie among citizens. Second, nationalist sentiments are likely to remain strong if there are frequent and visible public ceremonies or commemorations that affirm the history of the nation as a unit and portray the nation as a joint endeavor in which all can participate with a sense of shared responsibility. The repetition of associated ritual practices typically generates strong positive feelings that are shared, and this strengthens the meaning and impact of such public events for citizens (Collins 2004). Nationalism mitigates the problems of order associated with large social inequalities and creates the foundation for states to mobilize collective actions.

Rational-choice theory portrays nationalism as a collective good. Michael Hechter (2000) agrees with modernization approaches that nationalism is a recent phenomenon of the last two hundred years or so that was made possible by industrialization, improved communications technologies, centralized educational systems, and the like. However, he argues that such conditions do not provide an adequate explanation for the emergence of nationalism because they cannot answer questions such as: Why did large, "pan-local" associations develop? What motivated actors to form them? How were they different from large empires of the past? Nationalism, to Hechter, is a form of collective action designed to make the boundaries of a nation congruent with those of its governance (political) unit. The "governance unit" refers to a territorially defined entity responsible for producing the "bulk of" collective goods, including social order (Hechter 2000, 9). Hechter argues that nationalism solves the problem of social order generated by a disjuncture between the boundaries of the nation (cultural) and the governance (political) unit.

Hechter's theory makes several key points of relevance for our purposes. First, modern states need the capacity for "direct rule" of localized regions and groups from the center (the state institutional apparatus). The large, statelike empires of the past had to rely on indirect control (delegation) through intermediaries (leaders of localized units), and thus central authorities had limited means to monitor localized groupings. Industrialization and improved communication technologies in the eighteenth and nineteenth centuries made control from the center more feasible. Second, because of their capacity for direct rule (to control local units), modern states could more effectively mobilize around and solve collective action problems, and as a result citizens became more dependent on states for the production of valued joint goods. Third, the dependence of citizens on the state and the capacity for direct rule (monitoring) made national sovereignty an overarching collective good. In brief, Hechter (2000) argues that nationalism emerged when (1) there was a demand for sovereignty (autonomy, self-determination) and (2) the costs of the collective action necessary to generate and sustain that sovereignty were lower than the benefits of sovereignty.

Our theory of social commitments and Hechter's theory of nationalism are complementary in important respects. First of all, the capacity of the state for direct rule should bear on both the salience of the state to citizens in their everyday activity and the efficacy of the state at sustaining the production of collective goods valued by citizens. Second, the dependence of citizens on their state should enhance the importance or value they ascribe to their shared national identity. Third, state sovereignty and independence should strengthen the degree to which citizens credit the state for producing collective goods and perceive it as an important basis for collective efficacy. These three conditions therefore should enhance the degree to which a nation-state generates a sense of shared responsibility among its citizens and is a source of positive emotions that people want to reproduce. In other words, states should generate nationalist sentiments to the degree that citizens perceive the nation as a joint product for which they share responsibility and as a source of positive affect.[13]

If people have a greater sense of shared responsibility at the state level, the state's salience and efficacy should have stronger effects on nationalist sentiments. Pulling the threads together, figure 9.2 hypothesizes that the sense of shared responsibility is important because it determines when state salience and state efficacy are likely to have the strongest effects on nationalist sentiments—that is, shared responsibility moderates the effects of salience and efficacy on nationalist sentiments.

**Figure 9.2   Role of Shared Responsibility
in Nationalist Sentiments**

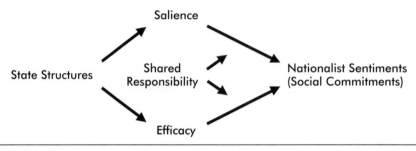

Source: Authors' compilation.

It is the combination of shared responsibility with salience and the combination of shared responsibility with efficacy that lay the firmest foundation for nationalist sentiments. The salience and efficacy of the state strengthen nationalist sentiments, especially if people perceive a shared responsibility for the collective results, because positive feelings from participation in joint activities then are likely to be attributed to the state. In sum, the figure portrays in a nutshell how the theory of social commitments contributes to an understanding of nationalist sentiments in modern nation-states.

CONCLUSIONS

There are important disagreements among political scientists and sociologists about the current plight of the nation-state as an institution. Some argue that the modern state, a fairly recent invention, reached its pinnacle of power in the twentieth century and has been in decline since that time, owing primarily to what has come to be known as globalization (Haas 2002; Fukuyama 2004). Others argue that states have adapted to changing international conditions, internally and externally, and preserved, if not enhanced, their role as principal mediators of international interdependencies and economic competition (Scharpf 2000; Rodrik 1997). Finally, still other scholars stress the subjective importance of the nation as a source of identity and a unifying force amid growing differences among people within modern states (Greenfeld 1992; Calhoun 2007; Laitin 2007). Nationalist sentiments are a plausible way in which states become and remain important objects of social commitment for citizens. Our theory suggests a micro-level affective mechanism by which this can occur.

Nation-states are the largest and most encompassing group or organizational affiliation for the vast majority of people. As such, states are removed, distant, and often disconnected from the everyday interactions and activities of people—or so it appears. By applying principles from our theory, we conclude that states create and sustain nationalist sentiments under three conditions. First, the state is salient as a national affiliation or identity owing to such structures as educational systems, political symbols or discourses, celebratory occasions, and interstate conflicts. Second, the state is a source of collective efficacy—that is, it generates joint goods that people cannot produce themselves or in other, generally smaller groupings (see Hechter 2000). When these goods are produced, they tend to generate positive emotions. Third, the state is perceived as a collective enterprise in which people have a shared responsibility for both good and bad results. This sense of shared responsibility leads them to attribute positive individual feelings from producing joint goods within the state to the state as an object. The overall message is that, if states meet these conditions, they are more important on a subjective level—and are likely to remain so even if recent arguments that the state is in decline turn out to have more merit than now appears to be the case.

Chapters 5 to 8 have pointed to several structural conditions that are likely to promote a sense of shared responsibility among members of a group, including interdependencies, equal power, dense network ties, and nested group affiliations. All of these are implicitly or explicitly involved in theories about nationalism. A central educational system, improved or expanded means of communication, ingroup-outgroup tensions (interstate conflict), and the capacity for direct rule from the political center suggest state structures that enhance the salience and efficacy of the state and thereby lay the groundwork for nationalist sentiments. Nationalist sentiments are built on structural interdependencies among a population, but then enhanced by the equalizing definitions of citizenship that overlay social inequalities, perceptions of direct, unmediated ties between the self and the state, and dense network ties within relative to outside the nation-state unit. Boiling down these structural conditions, we can see that nationalist sentiments reflect the degree to which structures and activities at the state level make the state not only salient as a source of efficacy but also a prime locus for joint action and shared responsibility. Under these conditions, people attribute individual feelings, experienced locally, in part to the larger national unit.

CHAPTER 10

Mechanisms of Social Order

The theory of social commitments is a theory about mechanisms of social order. By mechanism we mean a fundamental process or phenomenon through which social structures—micro and macro—produce social order in the form of stable, reliable practices, policies, and interactions. The principal mechanism for us is affect, grounded in the emotions people feel when they interact with others. This mechanism entails a micro-to-macro process wherein individual emotional experiences are associated with groups, organizations, communities, or nations. In chapters 3 and 4, we analyzed how and when the affective mechanism operates and showed its importance to social commitments in particular and, more broadly, to social order at micro and macro levels. Chapters 5 to 9 applied and used this affective mechanism to examine the commitment effects of a range of structural conditions that people often experience, from networks to nested groups to hierarchies to nation-states. This chapter compares the affective mechanism to several alternatives that also help to account for micro-to-macro effects, such as norms and trust. We argue that our affective mechanism is more fundamental than the alternatives.

There are many everyday examples of people creating or sustaining social orders. People establish unidirectional flows of movement on crowded sidewalks, form lines to theater ticket offices, and respect each other's space in subways. These are ordinary, micro-level routines that people take for granted and think very little about. Yet they are quite important to social order in large urban areas. Turning to work groups, people may regularly show each other respect, give each other opportunities, and assist each other despite personal costs. Group-oriented behaviors are standard practice in some groups, though not in others, and this has important effects on the larger organization. Finally, corporations may exceed the requirements of laws or obey ones that they could easily flaunt, and modern nations may observe international norms and treaties that they could violate with impunity. These actions affect social order at a larger level—for example, in an industry with many corporations or in an international region with many countries.[1] All of these behaviors reflect and affirm established practices or patterns of behavior. Each has an impact not just on a local order but also on social order within a larger group. Moreover, repetition is central in each case.

Repetition, regularity, and predictability are the sine qua non of social order (Berger and Luckmann 1966; Collins 1981; Wrong 1994). In fact, to Dennis Wrong (1994, 41) a society is an "immense series" of interconnected, interwoven social interactions that create and sustain the regularity and predictability of human actions. Macro social orders are social constructions grounded in the mutual expectations that people develop about each other when they repeatedly interact (see also Berger and Luckmann 1966; Collins 1981, 1989, 2004); repeated interactions forge enduring, reciprocal expectations. Thus, a macro-level social order should be resilient and stable to the degree that local, micro processes activate it and translate it in terms relevant to local situations, thereby reproducing macro structural and cultural patterns locally.[2] Yet, just as people may reproduce larger social patterns or practices in interaction with others, they also may generate alternative patterns or practices that are distinct from and undermine the larger order. Micro-macro consistencies are a fundamental source of social order, and micro-macro inconsistencies are a fundamental problem of order and a source of social change.

The commitment problem posed in this volume presumes a tendency toward disjuncture between the daily, micro interactions of people and the larger organizations and institutions that contextualize those local interactions. Sources of disjuncture include expanded opportunities for self-generated groups and organizations that compete with traditional social objects of commitment, such as work organizations, unions, and community groups. In the context of today's major social transformations, there are good reasons to posit a growth in opportunity for people to generate local emergent social orders that do not reflect or reproduce the larger order (see chapter 2). Repeated patterns of behavior and interaction therefore may generate consistency or disjuncture between local and larger social orders. An important question is how social order at the micro level affects social order at the macro level. To address this issue, we examine several fundamental mechanisms for repetition-to-social-order effects, comparing them to the affective mechanism of our theory and showing how they treat or resolve the micro-macro disjuncture. To set up this discussion, the next section places these comparisons in a broader context by contrasting economic and sociological (institutional) approaches to repetition as a source of social order.

REPETITION AS A SOCIAL FORCE

It is a virtual truism to say that mere repetition is a powerful force in human lives and an important foundation for social orders (see, for example, Berger and Luckmann 1966; Collins 1981). In psychology, the old saying is that "the best predictor of future behavior is past behavior." There is a strong tendency for people at the micro level to do what they have done in the past and for the organizations they populate to reveal a similar tendency at the macro level. Economic theories construe repeated patterns as rational, deliberative efforts to reduce uncertainties and achieve gains, whereas institutional theory from sociology construes repetition as habits or routines that are developed over time and taken for granted. Our theory of social commitments occupies a theoretical niche between these polarities of interpretation by connecting rational starting points or foundations with taken-for-granted institutional patterns or practices. Initial patterns may be purely rational and instrumental, and the resulting social ties therefore purely transactional; yet, when the same people repeatedly interact on joint tasks, an unanticipated result occurs: a relational tie with nonrational or noncontractual components. In this sense, it is difficult to prevent relational ties from occurring even in the most rationally oriented of social situations.

The standard approach in economics is to conceive of relational ties as a form of "stickiness" in a market (Williamson 1985; Fehr and Gintis 2007), whereas sociological approaches tend to interpret relational ties as incipient institutionalization or "taken-for-granted-ness" (see Berger and Luckmann

1966; DiMaggio and Powell 1983). Relational ties are known to emerge in and distort markets, just as institutional routines and habits are known to emerge in and create inertia in organizations (Hannan and Freeman 1977). Importantly, stickiness and take-for-granted-ness develop endogenously— that is, from the actions of people in interaction.[3] They have a micro foundation. From economic theorizing, stickiness develops because of the costs, risks, and uncertainties of finding better options, the likely improvements if such options are found, or the emergence of value specific or unique to their relation (Williamson 1985). Overall, economic theorizing transforms what appear to be nonrational attachments into a tractable, rationally based phenomenon (Williamson 1985), stressing the costs and benefits of repeated contracting and bounded rationality of decisionmaking in organizations (Simon 1957).

Institutional theory in sociology turns economics on its head, subsuming the rational under the nonrational (Berger and Luckmann 1966; Meyer and Rowan 1977). Stickiness here is normative and a basis for taken-for-granted practices or rules; it cannot be reduced to or effectively reinterpreted in purely instrumental market terms (DiMaggio and Powell 1983; Dobbin 1994). Berger and Luckmann (1966, 57) provide the classic statement on how easy and natural it is for institutional patterns to develop as a result of repeated patterns of interaction: "All actions repeated once or more tend to be habitualized to some degree." This is the initial step toward the institutionalization of a pattern. It occurs because people interpret and ascribe larger meanings to the fact that they are repeating an interaction pattern with the same others; in the process, group affiliations or larger social units become salient and are "objectified," which makes them a "third force" that people attend to, beyond self and other.[4] This institutionalization process leads people to treat their group affiliation as an objective reality and to orient their behavior in part toward it. Institutional theories in sociology provide a rich and deep analysis of what is often termed a "habit" or "routine," offering an alternative explanation for stickiness (see Dobbin 1994).

Economic notions of stickiness and institutional notions of taken-for-granted-ness are broad, orienting ideas about the results of repetition. The micro-level processes or mechanisms through which these effects occur are treated more unevenly and incompletely in these literatures. Similarly, other macro-sociological theories tend to posit that overarching top-down processes are prime sources of social order—including coercion (Hobbes, Marx), normative consensus (Durkheim), and collective interests (Locke, Weber)—but again, without much attention to the micro-level mechanisms that reflect or generate these processes locally. We contend that macro-level power and status structures (stratification), widely shared beliefs and values (culture), and larger community or group affiliations have important effects when these social dimensions are brought to and activated in the social interactions of people in local situations; otherwise, significant disparities and disjuncture between micro and macro conditions are likely to ensue. This is a key reason why we adopt a micro-mediation approach to the problem of social order. Let us now turn to the mechanisms through which repeated behaviors and interactions generate resilient social orders.

MECHANISMS OF SOCIAL ORDER

The affect mechanism is one of four primary micro-mediating mechanisms for repetition-to-social-order effects. The others are norms, trust, and identity. Some theories emphasize the role of normative constraints, asking how norms can emerge and acquire sufficient social force to constrain unbridled self-interest (see, for example, Coleman 1990). Other theories treat trust or uncertainty reduction as the prime way in which people solve problems of cooperation and social order (Kollock 1994; Cook, Hardin, and Levi 2005). Finally, still others emphasize the construction of identities, that is, how people arrive at and sustain shared conceptions of self and other that enable them to coordinate their behaviors (Stryker 1980; Burke 1991; Robinson and Smith-Lovin 2006; Hogg 2004). Distinct theoretical traditions have developed around each of these mechanisms. Each tradition contains implicit or explicit ideas about how local (micro) and larger (macro) structural and cultural conditions are interlinked, and also about how consistencies or disjuncture develop or are overcome at local, micro levels. The following sections elaborate each mechanism.

Norms

Dennis Wrong's (1994) theory is that normative expectations stem from and accentuate predictability. Mere predictability emerges whenever people interact with the same others, or even with different others in the same situation. They learn what to anticipate from others and adjust their own behavior accordingly; if everybody does this, a social situation quickly develops routines or rituals that come to be expected by those who enter that situation. Routine practices reduce the cognitive efforts that people have to expend to navigate a situation by enabling them to assume that past patterns will continue. Returning to the example from chapter 1 of a regular morning coffee shop, it takes very few visits before a customer has a sense of the overall environment of a coffee shop—the noise level, the lighting, and the mood, as well as the attitudes of the staff and the typical behaviors of other customers. Customers do not have to think about these things or wonder what the morning coffee shop will be like; they know before they get there.

At first, predictability involves only cognitive expectations—in other words, habits or routines without normative content or implied constraint on people. Wrong (1994) theorizes that these cognitive expectations become normative when people perceive that their own expectations complement those that others have of them in the situation. For example, if person A has expectations that person B will do y in a situation, this enables A to anticipate and successfully interact with B by doing x. This is the social impact or value of predictability per se (Wrong 1994). However, if A believes that B expects A to do x, and B believes that A expects B to do y, then behaviors x and y have become normative. One consequence is that violations of the expectations are salient, generate discomfort, and are subject to sanctions. An unusually noisy customer in a coffee shop with a predictably quiet, subdued mood that people expect, and expect others to expect, is likely to receive subtle sanctions such as frowns or quizzical looks.

In Wrong's (1994, 59) approach, social order entails "regularly fulfilled reciprocal expectations." His analysis of how purely cognitive expectations (predictability) become normative expectations (obligations) can be portrayed as a simple micro-institutional theory of how routines or habits develop normative content at the micro level, as in figure 10.1:

Figure 10.1   Wrong's Micro-Institutional Theory

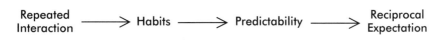

Repeated Interaction $\longrightarrow$ Habits $\longrightarrow$ Predictability $\longrightarrow$ Reciprocal Expectation

Source: Authors' compilation based on Wrong 1994.

In institutional theory (as in Wrong), normative expectations are unplanned. Emerging from repetition, such expectations become meaningful to people because they infuse these patterns with value (see also Selznick 1992). In Wrong's rendition of this process, mutual awareness plays a crucial role as the cognitive expectations become normative, but it then recedes into the background as the resulting practices or patterns are taken for granted and become more deeply embedded rituals in the social situation—that is, as the expectations become taken-for-granted realities associated with relations or groups (Berger and Luckmann 1966).

An alternative explanation for the emergence of norms is offered by rational-choice theories. James Coleman (1990) posits two conditions for norms to emerge and gain force in a situation. First, people experience costs from events they do not control, and they have a shared interest in overcoming or mitigating these costs. Costs here are negative externalities that people cannot control because they involve the actions of other people (Coleman 1990, 249). Second, a "demand for norms" emerges—that is, people look for ways to regulate individual behaviors in order to reduce the shared costs of negative externalities. Thus, norms emerge when people share an interest in having them and when they support sanctioning violators. In creating norms, people essentially relinquish some control over their own behavior in exchange for protection from negative externalities (Coleman 1990), a solution to the problem of social order generally reminiscent of Hobbes. Whereas recurrent interaction is not explicit in Coleman's analysis, norms are most likely to emerge with the repeated experience of negative externalities, and they are more effective in an ongoing network of ties or relations—that is, in conjunction with social capital (see Coleman 1990, chaps. 10 and 12). By implication, repeated interactions are an underlying condition for the formation of norms.

Norms produce social order because they invoke obligations to others or a community and are enforced by formal or informal sanctions. Complementing Coleman (1990), Hechter (1987) argues that a demand for jointly produced private goods underlies the shared interest in norms. The demand for norms is based, in turn, on the degree to which people are dependent on the group for valued outcomes. Hechter develops a theory of group solidarity that focuses on the capacity of groups to generate joint goods (excludable) from which people derive individual gain. Solidarity is essentially compliance due to obligation—in other words, contributing to the production of joint goods without an explicit quid pro quo. Obligations are likened to a tax that members of a group are willing to pay as the price of membership (Hechter 1987). The capacity of groups to generate joint goods is a function of how extensive (breadth, scope) the obligations (taxes) it can impose on members are and the degree of actual compliance with those obligations. Thus, solidarity—that is, person-to-group ties—is greatest when members are highly dependent on the group and the group has considerable capacity to monitor and sanction members who do not fulfill their obligations.[5]

To summarize, the literature on norms specifies two distinct routes through which people develop norms: norms can emerge unplanned and unintentionally, as a by-product of repeated social interactions; and they can emerge because people want to produce certain collective results and are unable to do this without some level of cooperation or collaboration with others. The first is the institutional route, and the second is the rational-choice route. It is important to note that these approaches are not mutually exclusive; in fact, either route may produce elements of the other. A quiet, peaceful coffee shop that begins to attract a noisier crowd may generate demand for a quiet norm and joint action among regulars or longtime customers to promote this. Alternatively, people who prefer quiet places may become regulars, and they may subtly and unintentionally communicate norms to those who are noisy and receive social support from other regular customers. Institutions can be unplanned and infused with value (Selznick 1992), or they can be purposive and imbued with instrumentality (Hechter 1990).

The theory of social commitments integrates themes from both theories about how norms emerge. It can explain how repeated patterns become infused with value and associated with a group affiliation—namely, because people experience positive feelings from the repeated patterns and these feelings are attributed to the group. Institutions have affective components because they are embedded in groups, are a source of successful joint activities, and become self-defining and identity-affirming. Thus, if interactions generate positive feelings that people associate with their group affiliation, (1) the demand for norms should be even stronger in the context of negative externalities; (2) the propensity to sanction informally should increase; and (3) contributions to a group-administered sanctioning system are likely to be greater. Affect-based norms reflect and sustain stronger person-to-group ties and generate more resilient social orders.

Trust

Relations of trust are a prominent recent answer to the Hobbesian question about social order. Here trust is the social "glue" or bond that enables people to reach out to and form new relations, to cross traditional cultural or social boundaries, and to find areas of joint benefit and collaboration with others (Cook, Hardin, and Levi 2005). Like a norm, trust entails an expectation, but in this case it is specifically a cognitive expectation about the likelihood of cooperation by others, their goodwill, or community regard (Pruitt and Kimmel 1977; Yamagishi and Yamagishi 1994; Fukuyama 1995; Cook, Hardin, and Levi 2005). Trust presupposes social uncertainty, that is, a social situation where people cannot confidently predict the course of events or each other's behavior and where misjudgments can be very costly. Trusting the untrustworthy will generate significant and unnecessary costs, whereas trusting the trustworthy will yield significant joint gains that would otherwise have been "left on the table." This is the dilemma faced by people in a trust situation or "trust game" (Coleman 1990).

The cooperative expectations involved in trust have been conceived in three primary ways. *Generalized trust* refers to expectations about people or humanity in general (Yamagishi and Yamagishi 1994; Yamagishi 2001). These are trans-situational predispositions that people carry from situation to situation. *Knowledge-based trust* refers to trust based on direct or vicarious interaction with the same others (Pruitt and Kimmel 1977). Here trust is a bet about the future behavior of particular others (Sztompka 1999). Knowledge-based trust is tantamount to a cognitive expectation or prediction. *Relational trust* is defined as trust of another based on the perception that not only do the other's interests favor cooperation, but also that the other takes account of the trustor's interests. This has been termed the "encapsulated interests" theory of trust (Hardin 2001, 2002; Cook, Hardin, and Levi 2005). We comment briefly on each of the three types and then give particular attention to the encapsulated-interests approach.[6]

Generalized trust varies across individuals within a culture and helps to distinguish cultures.[7] It implies an exogenous explanation for different types of social order, particularly high-trust and low-trust cultures, but generalized trust cannot explain the repetition-to-order effects of concern to us. This form of trust is not socially constructed from repeated interactions, and it does not imply a clear social mechanism. The knowledge-based concept of trust, on the other hand, indicates that trusting is an uncertainty reduction mechanism. Trust emerges from repeated interactions to the degree that people who interact with the same others over time gain more information about each other's intentions and orientations and are confident in their predictions about each other and about who is likely to be trustworthy. In this sense, trust is fed by predictability and regularity, as are norms, but it lacks the obligatory property of norms. Knowledge-based trust is a plausible cognitive mechanism, involving uncertainty reduction, through which repeated interaction generates and sustains order.[8]

The central message of theory and research on trust is that trust can solve the problems of uncertainty and vulnerability that are prevalent in social situations. Trust is complicated by the information required of others, the signaling of their intent, and so forth. Trusting others puts a person at risk, but it also is a condition that allows that person to form new relations and work with others to achieve joint gains he or she otherwise might forgo. In this sense, trust is a counterweight to tradition-based normative commitments because it has an "emancipating" effect on people within hierarchies, networks, and markets (Yamagishi and Yamagishi 1994; Fukuyama 1995). From such reasoning, it makes sense that trust would be particularly important as a source of social order in an individualized, market-oriented world. This conjecture helps to account for the very large body of theory and research on trust that has accumulated over the last fifteen years or so, given the major changes in the world during this period.

A recent analysis and reinterpretation of the voluminous research on trust by Karen Cook, Russell Hardin, and Margaret Levi (2005), however, argues that trust as a source of social order is relatively limited in today's world. Like us, Cook and her colleagues frame their theoretical argument with general observations about the major social transformations of the age—namely, that a greater proportion of people's relations today involve distant, "arm's-length" ties, and also that their ties are more instrumental. Trust ostensibly is declining in importance and is relevant to a smaller and smaller portion of human experience because people face serious deficits of information about each other. Adopting the encapsulated-interests notion of trust, the knowledge problem is that people (P) have difficulty making inferences about whether their own interests are subsumed within another's (O) interests—that is, whether O's cooperation is due to the fact that O's interests "encapsulate" P's.[9] Cook and her colleagues (2005, 196) argue that sufficient information about others is feasible only at an interpersonal or person-to-person level; thus, they state, "societies today are essentially evolving away from trust relationships toward externally regulated behavior." People must look beyond their ties to others for assurance that others will cooperate. Where do people look for and find such assurance?

The alternative theory, offered by Cook and her colleagues (2005), is that social order or widespread cooperation in a society is based on social and political institutions—specifically, the degree to which these institutions promote, sanction, and legitimize cooperation even in the context of interpersonal distrust. The formal institutions of a society explicate, enact, and enforce a normative framework that people can rely on. Thus, it is larger, macro-institutional structures rather than trust that enable people to take the risks necessary to develop new productive or collaborative relations with others beyond their very close ties, even with others who are strangers and whom they distrust. Person-to-group ties are implicit in this institutional framework, although these ties are purely instrumental and transactional, and the contemporary trends that Cook and her colleagues cite as background reflect what we have termed the individualization narrative of social transformations.

Overall, Cook and her colleagues (2005) offer a thoughtful and innovative analysis of the limited role of trust and trust relations, especially in the complex, changing societies of the contemporary era. Their institutional solution to the problem of order relies entirely on "externally regulated behavior" as the foundation of order. In commitment terms, their solution implies a combination of instrumental and normative commitment—namely, social order founded primarily on instrumentally based normative ties between people and their groups (see chapter 2). They posit a disjuncture or disconnect between local, micro contexts and larger social units, as we do, but in their analysis, macro-institutional structures bridge this divide. The affective component of commitment is missing from their analysis, as is the prospect of groups developing expressive, non-instrumental value. Their solution to the Hobbesian problem is essentially a refined and nuanced version of contemporary contractual solutions (see Hechter 1987; Coleman 1990).[10]

We have argued throughout this volume that instrumental ties are an inherently fragile and costly basis for widespread cooperation in a society. Shifts in incentives, intended or unintended, readily shift these ties if there is nothing other than individual benefits that tie people to groups. Affective ties to groups generate more widespread, more enduring, and lower-cost cooperation, because the expressive or intrinsic nature of the person-to-group ties makes people more willing to sacrifice their own interests for what they perceive as the collective good.

Both instrumental and affective ties can forge close connections between macro and micro realms, but only affective ties reduce the need for external mechanisms of monitoring and regulation. Instrumental ties necessarily involve greater transaction costs than affective ties. Self-monitoring and self-regulation on the local, micro level play a stronger role in the context of affective commitments to a society, and arguably these generate stronger ties between the micro and macro realms.

Identity

In social interactions, people construct and affirm identities, that is, definitions of self and other. Defined as "who" or "what" one is, an identity refers to the set of meanings attached to oneself by self and others (Gecas and Burke 1995, 42). Identities stem from *reflexivity,* that is, the fact that people look at themselves from the standpoint of others and interpret what another's behavior toward them means about who they are in a situation. They have both an exogenous macro and endogenous micro dimension, and these are intertwined at the local, micro level. In other words, identities emerge and evolve in the course of particular social interactions in particular social situations (Burke 1991), but they also are grounded in larger social structures and cultural beliefs. Identities, in this sense, are a locus of both order and change.

As a micro-mechanism of social order, identities enable people to reliably anticipate each other's behavior, thereby strengthening the force of normative or trust expectations. Consensual self-other identities enhance people's confidence that they and others will act in accord with expectations, but these identities also place local, regularized patterns of interaction in a larger macro-level context of meaning. For example, families are local orders in which parent-child interactions reveal predictable and expected family-specific patterns, but these are framed by the larger cultural definitions of parent, child, and family. Key identities in a family (parent, child, spouse, wife, husband, partner) create a direct link between the local, immediate interactions and larger structural or cultural conditions. Identities are therefore a crucial nexus linking the local (micro) and larger (macro) group context.

Two theoretical traditions, one from sociology and one from psychology, have important ideas about how locally created identities are tied to larger group or organizational affiliations. Structural identity theory emphasizes the ties between persons (P-P ties) in the context of larger structural positions or roles, such as daughter, cashier, social worker, or financial analyst (Stryker 1980;

Burke 1991; Stets 2006). In contrast, social identity theory emphasizes the ties between persons and the groups or social categories to which they belong or with which they are affiliated (P-G ties). Examples are gender, race, IBM employee, association member, or club member (Tajfel and Turner 1986; Turner and Reynolds 2004; Hogg 2004). Structural identity and social identity theories imply different pathways through which consistencies between micro and macro levels emerge and are maintained.[11]

The implication of structural identity theory is that social order is based on consensual self-other definitions, which are partly imposed by the exogenous structural roles and partly emergent through reciprocal behavioral adjustments in social interaction (Stryker 1980; Burke 1991). Self-other definitions emerge from "back and forth" processes in which people view their own behavior from the other's perspective, ascribe meaning to each other's behavior, and mutually adjust their actions to conclude a successful interaction episode. These processes occur at the micro level but are framed by a larger social structure and have the potential to solidify or change structurally defined roles. There is a two-way, reciprocal process between the micro and macro levels, in which role identities are the linchpin (Stryker 1980). The concept of a norm serves a similar purpose in rational-choice theories (see Coleman 1990), but an important difference is that identities involve the internalization of role meanings and render the micro-macro interconnections noncontractual. Structural identity theory explicitly connects locally enacted and established identities to larger structural roles and cultural meanings.

Sheldon Stryker's (1980) classic version of structural identity theory offers an elaboration of the ties between micro and macro levels. He notes that self-other identities attached to roles invoke shared cultural meanings simply through the common "names" used to refer to different roles (parent, worker, customer, or friend). These names are imbued with cultural meanings, such that the mere use of names activates culturally based normative expectations (to self and other) about the appropriate behavior for a person in role X interacting with a person in role Y. Yet, because people have multiple roles and identities, Stryker directs particular attention to how people select among identities. He theorizes that multiple identities are ranked in a salience hierarchy and that salience is determined by the commitment of people to particular identities. Identity commitment in turn is based on how extensive, dense, and close the network ties are that underlie and support that identity. The implication is that macro conditions make multiple identities available to people, but people choose among these and enact them in the context of local, micro situations, based in part on the network of ties in which the identities are embedded.[12]

Social identity theory, developed by European social psychologists, eschews concern with social interactions and structural roles and turns the spotlight on group affiliations. Social identities involve tacit or explicit group affiliations (such as clubs, neighborhoods, and professional associations) as well as common social categories (such as gender, ethnicity, and age). The theory starts from the notion that people simplify the world around them by categorizing events, objects, and persons and that, as part of this process, they compare themselves to others with reference to group or category affiliations, making inferences of similarity and difference. Social identity theory argues that shared social identities promote common shared expectations of behavior and norms that favor ingroup members over outgroup members.

Social identity theory conceives of groups and social categories in purely cognitive terms (see chapter 5 for elaboration). A social identity has two fundamental cognitive effects. First, it shapes perceptions of which other people are similar to oneself, specifically, who is affiliated with the same group or category; second, a social identity defines how oneself and those similar others are distinctive, namely, how they differ from other groups or categories (Tajfel and Turner 1986; Hogg 2004). Ingroup-outgroup perceptions are crucial to group identities. The theory argues that if two or more people perceive themselves as a group, they act in a group-oriented way—even without interacting with each other and without collective goals. It takes only a common, distinctive person-to-group tie to produce group-oriented behavior.

To elaborate, the main proposition is that mere social categorization (of self and others) is sufficient to generate a group identity and behavior oriented toward that identity, including bias in favor of ingroup members. Early experiments by Henri Tajfel and his colleagues (see, for example, Tajfel and Turner 1986) provided empirical support to this "mere categorization" hypothesis. In a context where subjects did not interact or see one another, categorization by nominal, meaningless labels (numbers, neutral colors) was sufficient to lead people to favor ingroup members over outgroup members in an allocation of rewards (see Tajfel 1969; Tajfel and Turner 1986). However, subsequent research showed further that categorization has stronger effects on ingroup cohesion and solidarity when the task is explicitly defined in collective terms (Ellemers, Spears, and Doosje 1997) or people are engaged in recurrent interaction with one another to achieve a common goal (Brown and Wade 1987).

The latter findings dovetail with our theory of social commitments, since repeated interactions and joint tasks generated stronger person-to-group ties.[13]

To conclude, these two traditions of identity theory address complementary facets of the problem of social order. Structural identity theory (Stryker 1980; Stets 2006) deals primarily with person-to-person ties in the context of larger role structures. Social interactions in concrete situations are the place where definitions of self are juxtaposed with the meanings attached to structural roles and where people choose identities to enact in light of how they and others view them, verifying who they are both to themselves and to others. Social order prevails to the degree that individuals share common understandings of who they are. Social identity theory deals explicitly with how people define themselves in light of their larger group or social category affiliations, arguing that a group identity shapes how people treat each other even if they are strangers who lack interpersonal ties. Even people at great social or physical distance from each other respond to shared group identities and treat fellow members with more "other regard" than otherwise. Applying our theory of social commitments, the affective mechanism suggests how and when P-P role behaviors strengthen P-G ties and, in turn, when the latter strengthen commitments to that role identity (see Lawler 2003). Thus, our theory specifies a way to connect the P-P focus of structural identity theory with the P-G focus of social identity theory.

AFFECT AND SOCIAL ORDER

The social mechanisms described here—norms, trust, and identity—are analytically distinct but complementary pathways to social order. Each captures a piece of the problem of social order. Norms define what is appropriate behavior, give people incentives to engage in this behavior, and provide assurance that others will do likewise. Trust enables people to overcome or transcend conflicts of interest by developing mutual expectations of cooperation. Norms may play an important role here (see Fukuyama 1995), but norms are not necessary to have trust (see Cook, Hardin, and Levi 2005). The expectations may be purely cognitive. Identities interweave and subsume cognitive and normative expectations within definitions of self and other, and self-other definitions are tied to roles (local or larger) or group affiliations (local or larger). Some of these mechanisms (social-dilemma norms and trust) have a contractual, transactional theme, whereas others (institutional norms and identity) have a noncontractual, relational theme.

We argue that the affect mechanism or pathway to social order, as proposed by our theory, is more fundamental than these other mechanisms. This argument is grounded in the implications of the neuroscience evidence on emotion. While this is a highly technical area, a well-founded generalization is that emotions are integrally involved in how the human brain receives and processes external events and stimuli; in fact, there is some evidence that in the human brain emotional processes start before cognitive processing (see, for example, Damasio 1999, 2003). In any case, it is virtually indisputable that any social interaction in any social context is likely to generate positive or negative emotions and that these involve internal, bodily sensations that constitute rewards or punishments (see chapter 4). Emotions are immediate and felt at a visceral level. Because they are internal rewards, people are motivated to reproduce positive feelings and avoid negative ones, and they try to understand where feelings come from and what produces them.

From the logic of our theory, it is reasonable to argue that positive feelings from repeated interactions tend to occur before norms emerge, trust develops, or self-other identities are affirmed. Thus, we hypothesize that the affective mechanism helps to explain (1) why purely cognitive expectations (predictability) evolve toward normative expectations; (2) why cooperative solutions to social-dilemma problems (negative externalities) become normative once the benefits of cooperation and related positive emotions are experienced a few times; (3) why informal, peer-based enforcement of norms is more likely if the norms sustain joint activities that foster positive emotions and feelings; and (4) why group identities come to have expressive, non-instrumental value beyond their instrumental benefits. Norms, trust, and identity can and do operate without an affective foundation, but there are good theoretical reasons for arguing that an affective mechanism, if present, strengthens (or weakens) normative, trust, and identity bases for social order. Figure 10.2 outlines the general argument.

Most normative solutions to the problem of social order imply a person-to-group tie that has an instrumental foundation. People ostensibly obey norms because of the rewards from doing so or the costs of violating them. In social dilemmas, the individual costs of violating norms are less than the rewards for free-riding unless groups have means of enforcing the norms. Formal enforcement mechanisms, built into the group structure, entail transaction costs and raise other free-rider problems (Hechter 1987; Fehr and Gintis 2007). Why would individually rational people contribute to such enforcement mechanisms, especially if they could reap the benefits of enforcement without paying

Figure 10.2   Mechanisms of Social Order

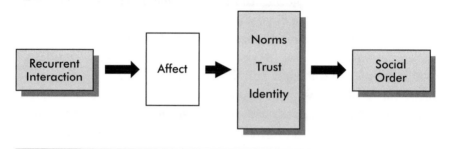

Source: Authors' compilation.

the costs? Enforcement represents a second-level public goods problem, requiring another layer of norms. Because of individual incentives to violate group norms, the effectiveness of norm enforcement is particularly problematic as groups become larger and more formal and as informal (peer) sanctions, such as expressions of disapproval, become less effective. Our affect mechanism of social order makes a very simple point about the enforcement problems involved in second-order public goods: to the degree that the person-to-group tie has an affective component, enforcement problems should be solved with less formal monitoring and lower transaction costs. People will obey norms voluntarily because "group regard" becomes a factor in their decision or an element of their utility function, owing to the affect mechanism.

From our theory, if trust relations generate positive feelings and social unit attributions of these feelings, they can be an important source of social order. Trust solutions to the problem of order, however, focus primarily on person-to-person ties rather than person-to-group ties. This makes it difficult to specify how trust at the local, micro level bears on or relates to social order at a higher or macro level (Cook, Hardin, and Levi 2005). One idea from this literature is that cultures that promote generalized attitudes of trust toward others produce more expansive network ties because generalized trust leads people to reach beyond their existing ties and form relations of trust with strangers (Fukuyama 1995; Yamagishi and Yamagishi 1994). If people are building bridges across traditional subgroupings within a larger social unit, denser and broader networks could strengthen order at the larger level—a micro-to-macro effect. Nevertheless, trust is a relatively weaker solution to the problem of social order, for reasons stated by Cook and her colleagues (2005): people lack sufficient information about others to be confident about whom they can trust, and thus trust is most relevant to order at the micro level. Our theory suggests, however, that people themselves could connect their trust relations to larger affiliations if those trust relations are a source of positive feelings and people view these feelings as "enabled" or fostered by a larger social unit within which the trust relations occur. Such micro-to-macro effects may be unintended by-products of efforts to build trust and trustworthiness at the local level.

Identity theories make fairly explicit connections between the micro and macro realms. In structural identity theory, roles foster shared definitions of self and other, but this requires substantial interaction at the micro level because larger structural roles have to be translated at the local level and the enacted roles may differ in important ways across role occupants. The larger context is clearer than in the case of trust, but like the trust approach to social order, the general focus of structural identity theory is on person-to-person ties rather than the ties to the groups or organizations within which the roles are enacted. In contrast, P-G ties are the central concern of social identity theory, but at the expense of downplaying the role of social interaction and P-P ties. Social (group) identities have the potential to organize and coordinate people in widely different local situations, but without regular social interaction with fellow members, it is not clear that these identities will remain salient and important, given the competition from other identities more directly tied to the immediate situations that people face. Our theory posits a connection between role structures and group identities by suggesting that the affective consequences of role-based interactions affect the strength of role occupants' ties to the group in which the roles are enacted.

CONCLUSIONS

Significant problems of social order are likely in a highly individualized world where traditional objects of commitment (local communities, work organizations, clubs) appear to be on the wane (Putnam 2000). One manifestation of this is disjuncture between local, micro social interactions and larger, macro conditions. The theory of social commitments notes that people themselves forge connections between micro and macro conditions. It specifies a micro-to-macro process that involves joint tasks or activities enacted at the local level but framed at the macro level and positive feelings experienced at the local level but attributed in part to larger social units. The central role of affect sets our theory apart from most others that approach the problem of social order from a micro-foundation, such as Coleman (1990) and Hechter (1987).[14] Historically, most theorizing about social order emphasizes how macro conditions constrain and shape individual orientations, behavior, and interaction (see Wrong 1994), and a much smaller corpus of work emphasizes the other side of the coin, micro-to-macro effects (Collins 1981; Coleman 1990; Ridgeway 1991; Lawler, Ridgeway, and Markovsky 1993). We offer a new way to connect micro to macro conditions by theorizing an affective mechanism that operates at the micro level and leads people to develop shared attachments to a group. If people associate their individual experiences at the micro level with larger, even quite removed organizations and communities, those collective units become salient, objective entities to which people orient their behaviors, from which they define themselves and others, and on behalf of which they enforce norms.

Large social units are likely to encompass a wide and diverse array of sub-units (see chapters 6 and 9). Such diversity may weaken or undermine social order. With this in mind, some scholars have explicitly asked how and when micro orders generate order at the macro level. Michael Hechter, Debra Friedman, and Satoshi Kanazawa (1992) argue that, in heterogeneous societies, the social order (solidarity) of a local group has a positive impact on social order at the societal level under three main conditions: (1) the local, micro group does not threaten the autonomy or ultimate authority of the larger unit (for example, the state); (2) the local group does not impose costs (negative externalities) on other groups that have the political clout to get authorities to intervene on their behalf; and (3) the local group integrates and controls marginal members of the society. These are the conditions under which heterogeneous states ostensibly have an interest in tolerating significant diversity of values, norms, and behavior. Stronger micro social orders, under such conditions, should indirectly strengthen macro orders rather than weaken the larger order.

David Laitin (2007), in an analysis of nation-states with diverse and powerful ethnic subgroups, comes to a similar conclusion, but with a different mechanism. He questions the standard hypothesis in political science that more heterogeneous states (ethnically and culturally) necessarily generate weaker, more fragile social orders than homogeneous states. This hypothesis assumes that diversity weakens the sense of common identity associated with state citizenship, makes communication difficult across ethnic subgroups of the state, and decreases the capacity of the state to generate collective action and sustain public goods (see also Putnam 2007). Laitin argues—and provides case evidence—that such problems of order (balkanization) are mitigated if states delegate autonomy to local cultural groups, safeguard that autonomy, and maintain liberal democratic institutions that give them equal rights of access to state resources and capabilities. The underlying mechanism is the development of multiple "layered identities" that promote complementary if not mutually supportive identifications with both the ethnic group and the larger state unit. The point is to develop social-political frameworks that encourage dual, interconnected identities for the state and ethnicity. Note that this solution implies nested group commitments in a decentralized context where local autonomy is supported and preserved by the larger unit, without unleashing excessive competition among local groups (see chapter 6).

Our theory of social commitments can be construed as a complement to the analyses of Hechter and Laitin, because it suggests a third process for micro-to-macro effects. For Hechter and his colleagues (1992), states grant autonomy or cede control to the local levels to the degree that groups at the local level do not threaten the larger order or impose excessive costs on it, and to the degree that they help control local populations. For Laitin (2007), ethnic groups choose collaboration and cooperation if states provide the necessary incentives for cooperation and a framework (liberal democratic institutions) for mutual assurance of cooperation by others. For us, these solutions are grounded in joint activities and a sense of shared responsibility for the results of these joint efforts. Both Hechter and his colleagues and Laitin posit a tacit or implicit bargain in which local groups enact and affirm their legitimized autonomy through freely undertaken joint tasks or activities that are likely to generate positive emotions. Repeated manifestations of the tacit bargain not only enhance the sense of shared responsibility at the local level but also generate perceptions that the state is a prime source of local autonomy and local order. The result, of course, is that people in the local group develop social commitments to the larger social unit, in part because the latter makes possible, promotes, or legitimizes the local order. Micro-level and macro-level commitments, therefore, are positively interconnected and mutually reinforcing.

CHAPTER 11

Conclusion

The "loss of community" has been a recurrent theme of the social sciences in the post–World War II era, a theme that harkens back to classic contrasts of agrarian communities (Gemeinschaft) and industrial societies (Gesellschaft). The general argument is that as human groups become larger, more complex, and differentiated, the sense of community suffers and depersonalization grows. Recent narratives about the changing world implicitly resurrect a loss-of-community theme without necessarily calling it that. In this contemporary narrative, human lives are becoming more private, individualized, and transactional, and thus it is difficult for people to develop and maintain relational ties, both to each other and to communities. This volume argues, in contrast, that social commitments to groups involving more than a transactional tie continue to develop and thrive even in a depersonalized world.

The capacity of people to develop emotionally based, person-to-group commitments is the key reason. We argue that people's commitments to small groups, work organizations, communities, and nations are a powerful, mobilizing force in their lives. People who are highly committed to a group are likely to devote more time to its activities; to work harder on behalf of the group; to defer immediate, individual gratification in service to longer-term collective goals; to weigh "other regard" and collective welfare over "self-regard" and individual interest when these conflict; to show disapproval to others who act contrary to the group's interest; and to cede greater power and control to legitimate authorities, representatives, or leaders of the group. Groups with highly committed members mobilize more widespread cooperation and collaboration and thus produce more predictable and stable social orders. In the global, individualized world we live in today, person-to-group ties are even more important sources of social order as person-to-person ties become more episodic, shallow, and fragile. Our theory of social commitments shows how and why micro-level interactions around joint tasks and activities promote people's affective commitments to groups.

A relevant anecdote about person-to-group commitments is provided in a *New York Times* article of March 10, 2008 (Richtel, Matt. 2008. "Going to the Company Elders for Help." *New York Times*. March 10, 2008) about a Hewlett-Packard (HP) program that recruits retired former employees to do significant, unpaid volunteer work for HP. The article indicates that HP is mobilizing "thousands" of retired employees to continue serving the company's needs in a variety of capacities, including sales, marketing, involvement in legislative issues of import to HP, and also in HP philanthropy. Many have joined this effort ostensibly because of their "affection for the company." One volunteer is quoted as saying: "I feel like I have two marriages: a wonderful marriage at home for 36 years and a wonderful marriage at HP." According to the article, for volunteers, continued involvement in the company is sufficient reward in itself because the volunteer work makes them "feel good" and allows them to retain their tie to the organization. The company thereby reaps significant benefits at minimal cost from the affective ties of retirees to the organization as a singular unit.

It is somewhat ironic that such strong commitments are being reported in Silicon Valley, "where long term company loyalty is as rare as a pinstripe suit; . . . [and where] people switch jobs and companies on Internet time, chasing the latest technology developments and the chance to cash in stock options or catch an initial public offering" (*New York Times*, March 10, 2008). Recent retirees developed their careers and these strong ties to HP in the "bygone era of paternalistic employers that promised lifelong employment." Nonetheless, this anecdote dramatizes the potential impact of affective ties or commitments by employees to an employer. This volume theorizes why affectively based commitments have stronger effects on such group-oriented behaviors than instrumentally based commitments.

The following sections broadly summarize the importance of person-to-group ties as a source of social order and outline our theory in an accessible way designed to convey the theory's implied practical advice on how to generate such social commitments. The chapter concludes with a final comment on the loss-of-community theme.

PERSON-TO-GROUP TIES
IN A CHANGING WORLD

A global, multicultural world has produced significant changes in how people relate to one another and how they are connected to groups and organizations (Putnam 2000, 2007; Haas 2000; McPherson, Smith-Lovin, and Brashears 2006; Laitin 2007). People increasingly work across cultural and national boundaries; corporations no longer make commitments to long-term employment; people move from job to job, organization to organization, and even career to career; union influence in the public sphere has diminished, as has the capacity of unions to protect the employment and benefits of members (Chaison and Bigelow 2002); people join fewer local, voluntary organizations (Putnam 2000); people have a smaller set of very close ties or others they can confide in (McPherson, Smith-Lovin, and Brashears 2006); and governments today face significant difficulties in meeting the demands and wants of citizens (Scharpf and Schmidt 2000b; Haas 2000). Across many areas of endeavor, not just economic ones, human contacts and ties reveal the properties of a neoclassical market, as the homo-economicus view of humanity has become virtually paradigmatic. These trends are generally consistent with classic loss-of-community themes.

In support, there is empirical evidence that standard, traditional network ties, organized around face-to-face contacts and interactions, are becoming looser, weaker, and less frequent (see Putnam 2000, 2007; Stolle and Hooghe 2004; McPherson, Smith-Lovin, and Brashears 2006). Putnam's (2000) "declining social capital" thesis is that people are experiencing a reduction or narrowing of their network ties within and across social boundaries, and that this is manifested in lower rates of participation and involvement in a wide range of voluntary associations, organizations, or group activities. Putnam offers a clear and coherent individualization narrative about how the social world is changing, but it is a narrative, not a reality. The empirical status of his thesis is controversial and open to debate on a number of grounds (for a review, see Stolle and Hooghe 2004). While we do find the observed decline in traditional types of memberships to be credible, we agree with many of Putnam's critics that the declining social capital thesis does not take sufficient account of new forms of social engagement that are more informal, fluid, flexible, and spontaneous (see Stolle and Hooghe 2004). New technologies (the Internet), for example, dramatically increase the capacity of people to make contact with more others in more contexts at more times and to sustain ties formed in face-to-face contexts (Katz and Rice 2002).

To study how the Internet affects social ties, James Katz and Ronald Rice (2002) conducted surveys between 1995 and 2000, the early period of Internet adoption. They observed that Internet ties or contacts tend to reflect and complement traditionally based ties by, for example, enabling more regular contacts among those who already have a relationship and increasing contact with neighbors, friends, and relatives. The introduction of the Internet did not promote isolation or reduce social ties (social capital), as many have argued, but rather enhanced the frequency of contact in existing networks and also helped to generate new social capital. The main inference of Katz and Rice's (2002) study is that the Internet acts primarily as a supplement to rather than a substitute for other social ties, while also expanding the opportunity to initiate new ties (see also Wellman and Haythornthwaite 2002). The conclusion of these authors posits a micro-to-macro process that dovetails with the implications of our theory:

> We can identify a cycle regarding individual use of the Internet, social interaction and collective social capital. Individuals follow their self-interest, which leads them to interact with others. This interaction leads to the creation of new information and forms of organization. This creativity in turn alters individuals' view of themselves and their relationships with others. This then enlarges . . . the "opportunity structure." (Katz and Rice 2002, 353)

Our theory is well suited to understanding the informal and emergent processes of group affiliation that dominate the lives of people today, in part because of such expanded opportunities and choices. The theory suggests how person-to-group ties can develop and become important forms of social engagement that unify people around shared activities and responsibilities even though their contacts with each other are frequently from a distance. The narrative about social transformations implicit in our theory is a social-relational narrative that stresses the capacity of people to jointly and endogenously create their own local or micro orders. The Internet enhances these capacities in particular when combined with traditional, face-to-face interactions and ties.[1]

Overall, the theory of social commitments suggests that person-to-group ties constitute a larger context of meaning and identity that frames and organizes social interactions in local situations; these ties enable people to do things together that they otherwise could not do and that in turn foster recurrent experiences of positive emotion or affect. We do not intend to suggest that person-to-group ties always have such effects. These effects occur only if the group ties have significant emotional and affective components, meaning that people have "gut-level" visceral feelings about their tie to a given group and cooperating or collaborating with fellow members affirms and strengthens such positive feelings. The stronger the affective component in group commitments, the more likely it is that people will define themselves with reference to that group affiliation, the group identity will be salient across social situations, people will act more often in accord with the expectations associated with that identity, and they will give it more weight when multiple identities are relevant in a social situation. Person-to-group ties or commitments need to be understood on their own terms and as distinct from the network and interpersonal ties between individuals.

In sum, the nature and the meaning of global trends are raising big questions and fostering debates that bear on the social, political, and economic dimensions of social order for the twenty-first century. What allows people in large diverse populations to cooperate and collaborate toward collective social, political, and economic ends? How can democratic political orders remain vital and efficacious if more and more people withdraw from or minimize their involvement in political matters? What enables culturally different people from different places in the world, with little direct contact, to define and work together toward common ends in a multinational corporation? How do people develop and sustain emergent virtual communities of interest from afar? How can the benefits of human differences or diversity (openness, tolerance, innovation) be repeatedly generated? What forces or structures might prevent the balkanization of human organizations? These are timely questions that suggest the need to reconsider how social order is generated and sustained. While we certainly do not claim to resolve all of these questions, the theory of social commitments addresses a neglected aspect of the social order problem that is implicated in them: the micro-foundations of person-to-group ties.

PERSON-TO-GROUP TIES AND SOCIAL ORDER

The issue of person-to-group ties is manifest in Thomas Hobbes's answer to his famous question: how is social order possible? He argues that, if people are left to their own devices, their relations descend into a "war of all against all." The Hobbesian solution is a contract between members of society through which they cede authority and control to a leviathan (governmental authority) that is capable of controlling the avaricious, malicious, aggressive, and competitive instincts of the human species. By implication, the problem of order for Hobbes is essentially a problem of generating and sustaining a contractual tie between the individuals and the state, and this contractual solution is purely instrumental and transactional. Echoes of this transactional solution are evident in much recent work recasting the problem of order as a social-dilemma problem (Hechter 1987).

Durkheim (1915) approaches the problem from different assumptions. He portrays social order as a more "natural" condition of the human species—in fact, as something that people create themselves but that then acts back on them (see also Berger and Luckmann 1966). Person-to-unit ties are explicit to Durkheim because a social order (society) is something that, to people within it, is "out there" external to themselves. It constrains people partly because they affirm its existence and importance, and it is fundamentally a moral force. Especially important for us, he observes that people sense this social unit especially when they are with others of the same society, meaning that their propensity to take account of this larger social unit is strongest when they are interacting with fellow members (see also Collins 1981, 2004). Durkheim (1915, 240–41) succinctly expresses this point:

> There are occasions when this strengthening and vivifying action of society is especially apparent. In the midst of an assembly animated by common passion, we become susceptible of acts and sentiments of which we are incapable when reduced to our own forces. . . . This is why all parties political, economic, or confessional, are careful to have periodical reunions where their members may revivify their common faith by manifesting it in common. To strengthen those sentiments which, if left to themselves, would soon weaken, it is sufficient to bring those who hold them together and put them into closer and more active relations with one another.

To Durkheim, person-to-unit ties are based not on a contract or force but on the moral and normative beliefs shared by members of the group. These ties are strongest when people are engaged in joint activities that not only make the society salient but also generate "collective effervescence" (uplift, elation) associated with the group affiliation.

Whereas person-to-group ties are central in classic versions of the problem of order, it is striking that most contemporary theory in the social sciences either ignores person-to-group ties or conflates them with person-to-person ties. The explosion of network imagery illustrates such an emphasis: it is conceived in terms of pairs or clusters of actors. The network is a unit, but not an object for actors as the state was for Hobbes or the society was for Durkheim. To some extent, this focus on person-to-person ties in much work in the social sciences may reflect the individual-centered history and culture of many Western societies, and to some extent it may reflect the failure and indeed the malevolence of prominent examples of twentieth-century societies founded on strong person-to-group ties, such as Nazi Germany and the Soviet Union. In addition, the individualization narrative underlying many analyses of contemporary social transformations suggests an interpretive framework that highlights individual opportunities and behavior, an economic concept of the human species, and person-to-person transactional ties.

The idea that person-to-person and person-to-group ties constitute a duality has long been recognized in sociological theory; examples are George Herbert Mead's (1934) seminal contrast of the specific others and generalized others as reference points for behavior and interaction, Talcott Parsons's (1951) treatment of the social system as a singular unit, and Peter Berger and Thomas Luckmann's (1966) classic treatise on the social construction of reality. Across such work, person-to-group ties generate the principal moral force of a larger community. Person-to-person interactions and ties certainly foster a semblance of order and stability; without the external moral force of shared person-to-group ties, however, these orders are not something people can readily rely on. Hobbes and Durkheim converge on this point, despite their differences. Nonetheless, in recent years the problem of order has been approached primarily from a person-to-person framework.

This volume treats people as an emotional, feeling species. People emote as much as they think—some would argue more so. In an individualized, transactional world, however, there is little place for emotion, or at least fewer and fewer places where feelings can be freely or openly expressed. Yet people invariably experience emotional ups and downs in their daily lives and in their interactions with others. An important theme of this volume is that even in highly transactional settings it is impossible to prevent people from feeling emotions and difficult to keep those feelings from having effects on people's relations and groups. This is why repeated transactions have relational effects. Whereas communities, organizations, and societies cannot prevent feelings from occurring, these groups do influence how people interpret and act on their feelings; what people do with their feelings and how they interpret them bears on their feelings and sentiments about group affiliations. If people associate their positive feelings and experiences with certain groups, they view that group affiliation as important in itself, intrinsically satisfying, and an expression of who they are and who they want to be. Groups that become objects of affective sentiment have enormous capacity to mobilize collective action and command sacrifice for the group's welfare—for good or ill.

THE THEORY OF SOCIAL COMMITMENTS

The theory thus reframes the problem of social order as an issue of how and when instrumental, transactional structures and interactions give way to relational, affective-normative, person-to-group commitments. It specifies a common underlying process for social commitments to groups of virtually any size, type, or function—from small groups to organizations to communities to nations. Even social commitments to large units like nations are based in self-generated, emergent micro processes; people themselves forge and sustain such micro-to-macro connections. In this section, we outline the theoretical argument in broad terms and suggest some practical implications of the theory.

Three central ideas of the theory interweave instrumental and non-instrumental conditions to explain social commitments. First, a social structure creates interdependencies among people and provides incentives for some to interact on a regular or repeated basis. This is the key instrumental component. Second, repeated interactions produce individual-level feelings (good-bad, up-down, elated-sad) that tend to be transitory or episodic but self-consciously felt or salient to those who experience them. This is the key non-instrumental component. Third, people interpret where those positive or negative feelings come from, which is the basis for more enduring affective sentiments about a group. This is the linkage between the instrumental and non-instrumental components. Social structures that produce a greater sense of shared responsibility lead people to interpret their individual feelings in collective terms, that is, as a manifestation of their group membership or affiliation. Thus, person-to-group social commitments become more affective to the degree that people in interaction not only experience positive feelings but perceive a shared responsibility for the results of their action; under these circumstances they attribute their feelings to the group.

Any theory requires a central mechanism, and affect is the mechanism in our theory. The sense of shared responsibility is in turn a key condition or linchpin that interconnects people's individual feelings in social interactions with their sentiments about a group. Shared responsibility is grounded in social structures that define the task as well as how individual behaviors contribute to it; a shared sense of responsibility determines whether people interpret their individual feelings as joint or collective products and thereby makes the group more salient and a stronger moral and normative force in the local situation.

Although abstract, the theory implies some practical advice—for example, on the use of teams and collective forms of accountability in the workplace; on how leaders can more effectively mobilize collective action; and on how social movements might sustain commitments to their cause. Here we once again identify key principles of the theory as we illustrate its practical implications.

First, there are certain conditions that promote a sense of shared responsibility:

- When repeated task interactions produce joint goods from which individuals receive benefits. For example, a manager putting together a project team or committee should make it clear that there are jointly produced results that they each value and will share in. This may be accomplished in the actual design of the team task or in the framing of it in a "charge" to the committee or team.[2]
- When it is hard for people to distinguish the contributions each makes to the task or the production of a joint good. This condition calls into question a premise of most approaches to work teams—specifically, the importance of well-defined individual responsibilities (Katzenbach and Smith 1993). From our theory, this sort of task design distracts attention from the collective nature of the endeavor and may balkanize task activities. More diffuse and overlapping responsibilities promote more contact, interaction, and negotiation among team members to accomplish the task because the task has more jointness. While a bit of disorder or even chaos may ensue under such conditions, the challenge posed is likely to strengthen the sense of shared responsibility if the task is accomplished.[3]
- When significant others (publics, authorities, leaders) hold those interacting to be collectively or jointly responsible for the consequences of their interac-

tion. Examples are managers or leaders who explicitly define the success of a team or organization in "we" terms as opposed to "I" terms; who carefully frame roles and responsibilities in conjunctive or shared terms; and who highlight what can be accomplished collectively rather than activities that are pursued individually. This may be done by conveying a compelling vision that resonates with the values and beliefs of group members or by emphasizing collective credit for organizational successes (Hackman 2002). This advice is similar to that of Lao-Tzu, who said that the best course is for leaders to take little credit: "When the best leader's work is done the people will say, 'We did this ourselves!'" (Hughes, Ginnett, and Curphy 2002, 23).

- When people are highly dependent on each other and have relatively equal power. To combat local-commitment problems in decentralized organizations, leaders or managers may place a premium on results that are produced by collaboration—specifically those that stem from sub-units exchanging unique information with each other and proactively producing results that none of the sub-units could have generated alone. Our theory suggests that cross-unit joint tasks are important, not only because of the benefits to the organization but also because they foster a sense of shared responsibility beyond particular sub-units. This helps to mitigate the nested commitments problem.

Second, there are certain conditions under which the sense of shared responsibility has the strongest effects:

- When the social interactions generate emotions (positive or negative) that people are motivated to either experience again or avoid in the future. Leaders, managers, or committee chairs can do many relatively small things that make members feel good—such as serving good refreshments at meetings, providing opportunities to participate in prosocial (philanthropic) activities outside of the workplace, and supporting pleasant work environments (with effective lighting, attractive decorations, comfortable furniture, and so forth). Also important is the explicit acknowledgment and celebration of group-level accomplishments in order to accentuate, when they occur, the positive emotional effects of success. Our theory affirms the importance of arousing positive feelings as often and widely as possible, and doing so tends to require paying attention to the "small" things that contribute to people's sense of respect and value in the organization.

- When a group or organization is perceived as causing, or making possible, the repeated interactions that lead (or fail to lead) to jointly beneficial goods. If people do tasks with shared responsibility and they experience positive feelings, group commitments may be directed at the local group rather than the larger group. In highly decentralized organizations in which local autonomy is critical to success, this may be a desirable state of affairs if the larger organization is highly dependent on the local units. Yet, if leaders need to mobilize coordinated efforts across the organization, it becomes more important that people perceive their autonomy at the local level as coming from, or being granted by, the center. To a large extent, this is a matter of how leaders frame and define the relationships between the central core and the sub-units of an organization. From our theorizing, the fundamental issue is how to ensure or heighten the saliency of the larger organization as a source of local autonomy.

- When a group or organization is perceived as an instrument of collective efficacy, enabling people to do things they otherwise could not do. This condition, again, is especially problematic in a decentralized organization. If a sub-unit has an important job opening and wishes to fill that position, central officials may resist allowing the sub-unit to recruit, or do so only grudgingly, or they may proactively encourage and support the effort. Assuming that the recruitment succeeds, does the center receive any credit for this success? In the former scenario, probably not; in the latter, probably so. It is often in the interest of the organizational center to establish some credit for success at the local level, and this is more likely if the center supports the local efforts and puts aside reservations whenever possible. Our theory points to some positive consequences when leaders just "get on board" and "go with it."

There appear to be many social arenas in which particular ideas from our theory might guide policies or practices, such as: (1) in designing and making the charge to committees, commissions, task forces, and work teams and designing their tasks; (2) in the framing by leaders of the organization's mission, the role members play throughout the organization, and the credit for organizational successes; and (3) in the balancing of autonomy and responsibility at the local level with oversight and accountability from the organizational center. These are pervasive policy and practice issues facing work organizations, NGOs, political organizations, and the like. Our theory, by emphasizing the emotions felt by people and the degree to which they perceive a shared responsibility for collective results, points in some directions that are not so apparent in other theoretical approaches.

The contributions of our theory center on how it integrates disparate ideas from different sources. The idea that social interactions involve joint activities or tasks is implicit in much prior work, as is the idea that people experience positive emotions from success and negative emotions from failure. Our theory of social commitments connects these two ideas in a new way, stipulating that joint activities produce affective sentiments about the groups within which people's interactions take place because the sense of shared responsibility makes them associate their feelings with the group affiliation. It is the combination of joint activities, common emotions, shared responsibilities, and social-unit attributions that generates person-to-group social commitments and imbues one or more groups with expressive, intrinsic value to people. This entails a micro-to-macro process that interconnects local, immediate social interactions with larger, more distant organizations, such as a multinational corporation or a nation-state.

THE MYTH OF COMMUNITY LOSS

It is a long-standing pastime of social commentators, journalists, and some social scientists to bemoan the "loss of community." Thoughtful, serious, and provocative analyses have viewed this as a problem of the contemporary age— and in nearly every other "contemporary age" since the full impact of industrialization became apparent in the second half of the nineteenth century. Social and economic changes in the second half of the twentieth century and at the dawn of the twenty-first have spawned analyses with somewhat similar loss-of-community themes. While such broad-sweeping interpretations have something of value to say about the conditions of human life at a given point, the "loss of community" appears to be more of a rhetorical device than a description of reality. Such analyses give little attention to the micro level and underestimate the (perhaps inevitable) capacity of the human species to construct community—and thereby person-to-unit ties.

Our theory of social commitments implies that the fountainhead of this capacity to create and sustain communities is emotional and affective. To be sure, people depend on each for valued outcomes, starting at birth, and there are many things that people can do or produce only in conjunction with each other; that is, people are interdependent in fundamental ways. Still, the foundational seeds of community, we argue, lie in the emotions that people feel when they interact with others and in what they do to understand and reproduce these affective experiences. Everyday feelings create or sustain ties to larger communities because people associate their feelings with these social units. The capacity to create and sustain communities, anchored so fundamentally in everyday interactions and emotional experiences, is too integral to and inherent in the human species for it to be lost in any real sense. We conclude that there is only one way people could suffer a generalized "loss of community": by first losing not only their capacity to find and engage in joint activities and tasks with others but also their capacity to emote and feel. In this sense, the loss-of-community themes of today are anchored not in the historical past but in illusion and myth.

NOTES

CHAPTER 1

1. In the end, Alex Rodriguez returned to the Yankees with a new contract. The press reported that he "crawled back" to the Yankee organization by initiating a face-to-face meeting with the Steinbrenner family in which he strongly proclaimed his allegiance and commitment to being a Yankee. Steinbrenner said: "Alex, at this point, wants to be a Yankee and is willing to make sacrifices. . . . He reached out to us through a third party and it appears he wants to be a Yankee." The end result was a contract comparable to the one he originally rejected, but with incentives that took account of his original market-oriented demands.

2. In these terms, a group can be a small, face-to-face group of friends or acquaintances, a local softball team, a professional association, a department in a corporation, a community (neighborhood, town, province), or a nation-state. The group is a social object that people perceive as "out there" as a force providing opportunities and constraints (Durkheim 1915; Berger and Luckmann 1966). At one extreme, a group may be a purely subjective entity, that is, the perception of an overarching affiliation among a set of people (Tajfel and Turner 1986; Brown 2000); at the other extreme, a group is formally established, recognized, and structured to achieve collective goals. With such variation in mind, our working definition of "group" is a perceived or "recognized" social unit or entity that encompasses a set of ongoing relations among the members and shapes their interactions with each other and with those outside the social unit or entity.

3. The distinctiveness and importance of person-to-group ties is documented empirically by an extensive body of research on social identity theory (Brewer and Gardner 1996; Turner and Reynolds 2004). That theory posits that the

mere categorization of people—simply giving a cluster of people a nominal label that contrasts with another cluster—leads them to treat those within their own group more favorably than those in a different group category. Such group-oriented behaviors occur even among anonymous strangers who are separated from one another and who do not individually benefit by treating similar others more favorably (Tajfel and Turner 1986; Hogg 2004). Social identity theory suggests the powerful effects that even minimal person-to-group ties can have on cooperation and collaboration with fellow members, as well as on hostility toward outsiders.

4. The Hobbesian problem of social order also was an important theme in classic theoretical works of sociology—in particular, the works of Marx, Weber, Simmel, and Durkheim. They aimed to understand the forces of order and disorder associated with the major social transformations of their time, particularly those in industrial societies. It is noteworthy that individual-society relationships (person-to-group ties) were their central concerns. We pick up this general theme and reframe it more explicitly as a person-to-group commitment problem.

5. By "micro" we refer to the regular interactions and experiences of people in social situations and local groups; by "macro" we mean the larger organizational contexts that are removed and somewhat distant from local interactions.

CHAPTER 2

1. These points of view are two sides of the same coin and are complementary. They reflect different starting points and emphases. We elaborate some of these in the course of this volume and return to Putnam's analysis at various points.

2. For more information, see "*Online Dating Magazine* Media Center: Abbreviated Online Dating Facts and Stats," available at: http://www.onlinedatingmagazine.com/mediacenter/onlinedatingfacts.html.

3. Frank Anechiarico and James Jacobs (1996) in fact found this to be true in a detailed historical analysis of governmental efforts in New York City to control corruption over the twentieth century. Anticorruption laws were generally ineffective for these reasons and made it more difficult and cumbersome to govern the city.

4. From this standpoint, the finding of McPherson and his colleagues (2006) that in the last decade of the twentieth century people had fewer confidants and their close ties were more kin-related may not suggest that they were socially isolated, but rather that person-to-group ties (professional identities, national affiliations) are more salient and require less direct, face-to-face social interaction to sustain, owing in part to wider access to others because of communication media.

5. We do not contend that person-to-group ties have to be continually generated or regenerated to have an effect on people. Once that tie forms, it may have effects without frequent person-to-person interaction. This seems most likely when the person-to-group tie is an important and valued source of personal and social identity, that is, an integral part of how people define themselves. Recall from chapter 1 that the causal order of person-to-person and person-to-group ties is two-way and contingent on the social situation.

6. The rational-choice principles underlying instrumental commitments could incorporate the group or organizational membership as a value or term in a utility function or as the determinant of actor preferences (see Hechter 1987; Elster 1986; Coleman 1990). However, this would transform the group object from an expressive entity to an instrumental one, which is important to our theorizing. In principle, one can subsume any item of value to individuals or any cause of a preference among choices (for example, to stay with or leave an organization) within a rational-choice framework. The question is whether this is useful for the given theoretical purposes. For our purposes, it is important and revealing to maintain a distinction between the instrumental and expressive, because we aim to examine certain connections between the rational and nonrational—specifically how the latter can emerge from the former.

7. See note 6.

8. Along with Ernst Fehr and Herbert Gintis (2007), we are essentially assuming that people have multiple, heterogeneous motivations or preferences; some are consistent with standard rational-choice principles, and some are not. Fehr and Gintis argue and demonstrate empirically that fairness and reciprocity preferences lead some people in a group to act in ways that depart from rational-choice theory; under some conditions (for example, where free riders are punished), they dominate purely self-interested actors and produce social order (in the form of collective goods). In our terms, preferences for fairness and reciprocity reflect a normative commitment that may stem from either an instrumental or an affective foundation.

CHAPTER 3

1. An earlier version of this chapter (Lawler and Thye 1999) was published in the *Annual Review of Sociology*.

2. The application of Sutton's Law in medicine instructs doctors to look for more common ailments before those that are more rare.

3. An emotion is an internal state of the human organism, centered in the nervous system and cascading through the body. A standard definition of emotion is: a

relatively short-lived positive or negative evaluative state with neurological, cognitive, and behavioral elements (Schachter and Singer 1962; Izard 1991). The terms *emotion* and *feeling* are used interchangeably here. *Affect* is a broader term that subsumes both emotion and feelings, and in some literatures it also includes mood states. We deemphasize mood states as such because they are diffuse, trans-situational, and lack a source or target. However, mood states are implied in our theorizing if they are connected to situational emotions and feelings and because of this, we do review some of the relevant literature on moods in this chapter.

4. Two contrasting models have emerged in psychological work. The circumplex model indicates that emotions lie on continua and can be reduced to a small number of dimensions, typically two (Guttman 1954; Russell 1980; Watson and Tellegen 1985; Russell, Weiss, and Mendelsohn 1989). One is emotional valence (pleasure-displeasure), another, perpendicular to the first, is the level of arousal. The second model adopts a differentiated approach to emotions, asserting that some emotions are more basic than others, but also that there are qualitative differences between some emotions; this is missed with a circumplex model (Clore, Ortony, and Foss 1987; Ekman 1980, 1992; Izard 1991; Batra and Holbrook 1990; Osgood 1966; Wierzbicka 1992). For example, anger and fear are very close to one another in the circumplex model, yet these emotions generate very different behaviors—fight or flight, respectively. We adopt elements of each of these approaches, as becomes clear later in the chapter.

5. People are known to vary in their capacity to read emotional cues. Recent work on "emotional intelligence" suggests that the ability to detect, understand, and manage emotions in interactions with others—that is, to give and receive emotional signals—is a crucial skill for people in positions of authority or management.

6. The six approaches are not necessarily independent of one another. They represent alternative orientations to how affect plays out in social interactions. Each points to a distinct set of questions or problems, and accordingly each illuminates certain aspects of emotion while ignoring or downplaying others. The metaphor "points of entry" is an apt construal for these six approaches and also is intended to communicate that there can be productive overlaps between them.

7. Erving Goffman (1959), who saw the world as a grand stage, theorized that, like scenes in a play, social situations entail scripts for acceptable behavior. A "script" is a recipe or set of rules that defines appropriate behavior in a given situation.

8. Kemper (1978, 1987) also attributes such effects to anticipatory emotions, which occur when a person expects a change in power or status whether or not it actually occurs.

9. Witness how changes in the cost and organization of health care, as well as internal changes in the field of medicine, are affecting doctor-patient relations. One can argue that transient impressions are more variable and changing significantly while fundamental meanings or sentiments about doctors are evolving more slowly. The result is more inconsistencies in the identity enactments of both doctors and patients, a potential reason for the growing number of malpractice suits.

10. There are at least four distinct models of judgment in the psychological literature. The priming model advanced by Bower (1981, 1991) suggests that positive or negative emotional states activate and make salient cognitive structures of the same valence. A second, but related, model suggests that mood-congruent social judgments result from efforts to maintain one's current mood state (Isen 1987; Wegener, Petty, and Smith 1995). Both of these models presume that emotions activate or serve to motivate certain cognitions more than others. A third model is based on the notion that people make decisions, in part, by sensing their current emotional reactions and using their reactions as data input (Schwarz and Clore 1983; Schwarz 1990; Clore and Parrott 1994). The fourth is the "reduced capacity" model. Here, emotional reactions are presumed to distract attention and burn cognitive energies and thereby attenuate a person's capacity for deliberative thinking (Eysenck 1977: Forgas, Williams, and Wheeler 2001; Wessel and Merckelbach 1997).

11. Research has supported this endogenous sequence across a significant number of experiments (for reviews, see Thye, Yoon, and Lawler 2002; Lawler and Thye 2006). More frequent exchanges produce more positive feelings (pleasure-satisfaction), and these in turn generate more cohesion. The effects of exchange frequency on cohesion are indirect and operate through the emotion mechanism.

CHAPTER 4

1. It is of course well known that people do not choose or stay in occupations purely on the basis of compensation. There are other benefits and incentives, such as interesting or satisfying work, that can be incorporated into an instrumental, rational-choice framework. What is new in our theory is the effort to understand when such individual feelings are associated so closely with the group that the group itself becomes an object of intrinsic or expressive value. While this may be incorporated into a rational-choice framework, we subscribe to the view that it is theoretically useful to distinguish the instrumental from the expressive. (For further comment on this point, see chapter 2, note 6.)

2. In fact, research on commitment to organizations suggests that those who are instrumentally committed stay because "they need to," those who are norma-

tively committed stay because "they believe they ought to," and those who are affectively committed stay because "they want to" (Mathieu and Zajac 1990).

3. It is important to note that there is empirical evidence, beyond our own work, supporting the idea that joint tasks and shared responsibilities make groups salient and weaken self-serving attributions in task situations. Stephen Zaccaro, Christopher Peterson, and Steven Walker (1987) studied quotes from athletes and coaches after wins and losses and found that self-serving attribution biases were weaker when the sport was group-based and involved joint, interdependent tasks (football, basketball) than when it was individual-based (tennis or golf). Donelson Forsyth and Karl Kelley (1996) did an experiment with a survival task and found that people experienced more positive affect when the group succeeded and gave the group more credit than themselves for its success. Overall, greater task interdependence and shared responsibility reduces self-serving attributions for group success, supporting a key point of our theory of social commitments (see also Dovidio, Gaertner, and Validzic 1998; Yzerbyt and Rogler 2001).

4. Job-switching and job rotation are other structures that generally should strengthen jointness and the sense of shared responsibility.

5. These distinctions bear a similarity to James Thompson's (1967) three types of task interdependence: pooled, sequential, and reciprocal. Under pooled task interdependence, each member or sub-unit makes an independent and separate contribution to a collective outcome; under sequential task interdependence, the results stem from interconnected sequential inputs; and with reciprocal task interdependence, there are complex contingencies among the outputs and inputs of members or sub-units. In table 4.1, these types of interdependence involve, respectively, personal, production-line, and team forms of shared responsibility.

6. Figure 4.1 also conveys how we integrate or interrelate the main principles of relational cohesion theory (Lawler and Yoon 1996; Thye, Yoon, and Lawler 2002) with those of the affect theory of social exchange (Lawler 2001; Lawler, Thye, and Yoon 2008). Shared responsibility acts as a moderator of the primary links posited by relational cohesion theory. Social-unit attributions of emotion mediate these effects of shared responsibility.

CHAPTER 5

1. This is implied by the key idea of social identity theory (Tajfel and Turner 1986) that groups may be purely psychological or cognitive, but they may also be

important sources of cooperative, group-oriented behaviors. This is referred to as a "minimal group." (See also chapter 1, note 3.)

2. Social identity is a non-instrumental, relational theory. It argues that social categorization (of self and others) is sufficient to generate group formation on a cognitive level, as well as behavior that favors members of one's own group over those of other groups (Hogg 2004). Social exchange is an instrumental, transactional theory. It suggests that relations and groups are based on individual incentives grounded in interdependencies and network ties (Molm and Cook 1995). We connect these two arguments by theorizing conditions and processes under which exchange structures generate social (group) identity effects.

3. This concept of the fundamental dimensions of social structure is informed in particular by a social-network (Burt 1992) or exchange-network (Emerson 1981; Willer 1999) point of view. Other approaches to fundamental dimensions can be found in the micro work on social identity and the macro work on stratification.

4. A similar concept underlies the Kevin Bacon game, which rose in popularity (in concert with his fame) during the early 1990s. The idea is to find actors who can be linked through their film roles to the actor Kevin Bacon. For instance, Robert De Niro has a "Bacon number" of 1 (De Niro was in *Sleepers* with Bacon), and John Leguizamo has a Bacon number of 2 (Leguizamo was in *Zig Zag* with Oliver Platt, who was in *Loverboy* with Bacon). Actors who have Bacon numbers of 7 or 8 are exceedingly rare in Hollywood since almost everyone has either worked with Kevin Bacon or with someone else who has worked with him. The structure of relations creates "closeness" in a very open and decentralized actor network.

5. These forms of exchange can be interwoven. Consider a work setting. The employment relationship is an instance of a negotiated exchange wherein each party agrees to the contractual terms of the relationship. At the same time, employees might build informal relationships with each other through reciprocal exchanges of small favors, advice, and drinks after work. They might engage in productive exchange by contributing their time or resources to produce a common good—such as a company picnic or family fund. Through generalized exchange, they might reflect and maintain organizational themes as well as interpersonal and community standards. Thus, the four forms of exchange are intertwined and can be recast as fundamental task structures within which people interact.

6. We should mention that these results contrast with the implications of some other theoretical and empirical work on social exchange—especially the fact

that generalized exchange produces the weakest social order (Ekeh 1974; Molm 2003; Molm, Collett, and Schaefer 2007). This other work assumes different structural conditions and emphasizes issues of risk and trust. For example, whereas our approach focuses on emotions and social commitments that emerge from objective task jointness and perceptions of shared responsibility, Molm and her colleagues focus on different structures and mechanisms, such as the salience of the conflict involved in the exchange. These approaches are actually complementary, and together they affirm how and when structures of exchange foster group perceptions and group behavior (see also Molm, Takahashi, and Peterson 2000).

7. By social networks here we simply mean the nature and pattern of relations that connect individuals in a larger system.

8. Richard Emerson (1972b) calls these "negatively connected" relations. More specifically, two dyadic relations are negatively connected when an increase in activity or magnitude in one relation implies a decrease in the other.

9. Emerson (1972b) develops a related idea termed "positively connected" relations. Two dyadic relations in a network are positively connected when an increase in activity or magnitude in one relation implies an increase in the other.

CHAPTER 6

1. Nested units imply at least one subgroup falling within or subsumed by another in the context of a structural hierarchy that ties them together. The issue of nested commitments is different from that of multiple commitments. Multiple commitments involve competing commitments to one's profession and organization, family and work, community and voluntary association, and so forth. Using "set theory" imagery, some group affiliations overlap; some are parallel, non-overlapping subsets within a larger set; some are parallel and independent of each other; and some are nested fully within another larger set. Our focus is on the last situation.

2. In the end, Welch's efforts appeared to pay off. The firm's revenues reportedly increased from $26.8 billion in 1980 to $130 billion by the time he left the firm in 2000 (Colvin, Geoffrey. 1999. "The Ultimate Manager." *Fortune,* November 22, 1999, p. 185). *Fortune* magazine named him "Manager of the Century" in 1999.

3. Much of the large body of research on organizational commitment emphasizes the commitment of employees to the organization as a unitary whole (Mowday, Porter, and Steers 1982; Mathieu and Zajac 1990; Meyer and Allen 1997) without regard to sub-unit commitments. This focus assumes that the organization as a whole is the most salient or important unit because sub-units are hierarchi-

cally organized and integrated under this umbrella. To be committed to one's department or local company is also to be committed to the larger unit within which this local unit is nested. However, the movement of work organizations toward greater diversification, decentralization, and employee participation in the 1960s and 1970s made the problem of nested commitments more apparent, and this has received more attention in recent years (see Morrow 1993; Morgan and Shelby 1994).

4. Universities are the prototype of "loose coupling," a relatively extreme form of decentralization. The concept of a loosely coupled organization was devised in more general terms to understand highly decentralized organizations in which each sub-unit has an independent role, separate activities, and a distinct identity within the organization. In universities, for example, it is not uncommon for each college to do its own fund-raising, generate its own budget, and even have a distinct logo. Richard Daft and Karl Weick (1984) and Douglas Orton and Weick (1990) offer incisive analyses of loosely coupled organizations, pointing to many positive benefits of loose coupling. One is that independent sub-units monitor and track particular issues and insulate the larger organizations from some classes of problematic events and uncertainties (see also March and Olsen 1975). From the proximal rule of the theory of nested commitments, loosely coupled organizations should be more efficient at generating order and cohesion in local independent units than in the organization as a whole.

5. This is a global treatment of the employability contract. In practice, its content and terms can vary widely across organizations, as can its impact on the commitment of employees. For example, Southwest Airlines is well known for its no-layoff policy and for the long-term mutual commitment between the company and its employees.

6. This states an implication of the theory; it is not an argument for centralized structures. Highly centralized structures may mitigate the nested commitment problem but have many other well-known problems. Also, from the theory of social commitments, highly centralized organizations are not likely to foster strong affective ties to the organization; the ties would be primarily instrumental.

CHAPTER 7

1. Williamson tends to assume a machine bureaucracy or command-and-control structure (Mintzberg 1979), and our discussion here does as well. A machine bureaucracy has very formalized rules and regulations, centralized authority, a chain

of command, and so forth. Another form of bureaucracy is exemplified by professionally based organizations such as hospitals, museums, libraries, law firms, and universities. Professional bureaucracies combine some forms of standardization, similar to a machine bureaucracy, with greater decentralization and delegation of decisionmaking authority to professionals. From our theory, professionally based bureaucracies have greater capacity to generate social commitments than machine bureaucracies because they may generate more collaborative forms of work (jointness), a greater sense of shared responsibility (collective efficacy), and more positive feelings about work activities.

CHAPTER 8

1. In terms of what they earn, the males and females may have been using different standards for comparison. The males may have been trying to "earn as much as possible," while the females may have sought to "reach agreement." This interpretation awaits further testing.

CHAPTER 9

1. Nationalist sentiments can be construed as the affective dimension of national loyalty, patriotism, and unity. In our theory, they represent a social commitment to the state.

2. In political science, "federalism" refers to how states distribute control and responsibility for public services between local and central political units (see Ferejohn and Weingast 1997; Rodden 2006). The underlying premise is that public functions are fulfilled more efficiently at the local level, with a few noteworthy exceptions, such as national defense. Over the last couple of decades, a "new federalism" school of thought has developed among political scientists and economists (Ferejohn and Weingast 1997), and in many countries this has spawned policies designed to move more control away from central states and toward local political units. The new federalism remains a subject of considerable debate (see Rodden 2006). Our theory suggests that federalism, new or old, creates a problem of commitment that is likely to affect the loyalty and responsiveness of people to the central state and thus the capacity of the state to mobilize collective action.

3. Arguments such as these about the decline of states implicitly adopt an individualization narrative about social transformations. People's ties to states are weaker and looser in part because their state cannot serve their needs and wants as it has done in the past, but also because people have more options to access

resources and opportunities. Individualization should be reflected in a disjuncture between the local, daily experiences of individuals and the nation-states of which they are citizens.

4. Identity-based arguments about nationalism are generally consistent with a social-relational narrative about major social transformations (see chapter 2).

5. Most of this research uses the Organization for Economic Cooperation and Development (OECD) data on eighteen countries.

6. It is worth noting that a recent, more comprehensive study by David Brady, Jason Beckfield, and Martin Seeleib-Kaiser (2005) compared a full range of hypotheses about globalization effects on the welfare state and found no overriding patterns, but did find comparatively stronger evidence for welfare state expansion (Rodrik 1997) than for welfare state decline (Fukuyama 2004).

7. "State" here refers to a nation-state. Nationalist sentiments can be generated in nations without states, but our focus here is modern nation-states.

8. Across both surveys, the response format was identical: "very close," "close," "not very close," and "not close at all." We compared the percentage who felt "very close" to their country versus the other units in each survey, as well as the means for closeness.

9. Specifically, for the 1995 survey the mean closeness (low numbers mean high closeness) are: 1.70 (N = 30038) for country; 2.06 (N = 29674) for county or province; 1.99 (N = 27420) for town/city; and 2.04 (N = 30053) for neighborhood. For the 2003 survey, the means for closeness are: 1.66 (N = 43285) for country; 1.96 (N = 42873) for county or province; and 1.83 (N = 43198) for town or city.

10. The intervening events between 1995 and 2003 may not have "pushed" the salience or efficacy of the state in the exact same direction. It is plausible, for example, that the events of 9/11 produced an upswing of nationalism especially in states threatened with terrorist attacks in the future. With this in mind, it is worth noting that of the six countries revealing an increase in closeness to country, two of them, the United States and the United Kingdom, have been highly threatened with terrorism, and Canada arguably may fit this criterion as well. These three countries, along with the Philippines, revealed the largest increases in mean closeness to nation among the twenty-one nations: 2.00 to 1.70 in Canada; 2.15 to 1.82 in the Philippines; 1.87 to 1.60 in the United States; and 2.14 to 1.92 in the United Kingdom.

11. Conclusions about the role of nested commitments or the conditions under which they are problematic for states would require a full-blown analysis with appropriate statistical controls. This is beyond the scope of the current volume,

but is a topic for future research. Comparisons across countries are difficult, but it should be possible to explain not only the cross-country patterns described here but also some of the differences in nationalist commitments across the countries. For example, it may be feasible to test whether more decentralized (federalist) states produce weaker nationalist sentiments about the state than centralized states, or how federalism in particular functional areas bears on such larger commitments to the state (Rodden, Eskeland, and Litvak 2003; Rodden 2006).

12. By "print capitalism," Anderson (1991, 2006) is referring to more widely available newspapers, periodicals, and pamphlets along with a dramatic increase in public conversations, dialogue, and ferment about the role, status, and responsibilities of people in human communities.

13. An implied hypothesis is that federalist (decentralized) state structures (see Rodden 2006) may enhance the efficiency of fiscal or public service functions and also promote nationalist sentiments if there is (1) monitoring without excessive constraint, that is, a balance of decentralization and centralization; (2) a sense of shared responsibility among citizens for the affairs of both the state and local political units; and (3) collective activities and rituals that generate positive feelings among citizens that they associate with the state.

CHAPTER 10

1. This macro example assumes that effects from lower (corporation) to higher (industry) levels of analysis can be interpreted as a micro-to-macro effect. Our theory portrays this as a nested commitments issue and traces ties to units at each level to the interactions of people in the lower-level unit (see chapter 6).

2. Recall that chapter 8 showed how and when local, micro interactions activate and mirror larger cultural beliefs about gender and race. When this occurs, social order at both levels is likely to be more stable. Discrepancies or slippage between micro and macro orders are a potential source of change.

3. If relational ties become valued objects, however, they then are exogenous forces or conditions that social interactions reproduce, strengthen, or weaken.

4. Berger and Luckmann (1966) identify two conditions that underlie the institutionalizing effects of repetition: habitualization, which is the tendency to repeat previous actions; and typification, which captures the idea that the larger meanings entail situational definitions of self and other.

5. A recent behavioral-economic approach to the normative foundation of social order provides a dramatic demonstration of the importance of micro processes to social order. Ernst Fehr and Herbert Gintis (2007) assume that any group has

people with at least three motivations: self-regard, other regard, or reciprocity. Those with reciprocity motivations are crucial to social order (public good provision), and they cooperate in a social dilemma only if cooperators have the capacity to punish noncooperators. The findings from a series of interesting experiments indicate that it takes only a minority of reciprocity-motivated actors to generate social order (a public good) as long as people can punish those who do not cooperate; without such a punishment capacity, it takes only a minority of self-regarding actors to undermine social order. The implication is that reciprocity norms become dominant when structural conditions allow those who cooperate to punish those who do not. The Fehr and Gintis (2007) approach is different from Hechter's (1987) in that they assume heterogeneous motivations, whereas Hechter assumes only self-interest or self-regard.

6.   There are other approaches to trust as well, some emphasizing individual characteristics (personalities, identities) and some the properties of institutions (see, for example, Kramer and Tyler 1996; Sztompka 1999; Cook 2001). Most emphases, however, can be subsumed within the categories of generalized, knowledge-based, and relational trust.

7.   For example, Toshio Yamagishi and Midori Yamagishi (1994) conducted a survey that compared generalized trust among Americans and Japanese and found that Americans have higher levels of generalized trust than Japanese. The implication is that Americans are more able and likely than Japanese to form business partnerships outside of their inner social circles. Yamagishi and Yamagishi term this an "emancipation effect" of trust (see also Yamagishi, Cook, and Watabe 1998).

8.   The role of uncertainty reduction was shown in an experiment on spot markets by Peter Kollock (1994). He found that repetitive transactions with the same others were more likely in markets where the quality of the product bought was uncertain than in markets where the product quality was known in advance. Repetitive transactions among the same buyers and sellers reduced uncertainty and set the stage for trust. In a related study, Lawler, Thye, and Yoon (2000) demonstrated that repeated exchange does make the other more predictable and that, when this occurs, actors are more likely to partake in a new joint venture (a social dilemma) involving significant risk. Thus, there is evidence that repeated interactions make partners more predictable to each other and produce a "bias" in favor of continuing to interact with the same others.

9.   This concept of trust (see also Hardin 2001, 2002) implies that trust requires the perception by a person (P) that another (O) has chosen cooperation because of "other regard" along with self-regard.

10. There is some recent work that conceives of trust as having both a cognitive and affective dimension, though here the affect tends to be directed at the other person rather than the individual or group. However, if encapsulated trust relations occur and the trust also entails positive feelings, tasks that generate a sense of shared responsibility should be more likely to produce this affective dimension of trust.

11. In addition to structural and social identity theories, there is a large body of theoretical and empirical work on the self, self-concept, and self-esteem in psychology and sociology (see Gecas and Burke 1995; Stets 2006). We exclude this work from the discussion here because it is less central to the question of how repeated interaction generates order.

12. Burke (1991) extends Stryker's theory by examining the moment-to-moment identity dynamics in which people compare their own behavior to an identity standard (for a comparison, see Stets 2006) and use the reactions of others as information. The identity standard can be construed as macro-cultural, but situational meanings are continuously affirmed or verified in social interactions. A strong identity commitment increases people's efforts to maintain consistency between their behavior and the relevant identity standards, reflected appraisals, and self-definitions (see Stets 2006). Whereas identity standards (self-meanings) are often grounded in structural roles, Burke's emphasis is on how people verify and adjust their identities in social interaction. Burke therefore elaborates in some detail how micro-macro consistencies are maintained.

13. It is also noteworthy that social identity theory supports the idea that person-to-group ties, once formed, should have effects on coordination among people who have little or no direct interaction with each other (Kramer 2006). Multinational corporations and associations, of course, make this a common experience of people in the contemporary world.

14. Hechter (1987) incorporates emotion by introducing the concept of "immanent goods," defined as "intrinsic pleasure." He treats this as a distinguishing feature of solidarity groups that can impose extensive obligations on members and exact substantial compliance. Immanent goods are intrinsic rewards that increase the dependence of members on organizations. A key difference between his approach and ours is that we theorize how and when such internal rewards are a source of expressive, non-instrumental ties to the group.

CHAPTER 11

1. We do not argue that virtual interactions have the same effects as face-to-face ties. The processes of our theory (felt emotions, sense of shared responsibility)

should be stronger in the face-to-face case. However, the same processes apply to virtual interactions, with the caveat that the emotional effects are likely to be weaker and harder to produce here, especially in the absence of periodic face-to-face contacts. The Internet, as a supplement to ties based on face-to-face interaction (Katz and Rice 2002), promotes the initiation of new ties that later produce face-to-face contacts. Thus, it has the potential to generate and sustain larger, self-generated communities of interest that include many others with whom a focal person has no direct contact.

2. This point is generally consistent with the theory-based applied literature on teams in the workplace (see especially Hackman 2002).

3. There is a trade-off here: assigning more diffuse responsibilities may produce coordination costs and reduce the likelihood of team success, yet it should heighten the positive feelings and affective sentiments about the group if the members are successful at the task. This may be especially helpful to an ongoing team that has future tasks to deal with.

REFERENCES

Abbott, Andrew. 2007. "Against Narrative: A Preface to Lyrical Sociology." *Sociological Theory* 25(1): 67–99.

Ackoff, Russell L. 1994. *The Democratic Corporation: A Radical Prescription for Recreating Corporate America and Rediscovering Success.* New York: Oxford University Press.

Adler, Paul S., and Seok-Woo Kwon. 2002. "Social Capital: Prospects for a New Concept." *Academy of Management Review* 27(1): 17–40.

Agnew, Jean-Christophe. 1986. *Worlds Apart: The Market and the Theater in Anglo-American Thought, 1550–1750.* New York: Cambridge University Press.

Alter, Peter. 1994. *Nationalism.* London: Edward Arnold.

Anderson, Benedict. 1991. *Imagined Communities: Reflections on the Origin and Spread of Nationalism.* London: Verso.

———. 2006. *Imagined Communities: Reflections on the Origin and Spread of Nationalism.* London: Verso.

Anechiarico, Frank, and James B. Jacobs. 1996. *The Pursuit of Absolute Integrity: How Corruption Control Makes Government Ineffective.* Chicago: Chicago University Press.

Anthony, Denise. 2005. "Cooperation in Microcredit Borrowing Groups: Identity, Sanctions, and Reciprocity in the Production of Collective Goods." *American Sociological Review* 70(3): 496–515.

Aoki, Masahiko. 1988. *Information, Incentives, and Bargaining in the Japanese Economy.* New York: Cambridge University Press.

Appelbaum, Eileen, and Rosemary Batt. 1994. *The New American Workplace: Transforming Work Systems in the United States.* Ithaca, N.Y.: ILR Press.

Arthur, Michael B., and Denise M. Rousseau, eds. 1996. *The Boundaryless Career: A New Employment Principle for a New Organizational Era.* New York: Oxford University Press.

Ashkenas, Ron, Dave Ulrich, Todd Jick, and Steve Kerr. 1998. *The Boundaryless Organization: Breaking the Chains of Organizational Structure.* San Francisco: Jossey-Bass.

Axelrod, Robert. 1984. *The Evolution of Cooperation.* New York: Basic Books.

Baker, Douglas D., and John B. Cullen. 1993. "Administrative Reorganization and Configurational Context: The Contingent Effects of Age, Size, and Change in Size." *Academy of Management Journal* 36(6): 1251–77.

Bales, Robert F. 1953. "The Equilibrium Problem in Small Groups." In *Working Papers in the Theory of Action,* edited by Talcott Parsons, Robert F. Bales, and Edward A. Shils. Glencoe, Ill.: Free Press.

Bandura, Albert. 1997. *Social Learning Theory.* Englewood Cliffs, N.J.: Prentice Hall.

Barney, Jay B., and Patrick M. Wright. 1998. "On Becoming a Strategic Partner: The Role of Human Resources in Gaining Competitive Advantage." *Human Resource Management* 37(1): 31–46.

Barsade, Sigal G. 2002. "The Ripple Effect: Emotional Contagion and Its Influence on Group Behavior." *Administrative Science Quarterly* 47(4): 644.

Bartel, Caroline A., and Richard Saavedra. 2000. "The Collective Construction of Work Group Moods." *Administrative Science Quarterly* 45(2): 197–231.

Batra, Rajeev, and Morris B. Holbrook. 1990. "Developing a Typology of Affective Responses to Advertising." *Psychology and Marketing* 7(1): 11–25.

Baumeister, Roy F., and Mark R. Leary. 1995. "The Need to Belong: Desire for Interpersonal Attachments as a Fundamental Human Motivation." *Psychological Bulletin* 117(3): 497–529.

Becker, Brian, and Barry Gerhart. 1996. "The Impact of Human Resource Management on Organizational Performance: Progress and Prospects." *Academy of Management Journal* 39(4): 779–801.

Beer, Michael, and Nitin Nohria, eds. 2000. *Breaking the Code of Change.* Boston: Harvard Business School Press.

Bell, Daniel. 1960. *The End of Ideology.* New York: Free Press.

Berger, Joseph, Bernard P. Cohen, and Morris Zelditch Jr. 1972. "Status Characteristics and Social Interaction." *American Sociological Review* 37(3): 241–55.

Berger, Joseph, M. Hamit Fisek, and Lee Freese. 1977. "Paths of Relevance and the Determination of Power and Prestige Orders." *Pacific Sociological Review* 19(1): 45–62.

Berger, Joseph, M. Hamit Fisek, Robert Z. Norman, and David G. Wagner. 1985. "Formation of Reward Expectations in Status Situations." In *Status, Rewards, and Influence,* edited by Joseph Berger and Morris Zelditch Jr. San Francisco: Jossey-Bass.

Berger, Joseph, Cecilia L. Ridgeway, M. Hamit Fisek, and Robert Z. Norman. 1998. "The Legitimation and Delegitimation of Power and Prestige Orders." *American Sociological Review* 63(3): 379–405.

Berger, Joseph, Cecilia L. Ridgeway, and Morris Zelditch. 2002. "Construction of Status and Referential Structures." *Sociological Theory* 20(2): 157–79.

Berger, Joseph, and Murray Webster. 2006. "Expectations, Status, and Behavior." In *Contemporary Social Psychological Theories,* edited by Peter J. Burke. Stanford, Calif.: Stanford University Press.

Berger, Peter, and Thomas Luckmann. 1966. *Social Construction of Reality.* New York: Anchor Books.

Biddle, Bruce J. 1986. "Recent Developments in Role Theory." *Annual Review of Sociology* 12(1): 67–92.

Bower, Gordon H. 1981. "Mood and Memory." *American Psychologist* 36(2): 129–48.
———. 1991. "Mood Congruity of Social Judgments." In *Emotion and Social Judgments,* edited by Joseph P. Forgas. Oxford: Pergamon.

Brady, David, Jason Beckfield, and Martin Seeleib-Kaiser. 2005. "Economic Globalization and the Welfare State in Affluent Democracies, 1975–2001." *American Sociological Review* 70(6): 921.

Brehm, Jack W. 1966. *A Theory of Psychological Reactance.* New York: Academic Press.

Brewer, Marilynn, and Wendi Gardner. 1996. "Who Is This 'We'? Levels of Collective Identity and Self-Representations." *Journal of Personality and Social Psychology* 71(1): 83–93.

Brief, Arthur P., and Howard M. Weiss. 2002. "Organizational Behavior: Affect in the Workplace." *Annual Review of Psychology* 53(1): 279–308.

Brown, Rupert. 2000. *Group Processes: Dynamics Within and Between Groups.* Oxford: Blackwell.

Brown, Rupert, and Gillian Wade. 1987. "Superordinate Goals and Intergroup Behavior: The Effect of Role Ambiguity and Status on Intergroup Attitudes and Task Performance." *European Journal of Social Psychology* 17(2): 131–42.

Brusco, Sebastiano. 1982. "The Emilian Model: Productive Decentralization and Social Integration." *Cambridge Journal of Economics* 6(2): 167–84.

Burke, Peter J. 1991. "Identity Processes and Social Stress." *American Sociological Review* 56(6): 836–49.

Burt, Ronald S. 1992. *Structural Holes: The Social Structure of Competition.* Cambridge, Mass.: Harvard University Press.

Byham, William C., Audrey B. Smith, and Matthew J. Paese. 2003. *Grow Your Own Leaders.* London: Financial Times/Prentice Hall.

Calhoun, Craig. 2007. *Nations Matter: Culture, History, and the Cosmopolitan Dream.* Oxford: Routledge.

Chaison, Gary, and Barbara J. Bigelow. 2002. *Unions and Legitimacy.* Ithaca, N.Y.: Cornell University Press.

Clark, Candace. 1990. "Emotions and Micropolitics in Everyday Life: Some Patterns and Paradoxes of Place." *Research Agendas in the Sociology of Emotions,* edited by Theodore D. Kemper. Albany: State University of New York Press.

Clore, Gerald L., Andrew Ortony, and Mark A. Foss. 1987. "The Psychological Foundations of the Affective Lexicon." *Journal of Personality and Social Psychology* 53(4): 751–66.

Clore, Gerald L., and W. G. Parrott. 1994. "Cognitive Feelings and Meta-Cognitive Judgments." *European Journal of Social Psychology* 24(1): 101–15.

Coase, Ronald H. 1988. *The Firm, the Market, and the Law.* Chicago: University of Chicago Press.

Coleman, James S. 1990. *Foundations of Social Theory.* Cambridge, Mass.: Harvard University Press.

Collins, Jim, and Jerry I. Porras. 1997. *Built to Last: Successful Habits of Visionary Companies.* New York: HarperCollins.

Collins, Randall. 1975. *Conflict Sociology: Toward an Explanatory Science.* New York: Academic Press.

———. 1981. "On the Microfoundations of Macrosociology." *American Journal of Sociology* 86(5): 984–1014.

———. 1989. "Toward a Neo-Meadian Sociology of Mind." *Symbolic Interaction* 12(1): 1–32.

———. 2004. *Interaction Ritual Chains.* Princeton, N.J.: Princeton University Press.

Condon, William S., and Louis W. Sander. 1974. "Neonate Movement Is Synchronized with Adult Speech: Interactional Participation and Language Acquisition." *Science* 183(4120): 99–101.

Cook, Karen S., ed. 2001. *Trust in Society.* New York: Russell Sage Foundation.

Cook, Karen S., Russell Hardin, and Margaret Levi. 2005. *Cooperation Without Trust?* New York: Russell Sage Foundation.

Daft, Richard L., and Karl E. Weick. 1984. "Toward a Model of Organizations as Interpretation Systems." *Academy of Management Review* 9(2): 284–95.

Dahrendorf, Ralf. 1959. *Class and Class Conflict in Industrial Society.* Stanford, Calif.: Stanford University Press.

Damasio, Antonio R. 1999. *The Feeling of What Happens: Body and Emotion in the Making of Consciousness.* New York: Harcourt Brace.

———. 2003. *Looking for Spinoza: Joy, Sorrow, and the Feeling Brain.* New York: Harcourt.

Damasio, Antonio R., Thomas J. Grabowski, Antoine Bechara, Hanna Damasio, Laura L. B. Ponto, Josef Parvizi, and Richard D. Hichwa. 2000. "Subcortical and Cortical Brain Activity During the Feeling of Self-Generated Emotions." *Nature Neuroscience* 3(10): 1049–56.

Deci, Edward L. 1975. *Intrinsic Motivation.* New York: Plenum Press.

DiMaggio, Paul, and Walter Powell. 1983. "The Iron Cage Revisited: Institutional Isomorphism and Collective Rationality in Organizational Fields." *American Sociological Review* 48(2): 147–60.

Dobbin, Frank. 1994. *Forging Industrial Policy: The United States, Britain, and France in the Railway Age.* Cambridge: Cambridge University Press.

Dore, Ronald. 1983. "Goodwill and the Spirit of Market Capitalism." *British Journal of Sociology* 34(4): 459–82.

Dornbusch, Sanford M., and W. Richard Scott. 1975. *Evaluation and Exercise of Authority: A Theory of Control in Organizations.* San Francisco: Jossey-Bass.

Dovidio, John F., Samuel L. Gaertner, and Ana Validzic. 1998. "Intergroup Bias: Status, Differentiation, and a Common In-Group Identity." *Journal of Personality and Social Psychology* 75(1): 109–20.

Durkheim, Émile. 1915. *The Elementary Forms of Religious Life.* New York: Free Press.

———. 1997. *The Division of Labor in Society.* New York: Free Press (originally published in 1893).

Eby, Lillian T., Marcus Butts, and Angie Lockwood. 2003. "Predictors of Success in the Era of the Boundaryless Career." *Journal of Organizational Behavior* 24(6): 689–708.

Eccles, Robert G., and Dwight Crane. 1987. "Managing Through Networks in Investment Banking." *California Management Review* 30(1): 176–95.

Ekeh, Peter. 1974. *Social Exchange Theory.* Cambridge, Mass.: Harvard University Press.

Ekman, Paul. 1980. *The Face of Man: Expressions of Universal Emotions in a New Guinea Village.* New York: Garland STPM Press.

———. 1992. "An Argument for Basic Emotion." *Cognition and Emotion* 6(3–4): 169–200.

Ellemers, Naomi, Russell Spears, and Bertjan Doosje. 1997. "Sticking Together or Falling Apart: Ingroup Identification as a Psychological Determinant of Group

Commitment Versus Individual Mobility." *Journal of Personality and Social Psychology* 72(3): 617–26.

Elster, Jon. 1986. "Introduction." In *Rational Choice,* edited by Jon Elster. New York: New York University Press.

Emerson, Richard M. 1972a. "Exchange Theory, Part 1: A Psychological Basis for Social Exchange Rules and Networks." In *Sociological Theories in Progress,* edited by Joseph Berger, Morris Zelditch Jr., and Bo Anderson. Boston: Houghton Mifflin.

———. 1972b. "Exchange Theory, Part 2: Exchange Rules and Networks." In *Sociological Theories in Progress,* edited by Joseph Berger, Morris Zelditch Jr., and Bo Anderson. Boston: Houghton Mifflin.

———. 1981. "Social Exchange Theory." In *Social Psychology: Sociological Perspectives,* edited by Morris Rosenberg and Ralph H. Turner. New York: Basic Books.

Evans, Paul, Vladimir Pucik, and Jean-Louis Barsoux. 2002. *The Global Challenge: International Human Resource Management.* New York: McGraw-Hill.

Eysenck, Michael W. 1977. *Human Memory: Theory, Research, and Individual Differences.* Elmsford, N.Y.: Pergamon.

Fehr, Ernst, and Herbert A. Gintis. 2007. "Human Motivation and Social Cooperation: Experimental and Analytical Foundations." *Annual Review of Sociology* 33(1): 43–64.

Ferejohn, John, and Barry R. Weingast, eds. 1997. *The New Federalism: Can States Be Trusted?* Stanford, Calif.: Hoover Institution Press.

Fink, Stephen L. 1992. *High-Commitment Workplaces.* New York: Quorum Books.

Firebaugh, Glenn, and Brian Goesling. 2004. "Accounting for the Recent Decline in Global Income Inequality." *American Journal of Sociology* 110(2): 283–312.

Forgas, Joseph P., Kipling D. Williams, and Ladd Wheeler, eds. 2001. *The Social Mind: Cognitive and Motivational Aspects of Interpersonal Behavior.* Cambridge: Cambridge University Press.

Forsyth, Donelson R., and Karl N. Kelley. 1996. "Heuristic-Based Biases in Estimations of Personal Contributions to Collective Endeavors." In *What's Social About Social Cognition? Research on Socially Shared Cognition in Small Groups,* edited by Judith L. Nye and Aaron M. Brower. Thousand Oaks, Calif.: Sage Publications.

Frank, Robert H. 1988. *Passions within Reason: The Strategic Role of Emotions.* New York: Norton.

———. 1993. "The Strategic Role of the Emotions: Reconciling Over- and Undersocialized Accounts of Behavior." *Rationality and Society* 5(2): 160–84.

————. 2007. *Falling Behind: How Rising Inequality Harms the Middle Class.* Berkeley: University of California Press.

Friedman, Thomas L. 2005. *The World Is Flat: A Brief History of the Twenty-First Century.* New York: Farrar, Straus and Giroux.

Fukuyama, Francis. 1995. *Trust: The Social Virtues and the Creation of Prosperity.* New York: Free Press.

————. 2004. *State-Building: Governance and World Order in the Twenty-First Century.* Ithaca, N.Y.: Cornell University Press.

Ganghof, Steffen. 2000. "Adjusting National Tax Policy to Economic Internationalization: Strategies and Outcomes." In *Welfare and Work in the Open Economy,* vol. 1, edited by Fritz Wilhelm Scharpf and Vivien Ann Schmidt. New York: Oxford University Press.

Gasper, Karen, and Gerald L. Clore. 2002. "Attending to the Big Picture: Mood and Global Versus Local Processing of Visual Information." *Psychological Science* 13(1): 34–40.

Gecas, Viktor, and Peter J. Burke. 1995. "Self and Identity." In *Sociological Perspectives on Social Psychology,* edited by Karen S. Cook, Gary Alan Fine, and James S. House. Boston: Allyn and Bacon.

Gellner, Ernest. 1983. *Nations and Nationalism.* Ithaca, N.Y.: Cornell University Press.

George, Jennifer M. 1995. "Leader Positive Mood and Group Performance: The Case of Customer Service." *Journal of Applied Social Psychology* 25(9): 778–94.

Giddens, Anthony. 1984. *The Constitution of Society: Outline of the Theory of Structure.* Berkeley: University of California Press.

Goffman, Erving. 1959. *Presentation of Self in Everyday Life.* Garden City, N.Y.: Doubleday/Anchor.

Gordon, Steven L. 1990. "Social Structure Effects on Emotions." In *Research Agendas in the Sociology of Emotions,* edited by Theodore D. Kemper. New York: State University of New York Press.

Granovetter, Mark. 1985. "Economic Action and Social Structure: The Problem of Embeddedness." *American Journal of Sociology* (91): 482–510.

Greenfeld, Liah. 1992. *Nationalism: Five Roads to Modernity.* Cambridge, Mass.: Harvard University Press.

Greenfeld, Liah, and Jonathan R. Eastwood. 2005. "Nationalism in Comparative Perspective." In *The Handbook of Political Sociology,* edited by Thomas Janoski, Alexander M. Hicks, and Mildred A. Schwartz. New York: Cambridge University Press.

Guibernau, Montserrat. 1999. *Nations Without States: Political Communities in a Global Age.* Cambridge, Mass.: Polity Press.

Guttman, Louis. 1954. "An Outline of Some New Methodology in Social Research." *Public Opinion Quarterly* 18(4): 395–404.

Haas, Ernst B. 2000. *Nationalism, Liberalism, and Progress,* vol. 2, *The Dismal Fate of New Nations.* Ithaca, N.Y.: Cornell University Press.

Hackman, J. Richard. 2002. *Leading Teams: Setting the Stage for Great Performances.* Boston: Harvard Business School Press.

Hall, Rogers. 1999. "The Organization and Development of Discursive Practices for 'Having a Theory.'" *Discourse Processes* 27(2): 187–218.

Hamel, Gary. 1991. "Competition for Competence and Inter-Partner Learning Within International Strategic Alliances." *Strategic Management Journal* 12(special issue on "Global Strategy"): 83–103.

Hannan, Michael T., and John Freeman. 1977. "The Population Ecology of Organizations." *American Journal of Sociology* 82(5): 929–64.

Hardin, Russell. 2001. "Conceptions and Explanations of Trust." In *Trust in Society,* edited by Karen S. Cook. New York: Russell Sage Foundation.

———. 2002. *Trust and Trustworthiness.* New York: Russell Sage Foundation.

Hatfield, Elaine, John T. Cacioppo, and Richard L. Rapson. 1993. "Emotional Contagion." *Current Directions in Psychological Science* 2(3): 96–99.

Haythornthwaite, Caroline, and Barry Wellman. 2002. "The Internet in Everyday Life: An Introduction." In *The Internet in Everyday Life,* edited by Barry Wellman and Caroline Haythornthwaite. Malden, Mass.: Blackwell.

Hechter, Michael. 1987. *Principles of Group Solidarity.* Berkeley: University of California Press.

———. 1990. "The Emergence of Cooperative Institutions." In *Social Institutions: Their Emergence, Maintenance, and Effects,* edited by Michael Hechter, Karl-Dieter Opp, and Reinhard Wippler. New York: Aldine de Gruyter.

———. 2000. *Containing Nationalism.* Oxford: Oxford University Press.

Hechter, Michael, Debra Friedman, and Satoshi Kanazawa. 1992. "The Attainment of Social Order in Heterogeneous Societies." In *Rational Choice Theory: Advocacy and Critique,* edited by James S. Coleman and Thomas J. Fararo. Newbury Park, Calif.: Sage Publications.

Heise, David R. 1979. *Understanding Events: Affect and the Construction of Social Action.* New York: Cambridge University Press.

Hobbes, Thomas. 1985. *Leviathan.* New York: Penguin Books (originally published in 1651).

Hobsbawm, Eric J. 1990. *Nations and Nationalism Since 1780.* Cambridge: Cambridge University Press.

Hochschild, Arlie Russell. 1979. "Emotion Work, Feeling Rules, and Social Structure." *American Journal of Sociology* 85(3): 551–75.

———. 1983. *The Managed Heart: Commercialization of Human Feeling.* Berkeley: University of California Press.

Hogg, Michael A. 2004. "Social Categorization, Depersonalization, and Group Behavior." In *Self and Social Identity,* edited by Marilynn B. Brewer and Miles Hewstone. Malden, Mass.: Blackwell Publishers.

Homans, George C. 1950. *The Human Group.* New Brunswick, N.J.: Transaction Publishers.

Hughes, Richard L., Robert C. Ginnett, and Gordon J. Curphy. 2002. *Leadership: Enhancing the Lessons of Experience.* New York: McGraw-Hill.

Hutchinson, John, and Anthony D. Smith. 1994. *Nationalism.* Oxford: Oxford University Press.

International Social Survey Programme (ISSP). 1995. "National Identity I." Available at: http://www.gesis.org/en/services/data/survey-data/issp/modules-study-overview/national-identity/1995.

———. 2003. "National Identity II." Available at: http://www.gesis.org/en/services/data/survey-data/issp/modules-study-overview/national-identity/2003.

Isen, Alice M. 1987. "Positive Affect, Cognitive Processes, and Social Behavior." In *Advances in Experimental Social Psychology,* edited by Leonard Berkowitz. New York: Academic Press.

Isen, Alice M., and Nehemia Geva. 1987. "The Influence of Positive Affect on Acceptable Level of Risk: The Person with a Large Canoe Has a Large Worry." *Organizational Behavior and Human Decision Processes* 39(2): 145–54.

Isen, Alice M., and Robert Patrick. 1983. "The Effect of Positive Feelings on Risk Taking: When the Chips Are Down." *Organizational Behavior and Human Performance* 31(2): 194–202.

Izard, Carroll E. 1991. *The Psychology of Emotions.* New York: Plenum Press.

Johnson, Eric J., and Amos Tversky. 1983. "Affect, Generalization, and the Perception of Risk." *Journal of Personality and Social Psychology* 45(1): 20–31.

Jones, Candace, William S. Hesterly, and Stephen P. Borgatti. 1997. "A General Theory of Network Governance: Exchange Conditions and Social Mechanisms." *Academy of Management Review* 22(4): 911–45.

Jones, R. Gareth. 2000. *Organizational Theory: Text and Cases.* Upper Saddle River, N.J.: Prentice Hall.

Kanter, Rosabeth Moss. 1968. "Commitment and Social Organization: A Study of Commitment Mechanisms in Utopian Communities." *American Sociological Review* 33(4): 499–517.

———. 1972. *Commitment and Community: Communes and Utopias in Sociological Perspective.* Cambridge, Mass.: Harvard University Press.

———. 1977. *Men and Women of the Corporation.* New York: Basic Books.

Katz, James E., and Ronald E. Rice. 2002. *Social Consequences of Internet Use.* Cambridge, Mass.: MIT Press.

Katzenbach, Jon R., and Douglas K. Smith. 1993. *The Wisdom of Teams: Creating the High-Performance Organization.* Boston: Harvard Business School Press.

Kelley, Harold H. 1967. "Attribution Theory in Social Psychology." In *Nebraska Symposium on Motivation,* edited by Donald Levine. Lincoln: University of Nebraska Press.

Kelley, Harold H., and John W. Thibaut. 1978. *Interpersonal Relations: A Theory of Interdependence.* New York: Wiley.

Kelly, Janice R., and Sigal G. Barsade. 2001. "Mood and Emotions in Small Groups and Work Teams." *Organizational Behavior and Human Decision Processes* 86(1): 99–130.

Kemper, Theodore D. 1978. *A Social Interactional Theory of Emotions.* New York: Wiley.

———. 1987. "How Many Emotions Are There? Wedding the Social and the Autonomic Components." *American Journal of Sociology* 93(2): 263–89.

Kohn, Melvin L., and Kazimierz M. Slomczynski. 1990. *Social Structure and Self-Direction: A Comparative Analysis of the United States and Poland.* Cambridge, Mass.: Blackwell.

Kollock, Peter. 1994. "The Emergence of Exchange Structures: An Experimental Study of Uncertainty, Commitment, and Trust." *American Journal of Sociology* 100(2): 313–45.

———. 1998. "Social Dilemmas: The Anatomy of Cooperation." *Annual Review of Sociology* 24: 183–214.

Komorita, Samuel S., and Craig D. Parks. 1996. *Social Dilemmas.* Boulder, Colo.: Westview Press.

Kornhauser, William. 1959. *Politics of Mass Society.* New York: Free Press.

Kramer, Roderick M. 2006. "Social Capital and Cooperative Behavior in the Workplace: A Social Identity Perspective." *Advances in Group Processes: Social Psychology of the Workplace,* edited by Shane R. Thye and Edward J. Lawler. Amsterdam, Netherlands: Elsevier.

Kramer, Roderick M., and Tom R. Tyler. 1996. *Trust in Organizations.* Thousand Oaks, Calif.: Sage Publications.

Laitin, David D. 2007. *Nations, States, and Violence.* Oxford: Oxford University Press.

Larson, Andrea. 1992. "Network Dyads in Entrepreneurial Settings: A Study of the Governance of Exchange Relationships." *Administrative Science Quarterly* 37(1): 76–104.

Lawler, Edward J. 1992. "Affective Attachments to Nested Groups: A Choice-Process Theory." *American Sociological Review* 57(3): 327–36.

———. 1997. "Affective Attachments to Nested Groups: The Role of Rational Choice Processes." In *Status, Network, and Structure,* edited by Jacek Szmatka, John Skvoretz, and Joseph Berger. Stanford, Calif.: Stanford University Press.

———. 2001. "An Affect Theory of Social Exchange." *American Journal of Sociology* 107(2): 321–52.

———. 2003. "Interaction, Emotions, and Collective Identities." In *Advances in Identity Theory and Research,* edited by Peter J. Burke, Timothy J. Owens, Richard T. Serpe, and Peggy A. Thoits. New York: Kluwar/Academic/Plenum Publishers.

———. 2006. "Exchange, Affect, and Group Relations." In *George C. Homans: History, Theory, and Method,* edited by A. Javier Treviño. Boulder, Colo.: Paradigm Publishers.

Lawler, Edward E., and Jay R. Galbraith. 1994. "Avoiding the Corporate Dinosaur Syndrome." *Organizational Dynamics* 23(2): 5–17.

Lawler, Edward E., III, Susan Albers Mohrman, and Gerald E. Ledford Jr. 1995. *Creating High-Performance Organizations: Practices and Results of Employee Involvement and Total Quality Management in Fortune 1000 Companies.* San Francisco: Jossey-Bass.

Lawler, Edward J., Cecilia Ridgeway, and Barry Markovsky. 1993. "Structural Social Psychology and the Micro-Macro Problem." *Sociological Theory* 11(3): 268–92.

Lawler, Edward J., and Shane R. Thye. 1999. "Bringing Emotions into Social Exchange Theory." *Annual Review of Sociology* 25(1): 217–44.

———. 2006. "Social Exchange Theory of Emotion." In *Handbook of the Sociology of Emotions,* edited by Jan Stets and Jonathan Turner. New York: Springer.

Lawler, Edward J., Shane R. Thye, and Jeongkoo Yoon. 2000. "Emotion and Group Cohesion in Productive Exchange." *American Journal of Sociology* 106(3): 616–26.

———. 2006. "Commitment in Structurally Enabled and Induced Exchange Relations." *Social Psychology Quarterly* 69(2): 183–200.

———. 2008. "Social Exchange and Micro Social Order." *American Sociological Review* 73(4): 519–42.

Lawler, Edward J., and Jeongkoo Yoon. 1993. "Power and the Emergence of Commitment Behavior in Negotiated Exchange." *American Sociological Review* 58(4): 465–81.

———. 1996. "Commitment in Exchange Relations: Test of a Theory of Relational Cohesion." *American Sociological Review* 61(1): 89–108.

———. 1998. "Network Structure and Emotion in Exchange Relations." *American Sociological Review* 63(6): 871–94.

LeDoux, Joseph E. 1996. *The Emotional Brain: The Mysterious Underpinnings of Emotional Life.* New York: Simon & Schuster.

Lepak, David P., and Scott A. Snell. 1999. "The Human Resource Architecture: Toward a Theory of Human Capital Allocation and Development." *Academy of Management Review* 24(1): 31–48.

Leung, Chi Kin. 1993. "Personal Contacts, Subcontracting Linkages, and Development in the Hong Kong–Zhujiang Delta Region." *Annals of the Association of American Geographers* 83(2): 272–302.

Lovaglia, Michael J., and Jeffrey A. Houser. 1996. "Emotional Reactions and Status in Groups." *American Sociological Review* 61(5): 867–83.

Mannix, Elizabeth A., and Margaret A. Neale. 2005. "What Differences Make a Difference? The Promise and Reality of Diverse Teams in Organizations." *Psychological Science in the Public Interest* 6(2): 31–55.

March, James G., and Johan P. Olsen. 1975. "The Uncertainty of the Past: Organizational Learning Under Ambiguity." *European Journal of Political Research* 3(2): 147–71.

Markovsky, Barry, and Edward J. Lawler. 1994. "A New Theory of Group Solidarity." In *Advances in Group Processes,* edited by Barry Markovsky, K. Heimer, J. O'Brien, and Edward J. Lawler. Greenwich, Conn.: JAI Press.

Markovsky, Barry, David Willer, and Travis Patton. 1988. "Power Relations in Exchange Networks." *American Sociological Review* 53(2): 220–36.

Marquardt, Michael J., and Lisa Horvath. 2001. *Global Teams: How Top Multinationals Span Boundaries and Cultures with High-Speed Teamwork.* Palo Alto, Calif.: Davies-Black.

Marx, Karl. 1967. *Capital: A Critique of Political Economy.* New York: International Publishers (originally published in 1867).

Mathieu, John, and Dennis M. Zajac. 1990. "A Review and Meta-Analysis of the Antecedents, Correlates, and Consequences of Organizational Commitment." *Psychological Bulletin* 108(2): 171–94.

McPherson, Miller, Lynn Smith-Lovin, and Matthew E. Brashears. 2006. "Social Isolation in America: Changes in Core Discussion Networks over Two Decades." *American Sociological Review* 71(3): 353–75.

Mead, George Herbert. 1934. *Mind, Self, and Society.* Chicago: University of Chicago Press.

Meyer, John P., and Natalie J. Allen. 1997. *Commitment in the Workplace: Theory, Research, and Application.* Thousands Oaks, Calif.: Sage Publications.

Meyer, John P., Natalie J. Allen, and Ian R. Gellatly. 1990. "Affective and Continuance Commitment to the Organization: Evaluation of Measures and Analysis of Concurrent and Time-Lagged Relations." *Journal of Applied Psychology* 75(6): 710–20.

Meyer, John, and Brian Rowan. 1977. "Institutionalized Organizations: Formal Structure as Myth and Ceremony." *American Journal of Sociology* 83(2): 340–63.

Mintzberg, Henry. 1979. *The Structuring of Organizations.* Englewood Cliffs, N.J.: Prentice Hall.

Molm, Linda D. 1987. "Extending Power Dependency Theory: Power Processes and Negative Outcomes." In *Advances in Group Processes,* edited by Edward J. Lawler and Barry Markovsky. Greenwich, Conn.: JAI Press.

———. 1997. *Coercive Power in Social Exchange.* Cambridge: Cambridge University Press.

———. 1994. "Dependence and Risk: Transforming the Structure of Social Exchange." *Social Psychology Quarterly* 57(3): 163–76.

———. 2003. "Theoretical Comparisons of Forms of Exchange." *Sociological Theory* 21(1): 1–17.

———. 2006. "The Social Exchange Framework." In *Contemporary Social Psychological Theories,* edited by Peter J. Burke. Stanford, Calif.: Stanford University Press.

Molm, Linda D., Jessica L. Collett, and David R. Schaefer. 2007. "Building Solidarity Through Generalized Exchange: A Theory of Reciprocity." *American Journal of Sociology* 113(1): 205–42.

Molm, Linda D., and Karen S. Cook. 1995. "Social Exchange and Exchange Networks." In *Sociological Perspectives on Social Psychology,* edited by Karen Schweers Cook, Gary A. Fine, and James S. House. Boston: Allyn and Bacon.

Molm, Linda D., Nobuyuki Takahashi, and Gretchen Peterson. 2000. "Risk and Trust in Social Exchange: An Experimental Test of a Classical Proposition." *American Journal of Sociology* 105(5): 1396–1427.

Moorman, Christine, Gerald Zaltman, and Rohit Deshpande. 1992. "Relationships Between Providers and Users of Market Research: The Dynamics of Trust Within and Between Organizations." *Journal of Marketing Research* 29(3): 314–28.

Morgan, Robert M., and D. Hunt Shelby. 1994. "The Commitment-Trust Theory of Relationship Marketing." *Journal of Marketing* 58(3): 20–38.

Morrison, Elizabeth Wolfe, and Sandra L. Robinson. 1997. "When Employees Feel Betrayed: A Model of How Psychological Contract Violation Develops." *Academy of Management Review* 22(1): 226–56.

Morrow, Paula C. 1993. *The Theory and Measurement of Work Commitment.* Greenwich, Conn.: JAI Press.

Mowday, Richard T., Lyman W. Porter, and Richard M. Steers. 1982. *Employee-Organizational Linkages: The Psychology of Commitment, Absenteeism, and Turnover.* New York: Academic Press.

Mullahy, John, Stephanie Robert, and Barbara Wolfe. 2004. "Health, Income, and Inequality." In *Social Inequality,* edited by Kathryn M. Neckerman. New York: Russell Sage Foundation.

Murnighan, J. Keith. 1994. "Game Theory and Organizational Behavior." In *Research in Organizational Behavior,* edited by Barry M. Staw and Larry L. Cummings. Greenwich, Conn.: JAI Press.

Myers, Scott. 1970. *Every Employee a Manager: More Meaningful Work Through Job Enrichment.* New York: McGraw-Hill.

Neckerman, Kathryn M., ed. 2004. *Social Inequality.* New York: Russell Sage Foundation.

Nee, Victor, and Richard Swedberg, eds. 2005. *The Economic Sociology of Capitalism.* Princeton, N.J.: Princeton University Press.

Nelson, Richard R. 2005. *Technology, Institutions, and Economic Growth.* Cambridge, Mass.: Harvard University Press.

Orton, J. Douglas, and Karl E. Weick. 1990. "Loosely Coupled Systems: A Reconsideration." *Academy of Management Review* 15(2): 203–23.

Osgood, Charles E. 1966. "Dimensionality of the Semantic Space for Communication Via Facial Expressions." *Scandinavian Journal of Psychology* 7(1): 1–30.

Osterman, Paul. 1994. "How Common Is Workplace Transformation and Who Adopts It?" *Industrial and Labor Relations Review* 47(2): 173–88.

Ouchi, William G. 1980. "Markets, Bureaucracies, and Clans." *Administrative Science Quarterly* 25(1): 129–41.

Parsons, Talcott. 1951. *The Social System.* Glencoe, Ill.: Free Press.

Pfeffer, Jeffrey. 1994. *Competitive Advantage Through People: Unleashing the Power of the Work Force.* Boston: Harvard Business School Press.

Podolny, Joel M. 1994. "Market Uncertainty and the Social Character of Economic Exchange." *Administrative Science Quarterly* 39(3): 458–83.

Podolny, Joel M., and Karen L. Page. 1998. "Network Forms of Organization." *Annual Review of Sociology* 24(1): 57–76.

Pohlman, Randolph A., Gareth S. Gardiner, and Ellen M. Heffes. 2000. *Value-Driven Management.* New York: AMACON.

Powell, Walter W. 1990. "Neither Market nor Hierarchy: Network Forms of Organizations." In *Research in Organizational Behavior,* edited by Barry M. Staw and Larry L. Cummings. Greenwich, Conn.: JAI Press.

Prentice, Deborah A., Dale T. Miller, and Jennifer R. Lightdale. 1994. "Asymmetries in Attachments to Groups and to Their Members: Distinguishing Between Common-Identity and Common-Bond Groups." *Personality and Social Psychology Bulletin* 20(5): 484–93.

Pruitt, Dean G., and Melvin J. Kimmel. 1977. "Twenty Years of Experimental Gaming: Critique, Synthesis, and Suggestions for the Future." *Annual Review of Psychology* 28: 363–92.

Pruijt, Hans D. 1997. *Job Design and Technology: Taylorism vs. Anti-Taylorism.* New York: Routledge.

Putnam, Robert D. 2000. *Bowling Alone: The Collapse and Revival of American Community.* New York: Simon & Schuster.

———. 2007. "E Pluribus Unum: Diversity and Community in the Twenty-First Century: The 2006 Johan Skytte Prize Lecture." *Scandinavian Political Studies* 30(2): 137–74.

Quick, James Campbell. 1992. "Crafting an Organizational Culture: Herb's Hand at Southwest Airlines." *Organizational Dynamics* 21(2): 45–56.

Rauch, James E., and Alessandra Casella, eds. 2001. *Networks and Markets.* New York: Russell Sage Foundation.

Richardson, George B. 1972. "The Organization of Industry." *Economic Journal* 82(327): 883–96.

Ridgeway, Cecilia. 1991. "The Social Construction of Status Value: Gender and Other Nominal Characteristics." *Social Forces* 70(2): 367–86.

Ridgeway, Cecilia L., and Shelley J. Correll. 2006. "Consensus and the Creation of Status Beliefs." *Social Forces* 85(1): 431–53.

Ridgeway, Cecilia L., and Kristan Glasgow Erikson. 2000. "Creating and Spreading Status Beliefs." *American Journal of Sociology* 106(3): 579–615.

Ridgeway, Cecilia, and Cathryn Johnson. 1990. "What Is the Relationship Between Socioemotional Behavior and Status in Task Groups?" *American Journal of Sociology* 95(5): 1189–1212.

Ritzer, George. 1995. *Expressing America: A Critique of the Global Credit Card Society.* Thousand Oaks, Calif.: Pine Forge Press.

Robinson, Dawn, and Lynn Smith-Lovin. 2006. "Affect Control Theory." In *Contemporary Social Psychological Theories,* edited by Peter J. Burke. Stanford, Calif.: Stanford University Press.

Rodden, Jonathan A. 2006. *Hamilton's Paradox: The Promise and Peril of Fiscal Federalism.* Cambridge: Cambridge University Press.

Rodden Jonathan, Gunmar Eskeland, and Jennie Litvak, eds. 2003. *Decentralization and the Challenge of Hard Budget Constraints.* Cambridge, Mass.: MIT Press.

Rodrik, Dani. 1997. *Has Globalization Gone Too Far?* Washington, D.C.: Institute for International Economics.

———. 1998. "Why Do More Open Economies Have Bigger Governments?" *Journal of Political Economy* 106(5): 997.

Rousseau, Denise M. 1995. *Psychological Contracts in Organizations: Understanding Written and Unwritten Agreements.* Thousand Oaks, Calif.: Sage Publications.

Russell, James A. 1980. "A Circumplex Model of Affect." *Journal of Personality and Social Psychology* 39(6): 1161–78.

Russell, James A., Anna Weiss, and Gerald A. Mendelsohn. 1989. "Affect Grid: A Single-Item Scale of Pleasure and Arousal." *Journal of Personality and Social Psychology* 57(3): 493–502.

Sabel, Charles F., Gary Herrigel, Richard Kazis, and Richard Deeg. 1987. "How to Keep Mature Industries Innovative." *Technology Review* 90(3): 26–35.

Savona, Dave. 1992. "When Companies Divorce." *International Business* 5(11): 48–51.

Schachter, Stanley, and J. Singer. 1962. "Cognitive, Social, and Physiological Determinants of Emotional State." *Psychological Review* 69(1): 379–99.

Scharpf, Fritz Wilhelm. 2000. "Economic Changes, Vulnerabilities, and Institutional Capabilities." In *Welfare and Work in the Open Economy,* vol. 1, edited by Fritz Wilhelm Scharpf and Vivien Ann Schmidt. New York: Oxford University Press.

Scharpf, Fritz Wilhelm, and Vivien Ann Schmidt. 2000. *Welfare and Work in the Open Economy,* vol. 1. New York: Oxford University Press.

Scheff, Thomas J. 1990. *Microsociology: Discourse, Emotion, and Social Structure.* Chicago: University of Chicago Press.

Scherer, Klaus R. 1984. "Emotion as a Multicomponential Process: A Model and Some Cross-Cultural Data." In *Review of Personality and Social Psychology,* edited by Phillip Shaver and Ladd Wheeler. Beverly Hills, Calif.: Sage Publications.

Schoderbek, Peter P., and William E. Reif. 1969. *Job Enlargement: Key to Improved Performance.* Ann Arbor: University of Michigan, Bureau of Industrial Relations.

Schwarz, Norbert. 1990. "Feelings as Information: Informational and Motivational Functions of Affective States." In *Handbook of Motivation and Cognition: Foundations of Social Behavior,* edited by Richard M. Sorrentino and E. Tory Higgins. New York: Guilford.

Schwarz, Norbert, and Gerald L. Clore. 1983. "Mood, Misattribution, and Judgments of Well-Being: Informative and Directive Functions of Affective States." *Journal of Personality and Social Psychology* 45(3): 513–23.

Selznick, Philip. 1992. *The Moral Commonwealth: Social Theory and the Promise of Community.* Berkeley: University of California Press.

Shott, Susan. 1979. "Emotion and Social Life: A Symbolic Interactionist Analysis." *American Journal of Sociology* 84(6): 1317–34.

Simmel, Georg. 1964. *The Sociology of Georg Simmel,* translated, edited, and with an introduction by Kurt H. Wolff. New York: Free Press of Glencoe.

Simon, Herbert A. 1957. *Models of Man: Social and Rational: Mathematical Essays on Rational Human Behavior in a Society Setting.* New York: Wiley.

Smith, Adam. 2007. "An Inquiry into the Nature and Causes of the Wealth of Nations" (1776), in *The Real Price of Everything: Rediscovering the Six Classics of Economics,* edited by Michael Lewis. New York: Sterling.

Smith, Amelia C. 1997. "Empowerment in New Zealand Organizations: Two Case Studies." PhD diss., University of Canterbury, New Zealand.

Smith, Anthony D. 2001. *Nationalism: Theory, Ideology.* Malden, Mass.: Polity Press.

Smith-Lovin, Lynn, and David R. Heise, eds. 1988. *Analyzing Social Interaction: Advances in Affect Control Theory.* New York: Gordon and Breach Science Publishers.

Stets, Jan E. 2006. "Identity Theory." In *Contemporary Social Psychological Theories,* edited by Peter J. Burke. Stanford, Calif.: Stanford University Press.

Stiglitz, Joseph E. 2006. *Making Globalization Work.* New York: W. W. Norton.

Stolle, Dietlind, and Marc Hooghe. 2004. "Inaccurate, Exceptional, One-Sided, or Irrelevant? The Debate About the Alleged Decline of Social Capital and Civic Engagement in Western Societies." *British Journal of Political Science* 35(1): 149–67.

Stryker, Sheldon. 1980. *Symbolic Interactionism: A Social Structural Version.* Menlo Park, Calif.: Benjamin/Cummings.

Swedberg, Richard. 2003. *Principles of Economic Sociology.* Princeton, N.J.: Princeton University Press.

Sy, Thomas, Stephane Cote, and Richard Saavedra. 2005. "The Contagious Leader: Impact of the Leader's Mood on the Mood of Group Members, Group Affective Tone, and Group Processes." *Journal of Applied Psychology* 90(2): 295–305.

Sztompka, Piotr. 1999. *Trust: A Sociological Theory.* Cambridge: Cambridge University Press.

Tajfel, Henri. 1969. "Cognitive Aspects of Prejudice." *Journal of Social Issues* 41(4): 79–97.

Tajfel, Henri, and John C. Turner. 1986. "The Social Identity Theory of Intergroup Behavior." In *Psychology of Intergroup Relations,* edited by Stephen Worchel and William G. Austin. Chicago: Nelson-Hall.

Tannenbaum, Arnold S., ed. 1968. *Control in Organizations.* New York: McGraw-Hill.

Thaler, Richard. 1980. "Toward a Positive Theory of Consumer Choice." *Journal of Economic Behavior and Organization* 1(1): 39–60.

Thoits, Peggy A. 1985. "Self-Labeling Processes in Mental Illness: The Role of Emotional Deviance." *American Journal of Sociology* 91(2): 221–49.

———. 1990. "Emotional Deviance: Research Agendas." In *Research Agendas in the Sociology of Emotions,* edited by Theodore D. Kemper. Albany: State University of New York Press.

Thompson, James D. 1967. *Organizations in Action.* New York: McGraw-Hill.

Thye, Shane R. 2000a. "Reliability in Experimental Sociology." *Social Forces* 78(4): 1277–1309.

———. 2000b. "A Status Value Theory of Power in Exchange Relations." *American Sociological Review* 65(3): 407–32.

Thye, Shane, and Edward J. Lawler. 2004. "Structural Cohesion and Group Formation in Networks of Exchange." Paper presented to the annual meeting of the American Sociological Association. August 23, San Francisco, Calif.

Thye, Shane R., Edward J. Lawler, and Jeongkoo Yoon. 2008. "Exchange and the Maintenance of Order in Status-Stratified Systems." In *Social Structure and Emotion,* edited by Jody Clay-Warner and Dawn I. Robinson. Amsterdam, Netherlands: Elsevier.

Thye, Shane R., Michael J. Lovaglia, and Barry Markovsky. 1997. "Responses to Social Exchange and Social Exclusion in Networks." *Social Forces* 75(3): 1031–47.

Thye, Shane, David Willer, and Barry Markovsky. 2006. "From Status to Power: New Models at the Intersection of Two Theories." *Social Forces* 84(3): 1471–95.

Thye, Shane, and Christine Witkowski. 2003. "The Status Value Theory of Power: The Effect of Status and Resource Differentiation on Power in Exchange." Paper presented to the annual meeting of the American Sociological Association. August 17, Atlanta, Ga.

Thye, Shane R., Jeongkoo Yoon, and Edward J. Lawler. 2002. "The Theory of Relational Cohesion: Review of a Research Program." In *Advances in Group Process,* edited by Shane R. Thye and Edward J. Lawler. Oxford: Elsevier.

Tichy, Noel M., and Stratford Sherman. 1993. *Control Your Destiny or Someone Else Will: How Jack Welch Is Making General Electric the World's Most Competitive Corporation.* New York: Currency/Doubleday.

———. 1994. *Control Your Destiny or Someone Else Will: Lessons in Mastering Change—from the Principles Jack Welch Is Using to Revolutionize GE.* New York: HarperBusiness.

———. 2001. *Control Your Destiny or Someone Else Will.* New York: HarperBusiness.

Tilly, Charles. 1990. *Coercion, Capital, and European States, AD 990–1990.* Cambridge, Mass.: Blackwell.

Turner, John C., and Katherine J. Reynolds. 2004. "The Social Identity Perspective in Intergroup Relations: Theories, Themes, and Controversies." In *Self and Social Identity,* edited by Marilynn B. Brewer and Miles Hewstone. Malden, Mass.: Blackwell Publishers.

Turner, Jonathan H. 2000. *On the Origins of Human Emotions: A Sociological Inquiry into the Evolution of Human Affect.* Stanford, Calif.: Stanford University Press.

———. 2002. *Face to Face: Toward a Sociological Theory of Interpersonal Behavior.* Stanford, Calif.: Stanford University Press.

———. 2007. *Human Emotions: A Sociological Theory.* New York: Routledge.

———. 2008. "Emotions and Social Structure: Toward a General Sociological Theory." In *Social Structure and Emotion,* edited by Jody Clay-Warner and Dawn T. Robinson. Amsterdam, Netherlands: Academic Press.

Turner, Ralph H. 1978. "The Role and the Person." *American Journal of Sociology* 84(1): 1–23.

Tyler, Tom R. 1989. "The Psychology of Procedural Justice: A Test of the Group-Value Model." *Journal of Personality and Social Psychology* 57(5): 830–38.

Ulrich, Dave, and Dale G. Lake. 1990. *Organizational Capability: Competing from the Inside Out.* New York: Wiley.

Uzzi, Brian. 1996. "The Sources and Consequences of Embeddedness for the Economic Performance of Organizations: The Network Effect." *American Sociological Review* 61(4): 674–98.

———. 1997. "Social Structure and Competition in Interfirm Networks: The Paradox of Embeddedness." *Administrative Science Quarterly* 42(1): 35–67.

Uzzi, Brian, and Ryon Lancaster. 2004. "Embeddedness and Price Formation in the Corporate Law Market." *American Sociological Review* 69(3): 319–44.

Wagner, David G., and Joseph Berger. 1993. "Status Characteristics Theory: The Growth of a Program." In *Theoretical Research Programs,* edited by Joseph Berger and Morris Zelditch, Jr. Stanford, Calif.: Stanford University Press.

Walker, Henry A., and Bernard P. Cohen. 1985. "Scope Statements: Imperatives for Evaluating Theory." *American Sociological Review* 50(3): 288–301.

Walker, Henry A., and Morris Zelditch Jr. 1993. "Power, Legitimacy, and the Stability of Authority: A Theoretical Research Program." *Theoretical Research Programs: Studies in the Growth of Theory,* edited by Joseph Berger and Morris Zelditch Jr. Stanford, Calif.: Stanford University Press.

Watson, David, and Auke Tellegen. 1985. "Toward a Consensual Structure of Mood." *Psychological Bulletin* 98(2): 219–35.

Watts, Duncan J. 2003. *Six Degrees: The Science of a Connected Age.* New York: Norton.

Weber, Max. 1968. *Economy and Society.* Berkeley: University of California Press (originally published in 1918).

Webster's Unabridged Dictionary. 1997. New York: Random House.

Wegener, Duane T., Richard E. Petty, and Stephen M. Smith. 1995. "Positive Mood Can Increase or Decrease Message Scrutiny: The Hedonic Contingency View of Mood and Message Processing." *Journal of Personality and Social Psychology* 69(1): 5–15.

Weiner, Bernhard. 1986. *An Attributional Theory of Motivation and Emotion.* New York: Springer.

Welch, Jack, and John A. Byrne. 2003. *Straight from the Gut: Jack Welch.* New York: Warner Books.

Wellman, Barry, and Caroline Haythornthwaite, eds. 2002. *The Internet in Everyday Life.* Malden, Mass.: Blackwell.

Wessel, Ineke, and Harald Merckelbach. 1997. "The Impact of Anxiety on Memory for Details in Spider Phobics." *Applied Cognitive Psychology* 11(3): 223–31.

Westcott, Malcolm R. 1988. *The Psychology of Human Freedom: A Human Science Perspective and Critique.* New York: Springer.

White, R. W. 1959. "Motivation Reconsidered: The Concept of Competence." *Psychological Review* 66(5): 297–333.

Wierzbicka, Anna 1992. "Defining Emotion Concepts." *Cognitive Science* 16(4): 539–81.

Wigley, Tom M. L., and Sarah C. B. Raper. 2001. "Interpretations of High Projections for Global-Mean Warming." *Science* 293(5529): 451–54.

Willer, David, ed. 1999. *Network Exchange Theory.* Westport, Conn.: Praeger.

Willer, David, and Bo Anderson. 1981. *Networks, Exchange, and Coercion: The Elementary Theory and Its Applications.* New York: Elsevier.

Willer, David, Michael J. Lovaglia, and Barry Markovsky. 1997. "Power and Influence: A Theoretical Bridge." *Social Forces* 76(2): 571–603.

Willer, David, and John Skvoretz. 1997. "Games and Structures." *Rationality and Society* 9(1): 5–35.

Williamson, Oliver E. 1975. *Markets and Hierarchies.* New York: Free Press.

———. 1981. "The Economics of Organization: The Transaction Cost Approach." *American Journal of Sociology* 87(3): 548–77.

———. 1985. *The Economic Institutions of Capitalism: Firms, Markets, Relational Contracting.* New York: Free Press.

———. 1991. "Comparative Economic Organization: The Analysis of Discrete Structural Alternatives." *Administrative Science Quarterly* 36(2): 269–96.

Wright, William F., and Gordon H. Bower. 1992. "Mood Effects on Subjective Probability Assessment." *Organizational Behavior and Human Decision Processes* 52(2): 276–91.

Wrong, Dennis H. 1994. *Power: Its Forms, Bases, and Uses.* New Brunswick, N.J.: Transaction Books.

Yamagishi, Toshio. 2001. "Trust as a Form of Social Intelligence." In *Trust in Society,* edited by Karen S. Cook. New York: Russell Sage Foundation.

Yamagishi, Toshio, Karen S. Cook, and Motoki Watabe. 1998. "Uncertainty, Trust, and Commitment Formation in the United States and Japan." *American Journal of Sociology* 104(1): 165–94.

Yamagishi, Toshio, and Midori Yamagishi. 1994. "Trust and Commitment in the United States and Japan." *Motivation and Emotion* 18(2): 129–66.

Yoon, Jeongkoo. 2001. "The Role of Structure and Motivation for Workplace Empowerment: The Case of Korean Employees." *Social Psychology Quarterly* 64(2): 195–206.

Yoon, Jeongkoo, and Edward J. Lawler. 2006. "Relational Cohesion Model of Organizational Commitment." In *Relational Perspectives in Organizational Studies,* edited by Olivia Kyriakidou and Mustafa Ozbilgin. Northampton, Mass.: Edward Elgar.

Yoon, Jeongkoo, and Shane R. Thye. 2002. "A Dual Process Model of Organizational Commitment." *Work and Occupations* 29(1): 97–124.

Yzerbyt, Vincent, and Anouk Rogler. 2001. "Blame It on the Group: Entitativity, Subjective Essentialism, and Social Attribution." In *The Psychology of Legitimacy: Emerging Perspectives on Ideology, Justice, and Intergroup Relations,* edited by John T. Jost and Brenda Major. Cambridge: Cambridge University Press.

Zaccaro, Stephen J., Christopher Peterson, and Steven Walker. 1987. "Self-Serving Attributions for Individual and Group Performance." *Social Psychology Quarterly* 50(3): 257–63.

Zelditch, Morris, Jr. 2006. "Legitimacy Theory." In *Contemporary Social Psychological Theories,* edited by Peter J. Burke. Stanford, Calif.: Stanford University Press.

Zelditch, Morris, Jr., and Henry A. Walker. 1984. "Legitimacy and the Stability of Authority." In *Advances in Group Processes,* edited by Edward J. Lawler. Greenwich, Conn.: JAI Press.

INDEX

ments); nested sub-units and (*see* nested commitments, theory of); noncontractual solutions to, 8, 29–30; person-to-group ties and, 190–93; relationship of macro and micro realms and, 8–9, 28–29, 167–68, 183–85; repetition and, economic *vs.* sociological approaches to, 168–70; social commitments and (*see* social commitments, theory of); status/ social inequality and (*see* status)

social structure: development of groups and, 74 (*see also* groups; structural foundations of groups); meaning and function of, 73–74

social ties: network, decline of, 13; person-to-person and person-to-group, distinction between, 3–4 (*see also* person-to-group ties); person-to-person and person-to-group, examples of interrelationships between, 5–7; relational (*see* relational ties); transactional (*see* transactional ties)

social transformation: as a disjuncture between micro and macro conditions of existence, 16, 29; historical and current, scholarship on, 12–13; narratives and (*see* narratives); person-to-group ties during current, 188–90; trends in the current, 14–16, 29

social-unit attribution of emotions, 46–47

Southwest Airlines, 105, 207*n*5

Spielberg, Steven, 125

spread of status value, 137–38

Starbucks, 141

state, the: conflict theories of state formation, 161–62; decline of, 145, 147–50; dimensions of, social commitments and, 152–54; ethnic groups and the problem of order in, 184–85; modernization theory and, 160–61; nationalist commitment to, question of, 145–47, 164–65 (*see also* nationalism/ nationalist sentiments); nation and, distinction between, 151–52; nested commitments in, 147, 154–59

status: beliefs, 136–37; definition of, 127–28; empirical experiment including considerations of, 132–36; expectation states theory and processes of, 136–39; inequality of and social commitment, 128–29; the problem of social order and, 129–32, 142–44; social exchange processes and, 139–42; stratification, explaining order in the context of, 136–42; zip code, signified by, 127–28, 138

Steinbrenner, Hank, 2, 199*n*1

structural approach to interaction context, 34, 36–38

structural condition for social-unit attributions of emotional experiences, 57–58

structural embeddedness, 123

structural foundations of groups, 73–77, 89–91; exchange, role of, 80–85; interdependence, role of, 78–80; networks as opportunity structures, 85–89; the social exchange orientation, 77–78

structural identity theory, 177–80, 183

structural interventions, 101